WITHDRAWN

MELVILLE'S MUSE

Melville's Muse

Literary Creation & the Forms of
Philosophical Fiction

JOHN WENKE

THE KENT STATE UNIVERSITY PRESS
Kent, Ohio, and London, England

© 1995 by The Kent State University Press, Kent, Ohio 44242
All rights reserved
Library of Congress Catalog Card Number 95-3560
ISBN 0-87338-527-6
Manufactured in the United States of America

Library of Congress Cataloging-in-Publication Data

03 02 01 00 99 98 97 96 95   5 4 3 2 1
Wenke, John Paul.
    Melville's muse : literary creation and the forms of philosophical fiction /
John Wenke.
        p. cm.
    Includes bibliographical references and index.
    ISBN 0-87338-527-6
    1. Melville, Herman, 1819–1891—Aesthetics. 2. Creation (Literary, artistic,
etc.) 3. Philosophy in literature. 4. Fiction—Philosophy. 5. Literary form. I. Title.
PS2388.A35W46 1995   95-3560
813'.3—dc 20   CIP

British Library Cataloging-in-Publication data are available.

To Sheila and our children,

Jacqueline Lillian, Joseph Hughes, and Benjamin Hughes

My lord, all men are inspired; fools are inspired; your highness is inspired; for the essence of all ideas is infused. Of ourselves, and in ourselves, we originate nothing. When Lombardo set about his work, he knew not what it would become. He did not build himself in with plans; he wrote right on; and so doing, got deeper and deeper into himself; and like a resolute traveler, plunging through baffling woods, at last was rewarded for his toils. "In good time," saith he, in his autobiography, "I came out into a serene, sunny, ravishing region; full of sweet scents, singing birds, wild plaints, roguish laughs, prophetic voices. Here we are at last, then," he cried; "I have created the creative."

—*Mardi*

What may man know?
(Here pondered Clarel;) let him rule—
Pull down, build up, creed, system, school,
And reason's endless battle wage,
Make and remake his verbiage—
But solve the world! Scarce that he'll do:
Too wild it is, too wonderful.

—*Clarel*

Contents

Preface

IN THE TURBID wake of years, Herman Melville came to feel an unjustified contempt for his auspicious and controversial debut in the genre of the travel narrative. He would always seem resentful that *Typee* (1846), of all his books, enjoyed some measure of ongoing popularity. What especially rankled him was his "horrible" reputation of having "lived among the cannibals" (*Correspondence* 193), as if this very rubric effaced or threatened his self-image. Melville felt pinioned within a reductive identity. In the public view, Melville's tale of cannibals marked the high point of his art; his refusal to supply works in the same line in favor of what Fitz-James O'Brien called "a trick of metaphysical and morbid meditations" (Leyda 565) was at best construed as perverse and at worst, insane. In 1853, following the publication of *Pierre* (1852), the same critic remarked that the stylistic simplicity of *Typee* stands in "wondrous contrast to Mardi, Moby Dick and Pierre. . . . Mr. Melville does not improve with time. . . . He totters on the edge of a precipice" (Leyda 466–67). Six years later, after Melville embarked on a thirty-year hiatus from fiction writing, *Typee* even haunted him at home. In Pittsfield, Melville was visited by two collegians, John Thomas Gulick and Titus Munson Coan, who had made a literary pilgrimage from Williams College. They came in hopes of hearing lively Polynesian yarns, a sort of oral anthropology laced with the titillation of romance. Perhaps flattered by the attention or made loquacious by liquor—Gulick noted that "His countenance is slightly flushed with whiskey drinking"—Melville was in an expansive mood. But to the young men's chagrin, he eschewed sunny tales of nude bathing with Fayaway and conjured the "shade of Aristotle," sermonizing on the decadence of modernity and extolling the splendors of antiquity. In his journal Gulick writes:

> Though it was apparent that he possessed a mind of an aspiring, ambitious order, full of elastic energy and illumined with the rich colors of a poetic fancy, he was evidently a disappointed man, soured by criticism and disgusted by the civilized world and with our Christendom in general and in particular. The ancient dignity of Homeric times afforded the only state of humanity, individual or social, to which he could turn with any complacency. What little there was of meaning in the religions of the present day had come down from Plato. All our philosophy and all our art and poetry was either derived or imitated from the ancient Greeks. (Leyda 605)

However pleased he was to have an audience, Melville was not disposed to give them what they wanted. As Coan remarked, "We have quite enough of Greek philosophy at Williams College, and I confess I was disappointed in this trend of the talk. But what a talk it was!" More concerned with "his theories of life," Melville was all too ready to disappoint his auditors and all too insistent upon scandalizing them with a "full tide of discourse on all things sacred and profane" (Leyda 605).

It is not so remarkable that this "cloistered thinker" had levied such judgments or betrayed such zest for philosophical disquisition (Leyda 606). After all, two years before Melville had delivered his most sardonic, iconoclastic, involuted, metaphysically dialogic novel, *The Confidence-Man: His Masquerade* (1857). What *is* remarkable is that his conversation with the Williams undergraduates offered an intensified rendering of those very ideas and predilections that drove him in 1847 and 1848 to remake himself as an artist. Even then, a young author on the rise, Melville betrayed an arch disdain for thrilling adventure narratives, which would pay, and worked up a voracious appetite for discoursing on "all things sacred and profane," which would never pay.

Melville's failures and successes in developing fictional forms to contain and express "all things sacred and profane" constitute the focus of this book. He was intent, as he put it in a letter to his father-in-law, Judge Lemuel Shaw, "to write those sort of books which are said to 'fail'—Pardon this egotism" (139); he was drawn to a commercially disastrous literary hybrid that provided a forum for his expansive intellectual inquiries. Crucial for Melville was the relationship between metaphysical speculation and its expression within a self-generated, protean fictional domain, a kind of slapdash fusion of disparate modes where one improvisation makes way for—and stands in dialectical relation to—the next. It was one thing to wish to be the great "sayer," the vatic Prometheus who storms the god-realm and steals the elemental fire. It was another thing to harness the combustion.

Melville's repudiation of popular adventure narrative in favor of philosophical romance led him to dramatize a host of amorphously confluent resources. He appropriated and transformed elements of his Calvinist-Lutheran heritage; his eclectic reading in ancient, Renaissance, and contemporary writers; his Romantic zeitgeist; and his cultural and political milieu. Melville's interest in philosophy offered a way to link topical concerns with what he frequently called "the Problem of the Universe" (*Correspondence* 180, 185, 186, 452). This grandiose approach may strike some as quaint and naive. But as Lawrence Buell notes,

> For the great [antebellum] writers as well as for the popular, the notion of art as a vehicle for the moral, philosophical, and religious imagination tended to come first and the problematization of this notion second. The sophistication of the latter idea was made possible by the former commitment. . . . [T]hat is a hard doctrine to impress upon the late twentieth-century mind, which tends to take moral relativism for granted. . . . [T]o the extent that we wish to think of our knowledge of these [antebellum] texts as

historical, however, we must also recognize their grounding in . . . such premises as the primacy of the moral imagination. (*New England Literary Culture* 82–83)

As far as Melville was concerned, literature offered a syncretic medium for dramatizing ultimate questions.

This study is not concerned so much with Melville's ideas, themes, or "meanings" but with the emerging forms through which "the moral imagination" achieves expression. One collateral purpose is to demonstrate how Melville's attraction to ancient and Renaissance writers became integral to his complex response to, and reformation of, Romanticism. Indeed, Melville's vexed Romanticism anticipates twentieth-century concerns with the indeterminacy of language, the displacement of logocentricism, the depiction of existential crisis, and the novel as forum for the collision of competing voices. I purposefully avoid contending with Melville's specific anticipations of Heidegger, Bakhtin, or Derrida, for this activity would require its own book. But it may prove interesting to those versed in these influential theorists to see how by reading, adapting, and reinventing the likes of Plato and Sir Thomas Browne, Melville found his own way into what seem peculiarly modern and postmodern dilemmas of identity and language.

Rather than situating my argument in relation to paradigms gleaned from Paul de Man or Hans-Georg Gadamer, I steadfastly attempt to engage Melville on his own terms—through biographical, historical, and cultural contexts—and with the help of source, influence, and textual scholarship. Such resources lead one to the exciting bottom line of close reading. Within less temperate zones on the current critical map, there is an unfortunate tendency toward gusty condescension—or even icy disdain—regarding attempts to base or initiate discourse on the eminently debatable ground of intention. As a host of documentary evidence indicates, and as major literary works affirm, Melville's reconstruction of himself as a writer emanated from a tour de force of intention. Theories that assert an author's irrelevance or death or disappearance, in my view, displace significant confusion. A deceased author's

bodily absence does not make away with the vestigial entanglements of untidy life and the traces they leave as textual residue.
Nevertheless, claims for intention should not serve as warrants for
critical reductiveness—the lockstep execution of an alleged master
plan. Within this critical narrative, my concern with Melville's putative intentions initiate, animate, and complicate discussion. What
becomes clear is that consciously articulated life choices led Melville
to create texts that are both dependent *and* revolutionary.

*Melville's Muse: Literary Creation and the Forms of Philosophi-
cal Fiction* is divided into three parts and eight chapters. Part One,
"*Mardi:* 'The Peculiar Theatre of the Romantic and Wonderful,'"
offers three chapters on *Mardi* (1849). "Making *Mardi*'s Patchwork"
explores Melville's repudiation of travel narrative in favor of what
he called "philosophic research" (*Omoo* xv). My examination of
Melville's reading extends Merton M. Sealts, Jr.'s great work on this
subject. Melville's immersion into Plato, Montaigne, Thomas
Browne, Robert Burton, and Coleridge, among others, helped him
develop his peculiar creative alchemy. "Narrative Self-Fashioning
and the Play of Possibility" details the evolution in *Mardi* of an
overreaching philosophical self, a narrator disgusted with quotidian existence and starved for experiences commensurate with his
frenzied visions. Melville develops two distinctly identifiable narrative voices that stand in dialectical tension—the genialist and
the solipsist. Chapter 3, "Perpetual Cycling," considers *Mardi*'s long
travelogue and Melville's dramatization of two distinct voyages into
"the world of mind" (557). Once Taji comes to inhabit an ontological realm outside the diachronic progression of the narrative,
his genial voice becomes diffused, as it were, through four allegorized characters representing Authority, Poetry, History, and Philosophy. Through these questers, Melville adapts the Platonic
dialogue and creates fables of identity. He also interpolates texts
within the text to engage the problematic issue of narrative authority and the self-exhausting nature of the philosophical quest.

Part Two, "The Absolute Condition of Present Things," contains one chapter on *Redburn* (1849) and *White-Jacket* (1850) and
two chapters on *Moby-Dick* (1851). Chapter 4, "*Redburn* and

White-Jacket: 'Concocting Information into Wisdom,'" examines Melville's debt to Pierre Bayle's *Dictionary* and then explores how ostensibly "straightforward, amusing" narratives contain "metaphysical ingredients" (*Correspondence* 131–32). Such elements as allusion, scenes of reading, and essayistic excursions rupture *Redburn* and permeate *White-Jacket.* Chapter 5, "*Moby-Dick* and the Impress of Melville's Learning," elaborates on the groundbreaking genetic implications of Harrison Hayford's "'Unnecessary Duplicates': A Key to the Writing of *Moby-Dick.*" I examine how works by Thomas De Quincey, Mary W. Shelley, Ralph Waldo Emerson, and Thomas Carlyle seem to have contributed to Melville's massive revision of his "whaling voyage" (*Correspondence* 162). Chapter 6, "*Moby-Dick* and the Forms of Philosophical Fiction," demonstrates the multilayered application of Ishmael's philosophical rhetoric, especially as it emerges in his process narrative, a fusion of past action and present-tense commentary. His admittedly provisional language experiment liberates him and allows him to proceed in two distinct but related directions—toward psychological examination of himself and others, and toward metaphysical speculation on phenomenal surfaces. Ishmael's concern with ontology, epistemology, and cosmology constitutes the narrative's sinuous philosophical architecture, especially as it fashions an approach to totality.

Part Three, "*Pierre* and *The Confidence-Man:* 'This Guild of Self-Impostors,'" considers two problem novels. Chapter 7, "Excursive Ponderings in *Pierre,*" examines an intentionally narrow focus: the third-person narrator's presentation of his increasing affective involvement with Pierre's "choice fate" (*Pierre* 5). In this novel, Melville peels back layer upon layer of social and psychological surface, extending the ontological and epistemological preoccupations in *Moby-Dick.* In the process, the narrator attacks philosophers as a "guild of self-impostors" (*Pierre* 208) and discounts literary influence. *Pierre* constitutes Melville's extended repudiation of the Taji-Ahab pursuit of the Absolute. Chapter 8, "*The Confidence Man: His Masquerade:* 'The Most Extraordinary Metaphysical Scamps,'" extends my earlier discussion of Melville's adaptation of the Platonic dialogue into this dialectical theater of changing players. The dialogue form focuses Melville's subversive exploration of self-possession and political power.

I have chosen to focus on those longer prose narratives that most clearly reveal Melville's attempts to marry fiction and philosophy. I do not extensively consider the ideational content of *Typee* and *Omoo* (1847); instead, I concentrate on Melville's movement away from these ostensible narratives of fact. While I comment on "Bartleby, the Scrivener" (1853) and *Benito Cereno* (1855) in passing, I do not systematically examine the short fiction. The nature of Melville's historical reconstruction in *Israel Potter* (1855) seems to make it tangential to my study. Since *Melville's Muse* explores his eleven-year evolution as a publishing fiction writer, the unfinished *Billy Budd* (1924) also stands outside the range of my endeavors. A consideration of this narrative's philosophical forms is not possible without a lengthy examination of Melville's poetry and poetics—clearly a project for another time.

Whether reading his fiction or his poetry, however, one must recognize that Melville was an artist, not a metaphysician. His books frequently betray strained and necessarily failed attempts to encompass the all-encompassing and resolve the irresolvable. In wrestling with "the Problem of the Universe" (*Correspondence* 186), he found neither a safe haven nor an "insular Tahiti" (*Moby-Dick* 274). Lacking neat systems or an easy faith, Melville's work offers a complex record of his repeated immersions into unsounded depths. In a letter to his friend Evert A. Duyckinck, Melville noted, "I love all men who *dive*" (121, Melville's emphasis), and to this extent, surely, he loved himself. Deep diving could not be assayed "without throwing oneself helplessly open" (*Pierre* 259). Melville courted this helplessness; the "world of mind" lay open (*Mardi* 557).

Acknowledgments

OVER THE MANY, many days that this book has found its way first into shape and now into print, I have had the good fortune to incur a number of debts. In 1982, John Bryant wrote asking me to contribute an essay on "Melville and Ancient Philosophy" to *A Companion to Melville Studies*. Because no one enlisted to do "Melville and Contemporary Philosophy," my charge became "Melville and the Rest of Philosophy." In the course of my research, my original, and naive, intention was simply to take many more notes than I could use and extend the remainders into a book. On the same principle that houses had better not be moved, essays had best not become books. In 1986, like Melville's poor pale Usher, I dusted off my unused note pile and found too many questions and too little clarification. Fortunately I had the luxury to reconstruct my foundation and to write and rewrite chapters. During this time other projects were started and finished, the Berlin Wall came down, our babies were born, inflation slowed, and the housing market picked up. Through it all, I was blessed to find kind and demanding readers who encouraged my efforts. Milton R. Stern read an early draft of the opening chapters and kept asking when I would finish. Later readers included James Duban, who published a version of Chapter 2 in *Texas Studies in Literature and Language* (1989), and Brian Higgins and Hershel Parker, who published part of Chapter 5 in *Critical Essays on Melville's Moby Dick* (1992). I am grateful to the University of Texas and G. K. Hall, respectively, for permission to present this material here in an altered form. My special thanks go out to Joel Kupperman, Thomas Riggio, Hershel Parker, and Sanford E. Marovitz, all of whom read the manuscript and made valuable suggestions for its improvement.

I am also grateful for the chance to mention other individuals and institutions who contributed in large and small ways to the completion of this project. These persons include Julia J. Morton, Linda K. Cuckovich, Gary Harrington, Michael Waters, Kathleen McWilliams, Patricia Howard, Maureen Barksdale, Anne Marie Orsini, Bernice Jones, Joseph J. Wenke, Jr., James Wenke, Robert Wenke, Michael Wenke, Bill S. Hughes, Albert J. Rivero, and my parents, Bernice C. and Joseph J. Wenke, Sr. These institutions include the University of Connecticut, Marquette University, Trinity College, Salisbury State University, and their respective libraries. I particularly appreciate the valuable time I spent in the University of Pennsylvania library. I am grateful to K. Nelson Butler and Thomas Bellavance for approving my 1990 sabbatical despite a constrained economic situation, and likewise to Salisbury State's Fulton School of Liberal Arts for reducing my fall 1992 load by one course.

Finally, I want to say thanks to Thomas Werge for introducing me to Melville's mysteries in 1972, when I was a sophomore at Notre Dame. And I cannot forget Sheila and all she has done.

PART ONE

Mardi:

"The Peculiar Theatre of the Romantic & Wonderful"

Making *Mardi's* Patchwork

> Weaker talents idealize; figures of capable imagination appropriate for themselves.
>
> Harold Bloom, *Anxiety of Influence*

As MOST MODERN readers recognize, *Typee* begins to chart the expansive perimeters of Melville's greatest work.[1] In deserting the *Dolly,* Tommo plunges into an alien but alluring geographical and psychological wilderness. Imprisoned within the Typee Valley, Tommo repeatedly confronts the limitations of his western point of view. Tommo "saw everything, but could comprehend nothing" (177). This nexus between visual clarity and interpretive ambiguity launches Melville into the deep. To see the world is by no means to read it from an authoritative perspective. In fact, Tommo is constrained most by his own system of cultural and semantic signification, the prison house of consciousness which provides unstable, inadequate points of investigative departure. Tommo's dilemma of sight without insight not only constitutes the epistemological center of *Typee* but also evokes the experiential condition that impels such later seekers as Taji, Babbalanja, Ishmael, Ahab, Pierre, Clarel, and Rolfe.

Upon completing *Typee,* Melville was at first understandably enthusiastic about reworking so productive a vein and more than happy to take up a task that would pay. Thus for the first and last time in his career, Melville penned a full-length sequel. In *Omoo* Melville's eye was fixed on extending his first success in terms that the public would applaud. The lurking epistemological dilemmas of *Typee* give way to virtually risk-free rebellion and lighthearted

3

escapade. D. H. Lawrence deftly encapsulates the nature of *Omoo*'s appeal—its ambience of lively humor and saturnalian adventure:

> *Omoo* is a fascinating book; picaresque, rascally, roving. Melville, as a bit of a beachcomber. The crazy ship *Julia* sails to Tahiti, and the mutinous crew are put ashore. Put in the Tahitian prison. It is good reading.
>
> Perhaps Melville is at his best, his happiest, in *Omoo*. For once he is really reckless. For once he takes life as it comes. For once he is the gallant rascally epicurean, eating the world like a snipe, dirt and all baked into one *bonne bouche*. (140)

Though renewing his assaults on the Christian missionaries, Melville avoids symbolic dark forests. As Lawrence suggests, *Omoo* is a literary romp, with Melville as lighthearted a writer as he would ever be.

Following the composition of his second book, Melville no longer viewed himself as a neophyte author, a publishing tyro grateful to have his words set into print. Writing the book solidified Melville's self-image as a literary artist, and in his correspondence with his publisher, John Murray, he clearly appreciated himself as such. On 29 January 1847, Melville wrote a boldly self-possessed letter concerning the recently completed narrative. Feeling no urge to puff his new work, Melville manifests a coy sense of self-assurance: "Of the book itself, of course, you will judge for yourself. So I will not say, what opinions of it have been given here by persons competent to judge of its merits as a work calculated for popular reading.— But I think you will find it a fitting successor to 'Typee'" (78). Melville goes on to offer a meticulous, legalistic set of instructions. Along with insisting that Murray not change the title, as Murray had with *Typee*, Melville demands that the publisher alter not a word except for routine proofreading: "I am desirous that the book shall appear in England, just as I send it: altho' there may be some minor errors—typographical—as the plates have been hurried in order to get them ready in time for the steamer. . . . However, there is no error, which any proof reader might not correct" (78). Melville took pains to assure Murray that *Omoo* had nothing in it that the publisher need worry about improving. If *Typee*'s amateur author, enthralled by the very fact of publication, was all too compliant in allowing the first American edition to suffer expurgation, then *Omoo*'s professional author, by now accustomed to the expectation of continued publication, was all too vigilant in preventing any edition from undergoing extra-authorial emendation.[2]

With the solidification of Melville's newfound vocational identity, however, came the problem of what to write next. In an 1851 letter to Hawthorne, Melville offered the paradigmatic articulation of the chronic unrest that drove him to see any achievement as mere prelude to the next venture. Fresh from writing *Moby-Dick*, Melville was on the hunt for larger quarry: "Lord, when shall we be done growing? As long as we have anything more to do, we have done nothing. So, now, let us add Moby Dick to our blessing, and step from that. Leviathan is not the biggest fish; — I have heard of Krakens" (213). *Omoo*, of course, was no *Moby-Dick;* but a similar process of disengagement took place after the second narrative's completion. Though Melville was growing increasingly impervious to his first narrative's rich symbolic power, the record indicates that he was fleeing not so much from *Typee* as from *Omoo*, especially as the second book assumed in his eyes the character of hackwork.[3] Composing *Omoo* was a self-educative process that, in the aftermath, led Melville to experience detachment from, and discontent with, the book.

Melville's devaluation of *Omoo* was as crucial to his artistic development as the composition of the narrative itself. In *Omoo*'s preface, written 28 January 1847, one day before the Murray letter cited above (Leyda 233), Melville dutifully identifies his range of subjects—the wildness of sailors in the South Pacific and the debasement of the Christianized Polynesians—citing his own wanderings as authority for his judgments. Melville adopts a matter-of-fact tone, at times even becoming defensive. He offers assorted disclaimers regarding his ridicule of natives and the absence of exact dates. Strangely, he warns the reader, "In no respect does the author make pretensions to philosophic research. In a familiar way, he has merely described what he has seen; and if reflections are occasionally indulged in, they are spontaneous, and such as would, very probably, suggest themselves to the most casual observer" (xv).[4] Melville makes modest claims, one feels, because he now sees *Omoo* as a modest book, a piece turned out in response to the exigencies—and euphoria—of his first publishing moment. *Omoo,* unsatisfying in its artistry, presented Melville with an exemplar of the sort of book he did not want to write. But the absence of "philosophic research" by no means makes *Omoo* a deficient book of its kind; indeed, such an absence contributes to its success. The reading public of Melville's day admired the adventurous exploits recounted in *Omoo* and shunned his expansive metaphysical narratives as aberrant, if not perverse, ventures.

The Murray letter and the Preface to *Omoo,* composed within a two-day period, initiated Melville's most crucial period of artistic transfiguration. But his first public (if oblique) act of critical self-definition finds issue in his review of J. Ross Browne's *Etchings of a Whaling Cruise.* Melville's announcement in that review of his affinity for the sea as the "peculiar theatre of the romantic and wonderful" generated the period of reading and writing that culminated in his wild attempt in *Mardi* to make the most out of his "philosophic research" (*Piazza Tales* 205).

By 2 February 1847 Melville had acquired J. Ross Browne's *Etchings of a Whaling Cruise* (1846), and he informed Evert A. Duyckinck, editor of the *Literary World,* that he would soon review it. *Etchings* tells the story of the author's naive initiation into the scurrilous world of autocratic seamanship. Like Melville's *Redburn,* Browne's narrator finds himself stripped of former pretensions to dignity; he must now prove himself in the brutal world of work. Along with providing a source and influence for parts of *Moby-Dick,* especially in Browne's depiction of the try-works and in his use of the "Town-Ho"-esque inset narrative called "Bob Grimley's Ghost," *Etchings* gives Melville the opportunity to meditate in print upon the relationship between the literatures of fact and imagination. As in his later review of Hawthorne's *Mosses from an Old Manse* (1850), Melville's review of *Etchings* discloses as much about Melville as it does about his ostensible subject. In what amounts to a literary manifesto, Melville articulates self-reflexive critical categories that both allow him to see his own achievement in *Typee* and *Omoo* through the matter-of-fact mirror of Browne's book and lead him to assert his allegiance to the "poetry of salt water" (*Piazza Tales* 205). Lamenting the demythification of sea yarns, Melville wrote:

> From time immemorial many fine things have been said and sung of the sea. And the days have been, when sailors were considered veritable mermen; and the ocean itself, as the peculiar theatre of the romantic and wonderful. But of late years there have been revealed so many plain, matter-of-fact details connected with nautical life that at the present day the poetry of salt water is very much on the wane. . . . Mr. J. Ross Browne's narrative tends still further to impair the charm with which poesy and fiction have invested the sea. It is a book of unvarnished facts. (205)

Though predominantly laudatory, Melville praises Browne for succeeding in a pedestrian endeavor.[5] To tell a remarkable story in a bland way is to avoid the exotic essence of the subject. However much Melville fictionalized the autobiographical centers of *Typee* and *Omoo*, he had already come to regard these works as mundane journalistic exercises. It irked Melville to be considered the romancer he truly was. Viewing himself through the filter of Browne, Melville takes the measure of his own accomplishment and finds it wanting. By packaging his materials within the conventions of the travel narrative, Browne stands guilty of deromanticizing the strange, the bizarre, the fantastic. By juxtaposing a narrative of "unvarnished facts" and the "poetry of salt water," Melville seems to be contemplating just what it might mean to revive the moribund poetics of sea life—to revel in, rather than domesticate, the exotic. In this review emerges the self-regarding critical complex that may well serve as the "germ" of *Mardi*.[6] The opening sequence of *Mardi*, for example, offers a literary critique of "long-drawn yarns

... [that are] Staler than stale ale" as well as a sweeping indictment of the routine life at sea (5). In jumping ship in midocean, the narrator, as actor and storyteller, repudiates the domain of quotidian experience in favor of plunging heart-and-head first into "the peculiar theatre of the romantic and wonderful."

In his review of *Etchings,* Melville not only offers a veiled manifesto, but he also demonstrates what will become a characteristic compositional practice in *Mardi*—that is, the appropriation, absorption, reinvention, and adaptation of his reading materials. Toward the end of the review, for example, Melville ostensibly paraphrases Browne's description of the chase and slaughter of a whale (*Etchings* 115–21). Nothing in Browne's treatment, however, approaches Melville's vibrant diction and imagistic sophistication. In what amounts to an act of literary upstaging, Melville uses Browne's scene and situation to frame his own reconstruction. Melville's reinvention achieves crescendo in "a mist, a crash,—a horrible blending of sounds and sights":

> We shudder at all realities of the career they will be entering upon. The long, dark, cold night-watches, which, month after month, they must battle out the best way they can;—the ship pitching and thumping against the bullying waves—every plank dripping—every jacket soaked. . . .
>
> Then the whaling part of the business.—My young friends, just fancy yourselves, for the first time in an open boat (so slight that three men might walk off with it) some 12 or 15 miles from your ship and about a hundred times as far from the nearest land, giving chase to one of the oleaginous monsters. . . . My young friends, just turn round and snatch a look at that whale—. There he goes, surging through the brine, which ripples about his vast head as if it were the bow of a ship. Believe me, it's quite as terrible as going into battle to a raw recruit.
>
> "Stand up and give it to him!" shrieks the boat-header at the steering-oar to the harpooneer in the bow. The latter drops his oar and snatches his "iron." It flies from his hands—and where are we then, my lovelies?—It's all a mist, a crash,—a horrible blending of

sounds and sights, as the agonized whale lashes the water around him into suds and vapor—dashes the boat aside, and at last rushes, madly, through the water, towing after him the half-filled craft which rocks from side to side while the disordered crew, clutch at the gunwale to avoid being tossed out. (*Piazza Tales* 209)

Melville thought so much of this passage that he recycled part of it into *Mardi*. In describing the wreck of the brig *Parki*, Melville's narrator depicts a storm that roars suddenly from the center of a calm: "It was all a din and a mist; a crashing of spars and of ropes; a horrible blending of sights and of sounds; as for an instant we seemed in the hot heart of the gale; our cordage, like harp-strings, shrieking above the fury of the blast" (117). Unlike the episode in the *Etchings* review, Jarl, the narrator in *Mardi*, and Samoa contend not with a wounded whale but a foundering ship. Melville personifies the *Parki* as "some stricken buffalo brought low to the plain, the brigantine's black hull, shaggy with sea-weed, lay panting on its flank in the foam."

Browne's *Etchings* stirred Melville's powers of criticism and invention; the review marks a significant moment in the evolution of his art. Not only does he declare allegiance to a genre of wild and fabulous fiction, but he also reinvents the very materials under examination. In this particular instance Melville reads a scene from Browne, reimagines and re-presents it in the review, then adapts selected elements of his reinvented material to an analogous scene in *Mardi*. This process of reinvention constitutes an instinctual and generative element of Melville's literary reflexes that was especially useful as his eclectic reading of 1847 and 1848 informed the composition of *Mardi*.

The making of *Mardi* looms as the most revolutionary event in Melville's creative life. For the first time he was trying to assimilate philosophical materials into an experimental piece of fiction. Pioneering scholars Merrell R. Davis and Merton M. Sealts, Jr., have done most to uncover the sources and influences that impinged upon Melville from the middle of 1847 through late 1848, when *Mardi* was completed.[7] Prior to this period, however, Melville was by no means ignorant of religious, literary, and ancient classics. His famous 1? June 1851 letter to Hawthorne—"Until I was twenty-five, I had no development at all. From my twenty-fifth year I date my life" (193)—must not be construed narrowly. Rather, it identifies Melville's self-conscious recognition of a recent intellectual flowering and his all-too-justifiable fears of exhaustion: "But I feel that I am now come to the inmost leaf of the bulb, and that shortly the flower must fall to the mould." Nor as a young boy was Melville a wild, untutored denizen of the woods. Instead, as David K. Titus demonstrates, he was exposed to a strongly classical curriculum at the Albany Academy School.[8] As Sealts suggests, Melville "possibly learned something of the old philosophers in 1830–1831 while enrolled in the Fourth Department . . . where the standard preparatory course included 'Universal, Grecian, Roman and English History'" ("Platonic Tradition" 280). In his father's well-stocked library, which was dispersed after Allan Sr.'s death, Melville probably had some acquaintance with Plutarch's *Lives*—which the narrator of *Redburn* mentions reading—and developed some familiarity with Shakespeare, Milton, and Coleridge, as well. The Bible, of course, was the primary text of his irregular schooling and, as Nathalia Wright has shown in *Melville's Use of the Bible,* provided a continuing resource for language, theme, image, and character.[9]

Following the completion of his first two books, Melville was itching to discover new intellectual worlds that could generate new artistic domains. Certainly it was not the reliance on reading that distinguishes the making of *Mardi.* In *Typee* and *Omoo,* Melville had supplemented and stimulated his memory and invention through copious, if somewhat random, research, most notably in travel narratives.[10] Melville continued this reading in preparation for his third book, examining such "unvarnished" narratives as Benjamin Morrell, *A Narrative of Four Voyages to the South Seas* (#372)[11]; Thomas Jefferson Jacobs, *Scenes, Incidents, and Adventures in the Pacific Ocean* (#293); Charles Darwin, *Journal of Researches. . . .during the Voyage of H. M. S. Beagle* (#175); Charles Wilkes, *United States Exploring Expedition, 1838–1842* (#532);

Jeremiah N. Reynolds, *Voyage of the United States Frigate Potomac* (#422).[12] What is most notable about this material is that it has so little to do with the substance and spirit of *Mardi*. More characteristic of *Mardi's* romantic departure, on the one hand, and Melville's pervasive preoccupation with intellectual play, on the other, were the two anomalous volumes Melville read in the spring and summer of 1847—the exotic La Motte-Fouque's *Undine, and Sintram* (#319) and a volume of extracts from Robert Burton's *The Anatomy of Melancholy* (#103).

By fall 1847, Melville was well into *Mardi* (Leyda 240). Undeniably, he had left pedestrian concerns behind. His 29 October 1847 letter to Murray reveals an artistic plan more in line with the literary leanings he expressed in his review of J. Ross Browne than with the matter-of-fact renderings of Morrell or Jacobs that Melville read. Melville testifies that the new South Sea adventure would be "continued from, tho' wholly independent of, 'Omoo' " (98). This letter must have left Murray feeling uncomfortable. Not only was Melville bargaining for better terms, but he provided a bewildering assessment of his plans: how could a new work be continued from yet wholly independent of its predecessor? More significantly, Murray had an utter distaste for fiction of any kind. The publisher even suspected that the name "Herman Melville" was part of a hoax got up by one or more professional writers. Murray found it hard to believe that a sailor could possess such erudition. And now here was this questionable presence dismissing his own earlier works as having "treated of subjects comparatively trite" (98). He now claimed to be working a "feild [sic] . . . troubled but with few & inconsiderable intruders . . . I only but begin, as it were, to feel my hand" (99).

Murray probably answered with a courteous, if puzzled, reply, questioning the market value of a third book in the same line. Nevertheless, to counter Melville's claims that he was being wooed by rival houses, Murray offered an advance. Melville's reply put Murray even more on the defensive. Melville's letter of 1 January 1848 reflects an "egotistical" act of economic and artistic self-assertion (102). Melville's demand that the advance be doubled might have been passed over as bartering among professionals. Melville, however, goes on to reject the generic limitations of *Typee* and *Omoo* in favor of the romantic aesthetic celebrated in the *Etchings* review, and in doing so, succeeds in describing exactly the sort of book that Murray would be least likely to publish: "[T]he plan I have pursued in the composition of the book now in hand, clothes the whole subject in new attractions & combines in one cluster all that is romantic, whimsical & poetic in Polynisia [sic]" (100). The project was indeed "a rathar [sic] bold aim" that sought to remake his Polynesian subject. He was preparing a "feild" on which to engage the shifting, elusive, alluring play of intellectual experimentation.

Melville pursued, it seems, the same grandiose scheme that later cashiers Pierre, the naive seeker after Truth. Melville was similarly inflamed by "the burning desire to deliver what he thought to be new, or at least miserably neglected Truth to the world" (*Pierre* 283). This is not to say that in 1848 Melville's sense of Truth was unified, simplistic, or discoverable: rather, Melville associated the word *Truth* with ostensible, or prospective, answers to irresolvable questions. He was not looking for the single key to resolve a particular conundrum but an entryway into an ideational domain of many rooms. Melville's inclination for using romantic fiction to pursue metaphysical Truth was but the form within which he made his commitment to an art based on mystery, dialectic, and irresolution. His search for a new artistic "feild" was the aesthetic response to his most expansive period of intellectual growth. As we will see below, *Mardi* depicts the explosive emergence of Melville's philosophical sensibility in its often unformulated or scattershot parts.

In composing *Mardi*, Melville infused the story of his questing narrator with ideational contexts gleaned and adapted from his ongoing and extensive "philosophic research." After his August 1847 marriage, Melville moved to New York City and there gained access to extensive library holdings, frequently borrowing books from Duyckinck and the New York Society Library, of which he became a member on 17 January 1848. In the following months, Melville was engaged in a reciprocal process of reading and writing. At times the writing echoed a source to the "length of ventriloquism" (Matthiessen 123).[13] More frequently, however, Melville reformed the prodigious materials that fed his invention.

During this period his reading betrayed an affinity divided between books of travel and books of romance and speculation. Narratives of the voyages of Bougainville (#85) and Barnard (#38) continued Melville's researches into the literature of exploration and discovery. Beginning in December 1847 and extending well into 1848, Melville pursued a self-developed curriculum that encouraged him to become a dedicated student of the "world of mind" (*Mardi* 557). Of a romantic and poetic cast were the Froissart *Ballads* (#158), the James Macpherson sagas of Ossian, especially the epic *Fingal* (#343), the plays of Shakespeare (#460a), Tegnér's translation of *Frithiof's Saga* (#500), Byron's *The Island* (Howard, *Melville*, 114), and Rabelais' *Gargantua and Pantagruel* (#417). According to Sealts, Melville was certainly reading Plato's *The Republic, Phaedrus,* and *Phaedo* ("Platonic Tradition" 279–81). But while Plato was, without question, the preeminent single influence on the philosophical themes of *Mardi* in particular and of Melville's career in general, Melville was also drawn at this time to a number of other writers whose work shares the protean, dialectical, and encyclopedic quality of Plato's dialogues. In the writings of Sir Thomas Browne (#89), Melville was fascinated by the shifting grounds of faith and doubt, especially as reflected in Browne's open-ended manner of address in *Religio Medici.* This speculative, dynamic, probing style informed Melville's lifelong penchant for setting into motion a complex play of competing voices. Browne's method provided a crucial model for Melville's attempt to translate the very process of thinking into the activity of writing. It must also be recognized that Melville encountered the same dialectical quality in the work of Coleridge (#154), Montaigne (#366), and Rabelais. With Plato in the lead, these writers essentially see the words on the page as an implicit or explicit dialogue in which language itself both releases and charts the permutations of thought.

Rhetoric and dialectic, therefore, assume high offices. To take the paradigmatic example from *The Republic,* a simple conversation between Glaucon and Socrates on a hot day leads to a magnificent inquiry into "nothing less than the rule of human life" (1:40). Among Melville's authors in this period, Plato was foremost in using dialectic to engage the multiple implications of any complex subject. In *The Republic,* for example, Socrates notes,

> Then dialectic, and dialectic alone, goes directly to the first prin-
> ciple and is the only science which does away with hypotheses in
> order to make her ground secure; the eye of the soul, which is
> literally buried in an outlandish slough, is by her gentle aid lifted
> upwards; and she uses as handmaids and helpers in the work of
> conversion, the sciences which we have been discussing. (1:293)

Melville was fascinated by this Platonic technique more because of its artistic versatility than its use as a conduit to a unified Truth. For Melville, dialectic—and the attraction of conversational metaphysics—has less to do with "the first principle" and more to do with "hypotheses." Melville's dialectic does not make one's ground secure; instead, it leads one directly *into* the "outlandish slough" that so exasperates his pondering heroes. Lacking the solace of Plato's absolute faith in the True and the Good, Melville applies the dialectical methodology of Socratic discourse to an open-ended inquiry into the mysteries of life. Like Thomas Browne, Melville loves the lure of mystery. Browne's declaration, "I love to lose my selfe in a mystery, to pursue my reason to an *o altitudo*" (14), finds expression in Melville's Babbalanja, *Mardi*'s philosophizing babbling angel.[14] In an early act of self-definition, Babbalanja describes himself as an improvisational seeker after "inscrutable" essences:

> I am intent upon the essence of things; the mystery that lieth be-
> yond . . . that which is beneath the seeming. . . . I probe the circle's
> center; I seek to evolve the inscrutable. . . . there is more to be

thought of than to be seen. There is a world of wonders insphered within the spontaneous consciousness; or, as old Bardianna hath it, a mystery within the obvious, yet an obviousness within the mystery. (352)

Babbalanja's chiasmus is no more revelatory than Keats' circular identification of Beauty and Truth.

Significantly, however, this passage demonstrates the syncretic quality of Melville's art. Though speaking in the manner of Thomas Browne through the Socratic technique, Babbalanja apparently adopts a Coleridge phrase—"spontaneous consciousness" (154)—from *Biographia Literaria* (#154). At issue here is not the matter of delineating specific influence. Rather, the presence of related multiple influences highlights the fusing power of Melville's imagination. He brought his own "spontaneous consciousness"—the mind moving in the process of thinking—to the task of reforming his reading materials. Like Bloom's figure "of capable imagination," Melville appropriated for himself without any concern for identifying his debts (*Anxiety of Influence* 5). If anything, he seemed intent on effacing the source of even his most obvious borrowings. Indeed, it is the "spontaneous consciousness" confronting life's mysteries—and the self then speaking of it—which attracted him most in other writers and which most reflects his own practice in *Mardi*. For Browne and Melville, the questions are all open; but for Browne, unlike Melville, protean creative dialectic subserves an unshakable religious orthodoxy. Despite this distinction, Melville admired the character of mind in Browne that could resolve denial into affirmation.[15] As Browne argues, it is an individual's responsibility to pay the "debt" of having reason. There is

> no *Sanctum sanctorum* in Philosophy: The world was made to be inhabited by beasts, but studied and contemplated by man: 'tis the debt of our reason wee owe unto God, and the homage wee pay for not being beasts; without this the world is still as though it had not been. . . . The wisedome of God receives small honour from those vulgar heads, that rudely stare about, and with a grosse rusticity

admire his workes; those highly magnifie him whose judicious en-
quiry into his acts, and deliberate research of his creatures, returne
the duty of a devout and learned admiration. (18)

Browne's attraction to pursuing elevated mysteries and
Coleridge's sense of the "spontaneous consciousness" dovetailed
with Melville's germinating sense of the truth-seeking possibilities
of literature. Melville's idiosyncratic and elusive Romanticism
emerges as his "deliberate research" into ancient, Renaissance, and
contemporary texts achieves eclectic reformulation. Indeed, assimi-
lation leads to translation. This book lover's search for unity and
integration finds puzzled expression in fictional delineations of
disunity and fragmentation; Melville thereby manifests the interplay between "reticulative" and "diasparactive" tendencies, the "two
consciousnesses, which define the Romantic mind—divided, but
confluent and necessary to each other's existence" (Lopez 94). Put
another way, Melville does not present a linear movement from
faith to doubt or doubt to faith but a dialectical process in which
faith is a concomitant to doubt. Melville demonstrates, as it were,
the dynamic activity of mediate, tenuous conclusions becoming
problematized and thus exciting new questions.

The predominantly unorthodox content of Melville's thinking
does not simply reflect the diasparactive nature of "De-Trans-
cendentalized" Romanticism but is actually closer to the skepticism of Montaigne and the iconoclasm of Robert Burton. While
Montaigne makes open-ended inquiries into a diverse array of subjects and Burton makes madly merry dissections of one controlling humor, both writers seemed to lead Melville "deeper and deeper
into himself" (*Mardi* 595). He found their probing intelligences
congenial to his own awakening unrest. Montaigne's articulation
of what Sir Thomas Browne calls the "flux and reflux" of experience reflects the spirit and substance of what Melville later refor-
mulates as "the pondering repose of If. . . . and Ifs eternally"
(*Moby-Dick* 406).[16] Montaigne writes, "Finally, there is no existence that is constant, either of our being or of that of objects. And

we, and our judgment, and all mortal things go on flowing and rolling unceasingly. Thus nothing certain can be established about one thing by another, both the judging and the judged being in continual change and motion" (455). Montaigne delineates the protean creative possibilities inherent in a destabilized self: "We are all patchwork, and so shapeless and diverse in composition that each bit, each moment, plays its own game" (244). These sentiments conform closely to a meditation by Babbalanja that also seems to be a reconstruction of the Heraclitean fragment that one "cannot step twice into the same river; for fresh waters are ever flowing in upon you" (Burnet 136). Such thoughts also resonate in Ecclesiastes, Seneca, and Sir Thomas Browne.

Certainly, this discussion is not meant to assert that Melville was responding to Coleridge more than Browne, or to one passage here more than to another passage there. What one finds when examining Melville's resources is an uncanny interplay of echoing themes. There is no point in pressing for the exclusivity of one source or influence over another. Rather, these multiple resources, all available to Melville at the same time and all apparently read with avidity, reinforce the very ideational substratum that he seems to have worked out on his own. Perhaps such passages struck resonant chords. Whether the encounter with such materials amounted to a discovery on Melville's part or confirmed the existence of a mysterious ur-complex, it becomes clear in *Mardi* that his passion for protean inquiry finds direct expression through representational characters, as in Plato and Rabelais; through the technique of direct address, as in Rabelais; and through the familiar, conversational, and speculative tones of Socrates, Montaigne, Browne, and Burton.

If Melville's intention was not to explain the totality of existence, as Plato for one sought to do, then Melville and his authors were at least trying to confront central questions of ontology and epistemology through active engagements with recognizable philosophical traditions. In every case, these writers drew on an eclectic, sometimes encyclopedic, range of materials. For example, Plato's dialogues routinely provide discussions of alternative points of view, as Socrates and his companions wrangle over the doctrines of Anaxagoras, Cadmus, Heraclitus, Parmenides, Pythagoras, and the Sophists. Browne's dazzling allusive technique transforms every page of *Religio Medici* into a debate among competing positions. Using the same allusive quality that characterizes the rapid-fire mental gyrations of Rabelais, Montaigne, and Burton, Browne makes graceful and precise reference to Plato, Aristotle, Pythagoras, Solomon, Epicurus, Seneca, Zoroaster, Moses, Cicero, Plutarch, and the Stoics, among many others. The allusive display in these writers and in Melville obliterates anachronism and has the effect of bringing the synoptic impress of various thinkers, schools, or movements directly into the debate in question. Melville's engagements with Plato, Rabelais, Montaigne, Burton, and Browne quickened his taste for philosophical discourse and encouraged his knack for wild invention. By fusing his newly discovered resources with the dictates of his liberated creative imagination, Melville thereby constructed a book that purports to depict an entire world, a geographical and metaphysical expanse that emerges, sometimes haltingly, with the author's germinating, spontaneous consciousness.

Because of the syncretic quality of Melville's imagination, the relatively few source and influence studies have concentrated on the localized function of incidental allusions. Such materials become most readily identifiable to the extent that they *have not* been transformed by Melville, though the more accomplished source studies of Sealts track the permutations of materials. One frequently confronts, then, the difference between the static and the organic, the unassimilated and the assimilated. For example, in an article on Melville's use of Proclus and "Neoplatonic Originals," Sealts argues that Melville merely lifted some abstruse terminology that he turned to satirical purposes in the Doxodox episode of *Mardi* (562–64). And in his monumental "Melville and the Platonic Tradition," Sealts juxtaposes parallel passages in order to render Melville's specific debts to Plato and Browne (282–87). William Braswell demonstrates how Melville directly copied from Seneca's *Morals By Way of Abstract.*

For the most part, however, Melville applied a method of intellectual appropriation that generates material which resonates
within an inclusive body of reading but which usually cannot be
identified from a particular passage or source. As Sealts conclusively demonstrates, Melville appropriates in *Mardi* the Platonic
theory of knowledge as recollection of truths which the soul discovered before birth (283). For example, Babbalanja explains,

> The catalogue of true thoughts is but small; they are ubiquitous;
> no man's property; and unspoken, or bruited, are the same. When
> we hear them, why seem they so natural, receiving our spontane-
> ous approval? why do we think we have heard them before? Be-
> cause they but reiterate ourselves; they were in us, before we were
> born. The truest poets are but mouth-pieces; and some men are
> duplicates of each other; I see myself in Bardianna. (397)

Sealts argues that Melville imbibed this liberating notion from
Thomas Browne, who derived it from Plato, probably in the *Phaedo*.
Browne writes,

> [F]or as though there were a *Metempsuchosis*, and the soule of one
> man passed into another, opinions doe finde after certaine revo-
> lutions, men and mindes like those that first begat them. To see
> our selves again wee neede not looke for *Platoes* yeare, every man
> is not onely himselfe; there have beene many *Diogenes*, and as many
> *Tymons*, though but few of that name; men are lived over againe;
> the world is now as it was in ages past; there was none then, but
> there hath been some one since that parallels him, and is, as it
> were, his revived selfe. (12)[17]

In discussing the practice of Lombardo, the epic poet and author
of *Koztanza*, Babbalanja combines the notion of ideational
metempsychosis *and* spontaneous discovery: "Of ourselves, and
in ourselves, we originate nothing. When Lombardo set about his
work, he knew not what it would become. He did not build himself in with plans; he wrote right on; and so doing, got deeper and

deeper into himself" (595). Obviously, Lombardo and his *Koztanza* provide self-reflexive versions of Melville and his book. What is not so apparent is that Melville formulates his aesthetic by drawing from and recasting parallel materials from his reading. Melville's own creative borrowings reflect the practices of earlier thinkers.[18]

By recognizing that all great thinkers draw from the same eternal source, Melville further legitimates the creative interplay between reading and writing. Babbalanja characterizes the artistic impulse as an autonomous principle of psychological necessity in which the buried thoughts of antiquity are resurrected through the self-driven creative act:

> And ere Necessity plunged spur and rowel into [Lombardo], he knew not his own paces. *That* churned him into consciousness; and brought ambition, ere then dormant, seething to the top, till he trembled at himself. No mailed hand lifted up against a traveler in woods, can so appall, as we ourselves. We are full of ghosts and spirits; we are as grave-yards full of buried dead, that start to life before us. And all our dead sires, verily, are in us; *that* is their immortality. From sire to son, we go on multiplying corpses in ourselves; for all of which, are resurrections. Every thought's a soul of some past poet, hero, sage. We are fuller than a city. (593–94, Melville's emphasis)

One builds a work of art not by following prescribed plans but by opening oneself to the buried forces. In order to experience the intuitional sources of creativity, the writer must eschew the rational limits of cognition. In a seemingly paradoxical way, one comes to "have created the creative" only by recovering what has been true—that is, hidden within the essential self—all along (595). The writer indeed is "not his own master." He is instead "a mere amanuensis writing by dictation. . . . [I]t was a sort of sleep-walking of the mind" (596). Melville was fascinated by the prospect of an abiding constancy in the deep structures of human consciousness that can only be discovered by intuition—an intuition that becomes expressed through the consequential activity of spontaneous creation. Paradoxically, Melville combines the romantic notion of art as unfolding process with a classicist sense that Truth is immutable, though not readily discoverable. Thus, ur-structures of human nature and the problematical notion of an abiding, possibly immanent, transcendent domain become expressed within an open-ended, dialectical, aesthetic process.

It must be emphasized that Melville did not necessarily *discover* in Plato or Browne this nexus between a commonalty of thought and art as process. Such notions seem to be part of Melville's sensibility as early as *Typee,* appearing explicitly through Tommo's discussion of the natural law that infuses the hearts of those ostensibly virtuous cannibals (200–202), and implicitly through Tommo's persistent epistemological uncertainty.[19] Nor was the concept of a genetic idea pool merely reinforced in Melville by his reading of Plato and Browne, alone. Other Renaissance and Romantic writers draw similar conclusions. Significantly, in the works of Burton and Coleridge, one finds an arresting cohesion on this point. Burton, for example, comically extends the concept of innate ideas into a principle of creative appropriation that seems to reflect, if not inform, Melville's practice:

> As a good house-wife out of divers fleeces weaves one piece of cloth, a bee gathers wax and honey out of many flowers, and makes a new bundle of all . . . I have laboriously collected this Cento out of divers Writers, and that without injury. . . . I have borrowed, not stolen. . . . The matter is theirs most part, and yet mine, whence it is taken appears (which Seneca approves), yet it appears as something different from what 'tis taken from; which nature doth with the aliment of our bodies, incorporate, digest, assimulate, I do dispose of what I take. (19–20)

To describe his own process of creative refashioning, Burton links homespun wit, classical allusion, and excremental imagery. Old thoughts become one's own when woven into one's own shape and size. It is the writer's context that makes such resources "mine." Context is all. Shortly thereafter, Burton offers a statement that could just as easily appear in Browne's *Religio Medici:* "We can say nothing but what hath been said, the composition and method is ours only, & shows a Scholar" (20).

A generative work that provided a conduit from German to American Romantics, Coleridge's *Biographia Literaria* presents the "primary imagination" as a mode of apprehension that functions "as a repetition in the finite mind of the eternal act of creation in the infinite I AM" (190).[20] But as Coleridge is quick to add, human creation does not exist in a vacuum; thus his "secondary Imagination" functions to rework the author's elemental materials: "It dissolves, diffuses, dissipates, in order to recreate; or where this process is rendered impossible, yet still at all events it struggles to idealize and to unify." Coleridge's description of creative consciousness offers at least an instructive paradigm of Melville's own attempts to synthesize disparate reading materials into an imaginative act that could truly be his own. Melville diffuses in order to fuse, discovers in order to recover, appropriates in order to recreate.

Melville's encounters with the works of Plato, Rabelais, Montaigne, Burton, Browne, and Coleridge contributed intellectual depth to the method Melville used in *Typee* and *Omoo* by giving him confidence to extend his mind within the elastic framework provided by his most admired teachers. Thus the activity of reading clarified and vindicated Melville's innately held beliefs; at the same time, it released him into a world of his own making, the very world in which his discoveries take place. The reading of Coleridge, then, would not only have been stimulating on its own terms, but it would also have reiterated the seminal Platonic theory of knowledge as recollection, a theory that also resonates in Burton and Browne. For Coleridge as well, the truth had been vocalized through numerous mouthpieces. Just as Coleridge says of his debt to Kant, "I regard truth as a divine ventriloquist: I care not from whose mouth the sounds are supposed to proceed, if only the words are audible and intelligible" (97), Melville would likewise have found liberating Coleridge's statement, "To admire on principle, is the only way to imitate without loss of originality" (55). Thus Melville found in his reading of early 1848 not only a creative primer but a symphony of echoes that corroborated his sense that the making of art emanated from a fusion of direct experience and acquired knowledge.

The nature of Melville's responses to his reading must initially be approached through influence study, but the primary method of influence study—the juxtaposition of related passages—must give way to a recognition of Melville's deeply rooted process of creative rehabilitation—"rehabilitation" because Melville's methods of research and composition in *Mardi* are critical extensions and intensifications of the instinctual method of bookmaking that he evolved in *Typee*. From its inception, Melville's literary activity was partly generated from his interaction with other books. At issue in *Mardi* is not so much the presence of "divine" or plagiaristic ventriloquism (Coleridge 97) so much as Melville's peculiar creative alchemy. By reading this host of encyclopedic writers, Melville was encouraged to imitate on principle, thereby convincing himself that he could create from these materials without loss of originality.

The "Time and Temples" chapter of *Mardi* distills what might be taken for the applied—or at least propounded—theory of artistic creation generated by the resource materials just examined. In *Mardi* three digressive chapters—"Time and Temples," "Faith and Knowledge," and "Dreams"—constitute detached centers of reflexivity, their digressions interrupting the diachronic progression of the narrative. Divorced from the ongoing action, these chapters provide summary assays on questions that the narrative sporadically addresses. "Time and Temples" examines the nature of the creative process; "Faith and Knowledge" explores the paradoxical relation of knowledge of the self to knowledge of the world; "Dreams" offers a self-portrait of the obsessed, exhausted, and imprisoned narrator, Taji, after the events of *Mardi* have ended. Unlike the rest of *Mardi*, these synchronous digressions are present-tense narrations that occur in the compositional moment and comment on the diachronic narrative.

In "Time and Temples" Taji begins his disquisition on the creative process by presenting an allusive collage of those builders who were able to construct prodigious temples that were "very long in erecting" (228). To forge structures that will endure throughout time, the builders must use ancient materials. As Taji points out, the elemental materials necessarily predate the building itself:

> For to make an eternity, we must build with eternities; whence, the vanity of the cry for any thing alike durable and new; and the folly of the reproach—Your granite hath come from the old-fashioned hills. For we are not gods and creators; and the controversialists have debated, whether indeed the All-Plastic Power itself can do more than mold. In all the universe is but one original; and the very suns must to their source for their fire; and we Prometheuses must to them for ours; which, when had, only perpetual Vestal tending will keep alive. (228–29)

Like the builder who must take granite from hills, Melville molds this passage from a wealth of potential sources. Sealts links elements of "Time and Temples" with Plato's *Timaeus,* where Socrates speaks of "the Plastic Artificer" ("Platonic Tradition" 294). The "All-Plastic Power" finds resonations in Coleridge and Goethe, while the "one original" suggests Plotinus' theory of the universe as constituting the diffusion through space of a once unified, now exploding, primary particle.

For Taji, then, the building of monuments offers an analog for the literary artist in general and the author of *Mardi* in particular. "Time and Temples" presents the previously discussed notion that poetic invention consists of the refiguration of preexisting literary materials. Melville was drawn to authors who do not simply evoke or allude to tradition but who actually subsume and transform the words of their predecessors. They build anew with ancient materials, most of which have reference to one original form. The artist, whether builder or writer, seeks to make a long-lasting structure out of stone or sign. *Time* constitutes the temporal continuum within which the elements of stone or language are transfigured by the principles of fire or mind. Thus the human artist becomes a Prometheus whose soul seeks expression in a "fine firm fabric" (229). As Taji insists, the longevity of the finished monument depends directly on the gestation of the artistic process: "And that which long endures full-fledged, must have long lain in the germ" (228). In "Time and Temples" Taji emphasizes stone rather than fire—"But let us back from fire to stone" (229)—and artistic product rather than artistic process, though in both cases the chapter depends on their reciprocity. The emphasis on "stone" is essentially an emphasis on time or duration. Melville uses an extended catalog of at least thirty negatives in order to insist that *no* human or natural structure was "raised in a day": "Nero's House of Gold was not raised in a day. . . . Nor was Virginia's Natural Bridge worn under in a year" (229). The catalog concludes with a celebration of the preeminence of the literary over the architectural: "Nor were the parts of the great Iliad put together in haste; though old Homer's temple shall lift up its dome, when St. Peter's is a legend" (229).

The progression from stone monument to literary monument leads Taji to a celebration of the eternal existence of the human soul and the deity. "Time and Temples" suggests that all human invention is, to paraphrase Coleridge, but the imitation of the divine act of creation within time. Longevity, however extensive, can never begin to be measured in relation to the eternal: "[S]o, in incident, not in essence, may the Infinite himself be not less than more infinite now, than when old Aldebaran rolled forth from his hand" (230). In "Time and Temples" Melville dissolves the distinction between the temporal and the eternal, thus indicating the possibility of transfer from one world to the next. Using a Platonic symbol, a figure from *Phaedrus*, Melville depicts the soul's transcendence and, by extension, the artist's creative transcendence of space, time, and matter: "Thus deeper and deeper into Time's endless tunnel, does the winged soul, like a night-hawk, wend her wild way; and finds eternities before and behind; and her last limit is her everlasting beginning" (230).[21] The artist-maker, figured as the "winged soul," flies beyond the limitations of material existence. Melville images an endless process of beginning that transcends the contextual entanglements of dialectic.

Though abstruse and, like the other digressions, betraying a sense of compositional frenzy, "Time and Temples" provides a gloss on some of the ideas about literary and philosophical invention that Melville was contemplating while composing *Mardi*. This chapter accentuates the process of creative self-fashioning on which Melville embarked in early 1847. Here Melville practices the theory of creative appropriation, while at the same time indicating how the artist's soul, like the Platonic nighthawk, might actually achieve transcendence. At the very least, this chapter suggests how Melville saw the work of art as the form within which ultimate questions could be propounded. "Time and Temples" depicts two forms of artistic activity: the Promethean builder forging durable structures from ancient materials becomes transformed into the soul bird on the wing. Taken together, these figures reflect the seminal conflict in Melville's work between the temporal and the eternal. Indeed, the dichotomy between the phenomenal and the noumenal and this dichotomy's concomitant formulation in conflicts between the many and the one, and between becoming and being, constitute the central philosophical complex animating Melville's writing. "Time and Temples" occupies a position in Melville's work similar to that which "The Artist of the Beautiful" occupies in Nathaniel Hawthorne's. For one moment at least, both writers affirm the successful artist's eventual transcendence. Melville's moment, however, is fleeting. Though the nighthawk soars into eternity, in the next paragraph the narrator calls the soul back: "But sent over the broad flooded sphere, even Noah's dove came back, and perched on his hand. So comes back my spirit to me, and folds up her wings" (230). Melville is more interested in the complex fusion of temporal and eternal realms than he is in resting with transcendence. In fact, the action of *Mardi* insistently places the quotidian self in frustrated, futile pursuit of absolute felicity. The direct entanglement of human quester and ideal form takes place only insofar as the narrator fabricates a tenuous and problematic deific identity. For Taji to "palm myself off as a god" is to locate himself at the very juncture between the phenomenal and the noumenal, the physical and the metaphysical (176).

2

Narrative Self-Fashioning and the Play of Possibility

And though essaying but a sportive sail, I was driven from my course, by a blast resistless.

—Mardi

As HE "wrote right on; and so doing, got deeper and deeper into himself" (*Mardi* 595), Melville became more confident of his purpose and less tolerant of any impingement on his designs. Irked by Murray's continuing suspicion that Herman Melville was "an imposter shade" and fixed on the right "determinations" of his self-vaunted instinct, Melville informed Murray of a design to be "blunt." Melville's third work would "in downright earnest [be] a 'Romance of Polynisian Adventure'—But why this? The truth is, Sir, that the reiterated imputation of being a romancer in disguise has at last pricked me into a resolution to show those who may take any interest in the matter, that a *real* romance of mine is no Typee or Omoo, & is made of different stuff altogether" (*Correspondence* 105–06, Melville's emphasis). Melville was intent upon engaging "that play of freedom & invention accorded only to the Romancer & poet," thereby mining Polynesia's "rich poetical material." In explaining his artistic evolution, Melville registered "invincible distaste" for his "narrative of *facts*":

Well: proceeding in my narrative of *facts* I began to feel an invincible distaste for the same; & a longing to plume my pinions for a flight, & felt irked, cramped & fettered by plodding along with dull common places. . . . My romance I assure you is no dish water nor its model borrowed from the Circulating Library. . . . It opens

27

like a true narrative ... & the romance & poetry of the thing thence grow continually, till it becomes a story wild enough I assure you & with a meaning too. (106)[1]

Even in this "blunt" manifesto, Melville fails to do justice to the extremity of *Mardi*'s departure. It does not, for example, open like a "true narrative." Rather, from the earliest chapters, Melville's "play of freedom & invention" issues in the narrator's wild, rhapsodic speculations. From the outset the overreaching philosophical self appears full-blown: the narrator takes center stage, decries his boredom, and vents his disgust with the everyday commonplace actualities of ship and crew. The way of the *Arcturion* was "a weary one ... Never before had the ocean appeared so monotonous; thank fate, never since" (4). Because of his education, the narrator is estranged from the crew; his "occasional polysyllable ... [and] remote, unguarded allusions to Belles-Lettres affairs" (14) make the narrator a learned outcast. Accepting his isolation, he repays the favor by dismissing the "flat repetitions of long-drawn yarns. ... Staler than stale ale." He eschews "Bill Marvel's stories" and "Ned Ballad's songs" (5). Melville projects his own impatience with high-sea adventure yarns into a narrator who distinctly defines his aspirations in terms of intellectual fulfillment. If Tommo in *Typee* deserts the *Dolly* because his belly is not satisfied, then the narrator of *Mardi* resolves to desert the *Arcturion* because his mind is malnourished. Even the captain, a fine nautical man in all respects, cannot "talk sentiment or philosophy." Nor can his shipmates "page [him] a quotation from Burton on Blue Devils" (5). No one on board is "precisely to [his] mind" (4).

Like Ahab in *Moby-Dick*, the narrator redefines the purpose of the voyage. While not heaped and tasked by the inscrutable malignity of brute forces, the narrator of *Mardi* is impelled by ennui to figure himself as an explorer on the high seas of consciousness and erudition. In a "willful mood" (7) he climbs the masthead, and in a passage that prefigures Ishmael's masthead reverie in *Moby-Dick,* the narrator divorces himself from the day-to-day concerns of life at sea. If "The Mast-Head" examines the death-dealing incompatibility between workaday actuality and mystical meditation, especially as the slip of an inch can bring one to plunge into "Descartian vortices" (*Moby-Dick* 158–59), then the "Foot-in-Stirrup" chapter of *Mardi* examines the exhilarating attraction of the mystical world of mind, especially insofar as the visionary lure provides an experiential displacement of the same old song of social contexts. In his frenzied vision, the narrator spins the materials of the ensuing fiction. His romantic vision counterpoints the forecastle yarns. The source of the succeeding tale is to be found more in mind than in extrinsic fact. In craving a world of expansive consciousness, he imagines a "dream-land" (*Mardi* 7) located on the magical margins of mind. Somewhere to the west, "loosely laid down upon the charts" (*Mardi* 7), this imaginary space displaces his present tedium. He imagines what the ship could never give him—a new, unexplored world exotic enough to engage, if not satisfy, his voracious appetite for the unknown.

Significantly, this visionary world ranges into view through a series of exotic images:

> In the distance what visions were spread! The entire western horizon high piled with gold and crimson clouds; airy arches, domes, and minarets; as if the yellow, Moorish sun were setting behind some vast Alhambra. Vistas seemed leading to worlds beyond. To and fro, and all over the towers of this Nineveh in the sky, flew troops of birds. Watching them long, one crossed my sight, flew through a low arch, and was lost to view. My spirit must have sailed in with it; for directly, as in a trance, came upon me the cadence of mild billows laving a beach of shells, the waving of boughs, and the voices of maidens, and the lulled beatings of my own dissolved heart, all blended together. (7–8)

As in the "Time and Temples" chapter, the moment of imagined transcendence is depicted through the Platonic image of a bird. Here the "low arch" through which the bird flies separates two competing experiential realms and two competing forms of narrative. The narrator's spirit soars with the bird, creating the spiritual imperative that will lead the body to follow. As in Rabelais's travelogue, one gets the sense in *Mardi* that new worlds are being spun out of the mind. Indeed, the narrator's visionary trance manifests how *ideas* determine not merely the exotic nature of place but the perimeters of behavior. Here Melville presents the creative moment of transfer. The quotidian is left behind, and the narrator figuratively loses hold, though he does not tumble into the Cartesian swirl but instead lifts into poetic rapture. For the narrator, the desire for philosophic vent cannot be dissociated from the mind-moving medium of poetic invention. What is most crucial here—and what will serve Melville in multiple ways not only in *Mardi* but in *Moby-Dick, Pierre, The Confidence-Man,* and *Clarel*—is the self-defining and self-realizing reach of the narrator's play of mind. His visionary experience both displaces the quotidian and imbues him with the psychological authority to pursue a life dedicated to his adventurous muse. The power of intuition makes pictures in the seer's mind. In this masthead moment, such visionary manifestations are peculiarly without foundation. Nevertheless, the vision supplies the narrator's imperative to desert, though each momentous step away from historical context creates its own ironic entanglement: he leaves a doomed ship but feels guilt; later he rescues the mysterious maiden Yillah but commits murder to do so; and, subsequently, Yillah's disappearance binds him as both pursuer and pursued.

The lesson deriving from the narrator's vision is clear: the imperatives of the starved philosophical self can only be answered by the narrator's attempt to estrange himself from his personal, cultural, and historical past. Even though this leap into romance leads frequently to the spinning out of tedious abstractions, Melville's great discovery in *Mardi* resides in the fictional possibilities inherent in the dramatization of ideas. Melville's career-long alternating expression or repression of this urge becomes a means for measuring his standing with the book-buying public. What Melville called *Mardi*'s "metaphysical ingredients (for want of a better term)" did in fact repel his audience. This was followed by his conscious, though not complete, suppression of "metaphysics ... [and] conic-sections" in favor of "cakes & ale" in *Redburn,* which allowed him to recapture the confidence of reviewers and readers (*Correspondence* 131–32). Similarly, following the commercial disaster of *Pierre,* Melville's success as, for the most part, an anonymous author in the relatively lucrative periodical market derived from his ability to contain his materials within the acceptable generic confines of sketch and tale.[2] In *Mardi,* Melville had trouble with his readers largely because he was trying to invent his own form: he sought to adapt the conventions of the exotic romantic voyage of search and discovery to the cause of metaphysical improvisation and satirical anatomy. In the resulting hybrid form—a compendium of competing if not self-defeating intentions—action and character were either subservient to, or representations of, the narrator's effusive, unfolding consciousness. *Mardi's* action essentially provides the excuse or point of departure for presenting the narrator's *experience* of his own consciousness, a concern that Melville successfully balances throughout *Moby-Dick,* especially in Ishmael's presentation of the cetology material as basis for analogy and symbol.

The early chapters of *Mardi* most fully depict the narrator's experience of consciousness as he confronts extreme physical situations. On the masthead, his elevated perspective and isolation lead him to mystical visions. Twice the narrator must contend with an oppressive meteorological condition, a calm at sea. While the narrator is still on the *Arcturion,* the calm induces a wildly skeptical flurry of thought; later adrift with Jarl in an open boat, the narrator meditates briefly on the relationship between objective and subjective frames of reference. As with the scene on the masthead, Melville uses these set pieces to explore the metaphysical implications of the narrator's circumstance. Each scene demonstrates the presentation of actions that exist solely to showcase the narrator's cogitations. Melville thus elevates the flux of consciousness itself to a principle of narrative self-fashioning; these moments offer extensions of his earlier preoccupation with Tommo's limitations of perspective in *Typee,* and they point ahead to Ishmael's inquisitive excursions in *Moby-Dick* and to the narrator's verbal gymnastics in *The Confidence-Man.*

A chapter in *Mardi*, "A Calm," succinctly dramatizes the fusion of the narrator's intellectual aspiration and the author's aesthetic experimentation. The dullness of workaday life at sea (and for Melville the banality of the travel narrative) stand in direct opposition to the possibilities for pursuing wild, speculative vistas (and for Melville the profundity of writing Truth). A calm at sea provides the quintessential intensification of all that the narrator most abhors. Its vacuity diametrically opposes his intellectual ferment. The calm appears as a static meteorological counterpoint to the involuted world of psychological flux. The physical locale ironically stirs a whirl of thought; the calm "unsettles his mind; tempts him to recant his belief in the eternal fitness of things; in short, almost makes an infidel of him" (9). In this suspended state, the narrator grows "madly skeptical" and begins to doubt his senses. In the face of the blank sea, he thinks of "Priestley on Necessity" and seeks the solace of philosophical determinism. Such a posture, however, is of no avail to the skeptic. He knows that the thing to do is to endure the calm; but he cannot bring himself to accept such a compromise. Indeed, the play of mind feeds on itself, frustrating the thinker with repeated admissions of his unacceptable impotence. This scene presents the first self-conscious expression in Melville's work of the tangled relationship between skepticism and stoicism, on the one hand, and the opposing psychological imperative to pursue a condition of absolute felicity, on the other. The calm functions as a foil for Melville to engage the complex he most wishes to consider: the metaphysical implication of an oppressive moment.

The second "trying-out" of the calm extends Melville's interest with placing his center of narrative consciousness in the experiential context of sheer vacancy and existential blankness. After deserting the ship, the narrator and Jarl become caught in the doldrums, an area conspicuously missing what Sir Thomas Browne calls "flux and reflux," the ebb and flow of process (20, 78–79). Here the natural world lacks gradation, distinction, dynamism: "Every thing was fused into the calm: sky, air, water, and all. Not a fish was to be seen. The silence was that of a vacuum. No vitality lurked in the air. And this inert blending and brooding of all things seemed gray chaos in conception" (48). Figuratively, the calm threatens the life of the intellect. Melville's fusion of fiction and philosophy depends not on "inert blending" but on an active interpenetration of extrinsic and cognitive realms. And that is what the narrator attempts as the tale develops: he takes an experiential dead end and brings it to intellectual life. The calm may originally be "gray chaos in conception," but the thinking mind re-forms such recalcitrant material and uses it to focus *Mardi*'s central concern: the revelation of the thinking mind, now in solipsistic isolation, later in a dialogue of projected intellectual abstractions.

What animates these two scenes, and provides unity not of execution but of purpose, is Melville's commitment to rendering the active play of intelligence. The narrating mind comes to know itself in the act of forging relationships that seem true or valid in the moment. In *Typee* such a process is implicit in Tommo's engagement with epistemological quandaries; the mystery surrounding Tommo's condition provides the basis of action and meditation. In *Mardi* the mind's very process of thinking constitutes the generative force of action. In *Mardi*'s paradigmatic scenes, the narrator's experience of a particular phenomenon suggests possibilities for thought, possibilities for reaction. As the scene changes, the thinker's very engagement with a new set of circumstances displaces the previous moment of insight. With these scenes on the calm, Melville has it both ways, for the encounter with nothingness is in itself an experience that stirs thought. Though there is a danger that the calm, by its very inertness, may never deliver the thinker to the next moment, a calm at sea partakes of an encompassing meteorological process and will eventually pass.

Nevertheless, Melville's interest in dramatizing the narrator's response to vacancy highlights the symbiotic relationship between phenomena and consciousness, with the preeminent focus on reaction over action. Later in the narrative, Taji's very phrase, "the world of mind" (557), suggests what has been implicitly true all along: there exists a vital link between object and subject, between the world of phenomena and the realm of perception.[5] Behind this strategy is the desire to make knowledge of the self through knowledge of the world the locus of interest. At stake here is Melville's ongoing attempt, first fully dramatized in *Mardi*, to present as an explicit fictional subject the protean qualities of human consciousness, with the distinct expectation that the formulation of one moment might be undone by the next. Melville's absolutists—among them Taji, Ahab, Pierre, Celio, Mortmain, Ungar, and possibly, Vere—become dangerous precisely because they refuse to adjust, or reformulate, the relation of subject to the changing world of objects. For Taji to insist that he must regain Yillah or for Ahab to insist that the White Whale has one fixed signification is for both men to preempt the potential validity of future experiences and future perceptions. Their kind of consciousness can be characterized as "inert blending" (*Mardi* 48). They eschew the challenge of what Redburn calls "a moving world" (157), in which the "flux and reflux" of experience presents repeated possibilities for reseeing the world and reconstituting the self. In *Mardi* the two depictions of the calm at sea, then, allow Melville to explore the reciprocity between phenomena and epistemology, brute fact and the pursuit of self-knowledge. The treatments of the calm are, in fact, early renderings of the epistemological centers of *Moby-Dick*—the "story of Narcissus" and "The Doubloon" chapter (5, 430–35). Any perception is one version of a multitude of self-reflecting configurations. The horror is that no further reading may be possible unless the world resumes its protean condition.

Early in *Mardi*, then, Melville was experimenting with developing techniques that would allow him to marry fiction and metaphysics. As we have seen, the narrator's trance on the masthead and the two renderings of a calm provide set pieces in which psychological reaction takes precedence over the complexities of the action itself. In fact, these scenes are bereft of dramatic activity, for instead Melville focuses on the mind's capacity to create meaning or, better yet, to create the speculative form within which meaning takes shape. Central is the critical intelligence responding to impressions from the human eye. For Melville the world is alive with teasing, though shifting and perhaps unknowable, signification;

without the assurance of transcendental beneficence, the perceiver is loosed into a realm of perceptual "flux and reflux."

The outgrowth of using narrative as a vehicle for rendering consciousness leads Melville to make consciousness itself the source of dialectic. In the early sequences of *Mardi*, Melville develops two distinctly identifiable narrative voices that stand in dialectical tension. The narrator oscillates between speaking as a fraternal genialist and a solipsistic isolationist. Prior to the narrator's loss of Yillah, both voices appear intermittently. A moment's mood tends to determine one's perceptions; one's reading subsequently informs behavior. While the narrator's fraternal strain, which links him to communal life in a historical and social context, appears in his highly selective federation with Jarl, his solipsistic strain, which reflects anticommunal life in an ahistorical absolutistic context, becomes manifest in his bitter estrangement from ship life.

The narrator's genial voice celebrates the unifying nature of humor and verbal play. At one point the narrator, gushing effusively over the amiable side of a shark, brings his meditation to a joyous close: "Now hate is a thankless thing. So, let us only hate hatred; and once give love play, we will fall in love with a unicorn" (41). The narrator also engages in a whimsical display of learning. Commenting on Jarl's grave demeanor, the narrator reflects, "But how account for the Skyeman's gravity? Surely, it was based upon no philosophic taciturnity; he was nothing of an idealist; an aerial architect; a constructor of flying buttresses" (36). Later the narrator forces a comparison between Jarl and Bishop Berkeley, thereby debunking an idealist who also keeps a matter-of-fact eye on the main chance: "[H]onest Jarl was nevertheless exceedingly downright and practical in all hints and proceedings concerning [the ship]. Wherein, he resembled my Right Reverend friend, Bishop Berkeley—truly, one of your lords spiritual—who, metaphysically speaking, holding all objects to be mere optical delusions, was, notwithstanding, extremely matter-of-fact in all matters touching matter itself" (63).

The narrator is at other times given to visionary and self-isolating fulminations. Related to his solipsism is the desire to assert his will and thereby dominate others. He takes control of the *Parki* and turns Jarl, Samoa, and Annatoo into subservient crew members. He speaks in the

> mild, firm tone of a superior; being anxious, at once to assume the unquestioned supremacy. . . . Our course determined, and the command of the vessel tacitly yielded up to myself, the next thing done was to put every thing in order. . . . I felt no little importance upon thus assuming for the first time in my life, the command of a vessel at sea. The novel circumstances of the case only augmented this feeling . . . I was owner, as well as commander of the craft I sailed. (96–97)

In *Mardi*, Melville does not maintain anything approaching consistency of voice. Instead, these conflicting voices help him to extend the possibilities of fictional form, especially as the genialist or the solipsist come to suggest metaphysical qualities of consciousness. Exemplifying this are two parallel narrative excursions—articulations of the genialist and the solipsist, respectively—each dealing with states of existence outside the diachronic movement of the narrative. In each instance, the narrator employs the allusive catalog to show his relationship to the great thinkers of the past.[4] In both cases Melville uses the present tense to separate his materials from the ongoing retrospective narrative. In the chapter "A King for a Comrade," the narrator presents a vision of a congenial afterlife. The contrasting case occurs in the "Dreams" chapter, where the solipsistic narrator, by now named Taji, suffers miserably in a prison. The scene could only take place sometime after the narrative concludes with Taji being chased "over an endless sea" (654).

In a fascinating passage in "A King for a Comrade," which echoes elements of style and theme in *Religio Medici*, the genial narrator seeks to merge (rather than dissociate) the immediate time-bound world of sense experience with the exotic, rhapsodic world of transcendent thought. Rather than trying to escape the commonplace, the narrator takes the strange and invests it with the homely and familiar. In effect he personalizes an imagined afterlife.[5] The narrator's meditation on Jarl's ancestry and the interrelationship among mortals culminates with a densely allusive vision of a federated and congenial afterlife, replete with cameo appearances by many of the great dead:

> All of us have monarchs and sages for kinsmen; nay, angels and archangels for cousins. . . . Thus all generations are blended: and heaven and earth of one kin. . . . All things form but one whole; the universe a Judea, and God Jehovah its head. Then no more let us start with affright. In a theocracy, what is to fear? . . . No custom is strange; no creed is absurd; no foe, but who will in the end prove a friend. In heaven, at last, our good, old, white-haired father Adam will greet all alike, and sociality forever prevail. Christian shall join hands between Gentile and Jew; grim Dante forget his Infernos, and shake sides with fat Rabelais; and monk Luther, over a flagon of old nectar, talk over old times with Pope Leo. . . . Then shall the Stagirite and Kant be forgotten, and another folio than theirs be turned over for wisdom; even the folio now spread with horoscopes as yet undeciphered, the heaven of heavens on high. (12–13)

This vision of a happy afterlife finds an experiential counterpoint in the "Dreams" chapter. "Dreams" is a digressive chapter that functions as a set-piece divorced from the ongoing action. By offering a self-portrait of Taji, "Dreams" succinctly presents the culmination of Melville's use of the solipsistic, absolutistic voice in *Mardi*. Taji's self-exhaustion has derived explicitly from his overindulgence in philosophical speculation. The unrestricted search for Truth, which initiated his flight from the *Arcturion*, not only leaves him physically imprisoned but psychologically wasted. Indeed, Melville's first philosophical narrative demonstrates the danger of the unimpeded metaphysical quest, a danger emphatically reinforced in *Moby-Dick* and *Pierre*. Taji's extreme dedication to learning comes at the expense of his relationship to the limited, but life-sustaining, domain of social contexts. Whirled by the hyperactive flights of his

soul, the megalomaniac Taji experiences panoramic vistas that paradoxically become self-restricting:

> And my soul sinks down to the depths, and soars to the skies; and
> comet-like reels on through such boundless expanses, that
> methinks all the worlds are my kin, and I invoke them to stay in
> their course. Yet, like a mighty three-decker, towing argosies by
> scores, I tremble, gasp, and strain in my flight, and fain would cast
> off the cables that hamper. (367)

Falling prey to the competing claims of contentious, unintegrated voices, Taji journeys into the world of mind and gains access
to many nations, times, places, and authors.[6] Consequently, he not
only "reels on through such boundless expanses" but comes to identify with the sources of all knowledge. He becomes, as it were, lost
in an intellectual vortex. "[F]ull with a thousand souls," Taji struggles
with a library of voices. The theater of the mind engages in an endless, self-defeating drama of dialectic. It is here that Melville's use
of the allusive catalog becomes more than a technique for learned
display, a means of evoking a litany of ideational contexts, for here
Melville dramatizes the debilitating psychological effects of the solipsistic and absolutistic intellectual pursuit. Taji winds up talking
interminably to himself in a grim repetition of ruminative thought.
Such broad knowledge becomes in itself the imprisoning force. Taji
consorts with Homer, Anacreon, Hafiz, Shakespeare, Ossian, Milton,
and Petrarch. In his mind "St. Paul ... argues the doubts of Montaigne;
Julian the Apostate cross-questions Augustine; and Thomas-a-
Kempis unrolls his old black letters for all to decipher" (367). His
play of mind includes such figures as Zeno, Democritus, Pyrrho,
Plato, Proclus, Verulam, Zoroaster, Virgil, and Sidney. Taji's "memory
is a life beyond birth; my memory, my library of the Vatican, its
alcoves all endless perspectives" (367–68). In this remarkable chapter
Melville reveals that Taji's mind has become self-restrictive, his intellectual absolutism self-exhausting. His mental growth, while perhaps stunning in its allusive reach, succeeds finally in accentuating
Taji's estrangement from other human beings. Total immersion in
the "Vatican" of knowledge severs him from social experience.

Melville's congenial and solipsistic narrative voices reflect polarized attributes of being. In the two cases just examined, the narrator constructs a world that mirrors his informing psychological disposition. His vision of the afterlife depicts a socially democratizing world in which great differences in viewpoint become the prelude to an all-encompassing communalism. Taji's imprisonment in "Dreams" derives from a paradoxically willed necessity. He becomes the victim of what he most longed to be: "My cheek blanches white while I write; I start at the scratch of my pen; my own mad brood of eagles devours me; fain would I unsay this audacity; but an iron-mailed hand clenches mine in a vice, and prints down every letter in my spite" (368).

Throughout his career, Melville refined his ability to bring into dialectical relationship characters that can be identified through voices and visions that are, on the one hand, genial and relativistic and, on the other, solipsistic and absolutistic. The narrative voices of *Mardi* prefigure the more finely realized conflicts in voice and vision that are later expressed in Ishmael and Ahab, young Pierre (with Lucy) and the older Pierre (with Isabel), the lawyer and Bartleby, Clarel and Nathan, Rolfe and Ungar. Through these distinct voices, Melville makes character, perception, and behavior sources for dialectic. In "Bartleby, the Scrivener," for example, the mystery underlying Bartleby's naysaying absolutism releases in the lawyer a nagging series of interpretations, no one of which answers, any one of which conducts him to the next unsatisfying attempt.[7]

While Melville's experiments in *Mardi* with the ideational play of possibility and the dramatization of competing voices can certainly be viewed as part of the emerging intellectual process that later generates Ishmael and Ahab, we are nevertheless closer to Melville's creative rhythms in *Mardi* if we see these voices as emerging from spontaneous, unintegrated impulses seeking expression in narrative form. The competing voices are attempts to dramatize distinctly philosophical moods. In *Mardi*, Melville grafts philosophical aspirations to his tried technique of the first-person narrative, persistently accommodating philosophical concerns to the demands of his plot. Whereas in the early sequences of *Mardi* the narrator inhabits a state of psychological free fall between the demands of geniality and solipsism, Melville moves the plot to the moment at which the two voices will no longer be reflected in the narrator's diachronic rendering of events.

In presenting *Mardi*'s major dramatic action—the discovery and rescue of Yillah—Melville allows his narrator to undergo a self-generated and self-fashioned ontological revolution that estranges him from the social world and its rhetoric of fraternal interactions. In repudiating his historical past, the narrator aspires to cosmic status. Melville's presentation of the Yillah episodes can be seen as the means whereby he brings his first absolutist into full figure. If the narrator's boredom on the *Arcturion* launches his philosophical quest and Taji's incarceration in "Dreams" stands as a paradoxically never-ending ending of this process, then the irreversible moment of ontological, intellectual, and rhetorical transfer begins when the narrator meets the high priest Aleema, who is conducting the mysterious Yillah toward sacrificial death. The narrator intervenes, kills Aleema, and rescues the maiden.

The creation of Yillah marks a crucial moment in Melville's career. The figure of Yillah fuses a host of literal and symbolic attributes. Merrell R. Davis links Yillah's literary antecedents with La Motte-Fouqué's Undine, Moore's Lily, Von Hardenberg's Mathilde, Southey's Oneiza, Coleridge's Geraldine, Keats's Lamia, and also the enchanting fays of medieval legend (75–76). With her "reminiscences of her shadowy isle" (158), Yillah represents the Platonic realm of the soul's preexistence (Sealts, "Platonic Tradition" 291). Yillah can also be seen as an all-alluring ideal, a symbol of the Absolute, a sign of primordial perfection—once enjoyed, now regained, soon to be lost.

This reading of Yillah's symbolic attributes, however reflective of Melville's expansive learning, tends to make her little more than an abstract lure for the four questers to pursue. What tends to be overlooked, and what characterizes Melville's fictionalization of the philosophical ideal in Yillah and later in Moby Dick and Isabel, is that these romantic, religious, and philosophical entities have no intrinsic supernatural qualities whatsoever. The ideal attributes of Yillah, Moby Dick, and Isabel generate explicitly from *stories* told by human beings on the hunt for mythic patterns that will explain the unusual and mysterious. Yillah's tale of deific origin, for example, derives from Aleema's religious contexts; Moby Dick's putative ubiquity in time and space evolves from the fertile speculations of superstitious mariners; Isabel's legend falls from her own lips. Quite possibly a lunatic, Isabel gives narrative form to images of her shadowy past. Her controlling desire is to regain the figure of a lost father through entanglements with a supposed half brother. In *Mardi*, Yillah believes Aleema's stories; she relates these tales to the narrator, who not only seconds but embellishes them, writing himself into the script of her biographical delusions. Thanks to Aleema's sons, we discover that the biological and historical creature yclept Yillah is the daughter of adventuring missionaries of European descent who were slaughtered by islanders after these missionaries slew three suspected thieves (307–08). Aleema, however, obliterates her cultural origins. All she has left are vague memories of Taji's language and the creation myth imposed on her by Aleema.

Yillah purports to be "more than mortal, a maiden from Oroolia, the Island of Delights." One day, she became entangled in a vine and transformed into a flower, her "conscious soul folded up in the transparent petals" (137). In due time, the blossom found its way to Aleema, who "by a spell" returned Yillah to maiden form. According to Aleema, the exiled spirit was then called home to Oroolia. She was to travel there by way of the vortex at Tedaidee. Significantly, in Aleema's tale Melville draws on Platonic and Cartesian complexes, bringing them directly into collision. On the one hand Yillah symbolizes the ideal, the Absolute, the ethereal soul cast temporarily into earthly form; on the other, Yillah's fate is prefigured by the "whirlpool" (138). She must plunge into the vortex and thus be purged of mortal qualities. According to Aleema, Yillah would "follow thy bird" and enter the "vortex on the coast of Tedaidee" (157). Melville links Yillah not only to the Platonic image of the soul's preexistence but also to the Platonic figure that depicts the soul's transcendence. As the bird enters the whirlpool, Platonic and Cartesian, ideal and material entities collide. Like the young Platonist on the masthead in *Moby-Dick*, who hovers over

"Descartian vortices" (159), Yillah stands to be killed by the brute facts of material existence.

The narrator originally sees Yillah as a poor manipulated victim. He "was almost persuaded that the luckless maiden was some beautiful maniac" (137). At the same time he has no trouble seeing Aleema as a fiction-making charlatan who acts for "ulterior purposes connected with . . . sacerdotal supremacy" (139). Not only does the narrator understand that Yillah's metaphysical identity was applied from without, but he clearly recognizes that this fiction undermines her essential humanity. As the narrator points out, the Aleemas of the world kidnap infants and

> craftily delude them, as they grow up, into the wildest conceits.
>
> Thus wrought upon, their pupils almost lose their humanity in the constant indulgence of seraphic imaginings. . . . Beguiled with some fairy tale about revisiting the islands of Paradise, they are led to the secret sacrifice, and perish unknown to their kindred. (139)

Put simply, the narrator comprehends fully the extent to which Yillah fell victim to a religious confidence game. Her deliverance could be accomplished, the narrator realizes, by weaning her from the fiction of godliness. And he has every opportunity to restore her to herself. Yillah has distant recollections of her native tongue: "She started, and bending over, listened intently, as if to the first faint echo of something dimly remembered. . . . [W]ith much earnestness, she signed to me to address her as before " (137). Later, the narrator reports, "Often she entreated me to repeat over and over again certain syllables of my language" (152). In an instinctual attempt to recapture her lost identity, Yillah pronounces these words "even as if recalling sounds long forgotten." Instead of telling her the historical facts of her past—"she had not the remotest conception of her real origin" (153)—the narrator appropriates and extends Aleema's fiction:

> In relating her story, the maiden frequently interrupted it with questions concerning myself:—Whence I came: being white, from

Oroolia? Whither I was going: to Amma? And what had happened
to Aleema? For she had been dismayed at the fray, though knowing not what it could mean. . . . These questions for the time I
endeavored to evade; only inducing her to fancy me some gentle
demi-god, that had come over the sea from her own fabulous
Oroolia. And all this she must verily have believed. For whom, like
me, ere this could she have beheld? Still fixed she her eyes upon
me strangely, and hung upon the accents of my voice. (140)

When the narrator fashions a fiction of their past acquaintance,
Melville is again drawing on the Platonic notion of knowledge as
reminiscence of primordial spiritual unity. The narrator tells her,
"Those little spirits in your eyes have seen me before. They mimic
me now as they sport in their lakes. All the past a dim blank? Think
of the time when we ran up and down in our arbor, where the
green vines grew over the great ribs of the stranded whale" (143).
Using distinctly Platonic figures, the narrator identifies her as "the
substance of this spiritual image. . . . the earthly semblance of that
sweet vision, that haunted my earliest thoughts" (158). Just as they
were married, so should they *now* marry.

The narrator, however, realizes that this fictionalized, metaphysical kinship is inimical to his desire for earthly, physical love. He
finds himself in a quandary: how can he continue to impose his
self-deifying fiction while at the same time leading her to love him
with the repressed passion of her buried human nature? He wants
Yillah to think of him as a fellow god, but to do so might also
"teach her to regard him as some frigid stranger from the Arctic
Zone, what sympathy could she have for him? and hence, what
peace of mind, having no one else to cling to?" (142). This dilemma
characterizes Melville's metaphysical questers: self-identification
with the Absolute freezes the emotions and destroys human sympathy. To what limits, then, should the narrator carry the fiction?
And what are the contingencies of becoming trapped within the
deific terms of his self-dramatization? At first, Yillah "had wildly
believed, that the nameless affinities between us, were owing to

our having in times gone by dwelt together in the same ethereal region. But thoughts like these were fast dying out" (158). She begins to look into his human eyes and listen to the sound of his human voice. Falling in love would demythify their divine status; but in order to enhance his stature, the narrator feels he must "prop my failing divinity; though it was I myself who had undermined it. . . . I perceived myself thus dwarfing down to a mortal" (159).

In adopting the identity of Taji, a demigod from the sun, the narrator effectively renounces his place among fellow mortals. Like Yillah's fabled deification, the fictional status of demigod generates from self-serving imperatives. Its fundamental purpose is to magnify the self, thus providing ontological warrant for his claim to special privilege. As revealed on the *Arcturion,* the narrator essentially longs for an idealized state (7–8). Consequently, his fiction making with Yillah serves his narcissistic self-love. He does not so much love Yillah the maiden as he loves the concept of a fit companion for his invented god-self. In *Mardi,* Melville does not directly engage the tensions between the demands of Taji's absolutistic yearnings and his sensual compulsions. Instead, he dissociates the romance and philosophical plots into elements of his quest saga. The missing Yillah becomes no more than a lost ideal; the moral and sexual contingencies of Taji's rescue of Yillah erupt only when Aleema's avenging sons and Hautia's seductive heralds occasionally appear. As a character, Taji virtually disappears. The play of philosophical rumination no longer has its center in the tension between his genial and solipsistic voices. In effect, the disappearance of Yillah completes Taji's estrangement from the realm of commonplace experience—a process that began with his boredom on the *Arcturion.*

Since mythic Yillah reflects a narcissistic projection of Taji's deific aspirations, and his physical love is inimical to his desire for transcendent status, then Yillah's disappearance eradicates Taji's place in the narrative. For Taji, to have lost Yillah is to have lost the capacity for presenting himself through the tension between two voices and two modes of existence. The congenial voice, figuratively speaking, becomes lost in the vortex that presumably swallows flesh-and-blood Yillah. In the post-Yillah chapters, Taji *never* engages his companions in their seemingly endless discourses. Seldom do his companions speak to him. With the unpredictability of a spirit rapper, he makes long declamatory speeches in the interpolated digressions. As a third-person narrator he records the conversations of his companions, every now and then duly noting that Yillah is not to be found.

Having eschewed the social axis, Taji finds himself condemned to solipsism; he then adopts the appropriate rhetorical mode of soliloquy. In his most self-revealing monologue, "Sailing On," Taji sums up the uncompromising single-mindedness of the absolute idealist:

> Oh, reader, list! I've chartless voyaged. With compass and the lead, we had not found these Mardian Isles. Those who boldly launch, cast off all cables; and turning from the common breeze, that's fair for all, with their own breath, fill their own sails. Hug the shore, naught new is seen. . . .
>
> And though essaying but a sportive sail, I was driven from my course, by a blast resistless; and ill-provided, young, and bowed to the brunt of things before my prime, still fly before the gale. (556–57)

In this moment of reflexivity, Taji depicts his "bold quest" both in terms of his protean compositional method and his attending intellectual exhaustion:

> But this new world here sought, is stranger far than his, who stretched his vans from Palos. It is the world of mind; wherein the wanderer may gaze round, with more of wonder than Balboa's band roving through the golden Aztec glades.
>
> But fiery yearnings their own phantom-future make, and deem it present. So, if after all these fearful, fainting trances, the verdict be, the golden haven was not gained;—yet, in bold quest thereof, better to sink in boundless deeps, than float on vulgar shoals; and give me, ye gods, an utter wreck, if wreck I do. (557)

This passage specifically points ahead both to "The Lee Shore" chapter of *Moby-Dick* and to the more extreme megalomaniacal rants of Ahab and Pierre.

In *Mardi,* however, Melville's interest is focused more on exploring "the world of mind" than on depicting the "utter wreck" of the Promethean quester. Ironically, except in the digressions, Taji reveals very little of what he discovers on his sallies through intellectual space. Given the fact that his actions and thoughts have the same focus—regaining Yillah—Melville must invent a strategy whereby the narrator's futile quest can impel Melville's preoccupation with intellectual play, improvisation, and dialectic. Though Taji has one thing on his mind, Melville has many. Melville displaces Taji as the center of consciousness and focuses his ideational concerns through the questers—four characters who represent four distinctly adumbrated modes of knowledge and being: Media is Political Authority; Babbalanja is Philosophy; Yoomy is Poetry; Mohi is History. Each character speaks for his own special interest. Wrangling over abstract issues as they encounter a multitude of allegorical contexts, Taji's four companions allow Melville to explore the "chartless . . . world of mind" (556–57). The narrative's dramatic action thus provides a series of counterpoints to the dead-end issue of Yillah's discovery. The journey through *Mardi,* ostensibly a quest for the maiden, provides both form and forum through which Melville can try out narrative techniques capable of containing his speculations.

3

Perpetual Cycling

Wherefore, it is a perpetual cycling with us, without progression;
and we fly round, whether we will or no. To stop, were to sink into
space.

—*Mardi*

In *Mardi*'s long travelogue, Melville dramatizes the effects of two
distinct voyages into "the world of mind" (557), each developing
and intensifying the narrator's earlier voices—the angry solipsist
and the effusive genialist. As we have seen, Taji inhabits an ontological realm outside the diachronic progression of the narrative.
Once Taji absents himself, his genial voice becomes diffused through
the multiple perspectives of the four questers. Ostensibly search-
ing for Yillah, these questers actually explore the zany, sometimes
brutal, expanses of Mardi. Appropriating the structure of Rabelais's
Gargantua and Pantagruel, Melville devises dramatic situations that
seem to proliferate from the mind. While Pantagruel and Panurge
seek the Oracle of the Holy Bottle and visit such places as Nowhere
Island, Sneaks' Island, the Isles of Vacuum and Void, and many
others, Melville's questers stop at sixteen islands, among them
Valapee, Juam, Maramma, and Vivenza.

Mardi depicts the evolving creation of an open fictive world.
Indeed, as the questers go forth, Yoomy echoes the ending of *Paradise Lost:* "The dawn of day is passed, and Mardi lies all before us"
(200). *Mardi* is more notable for its tour de force of intellectual
display than its originality. Particular ideas are eminently expendable, as easily left behind as the island of Nora-Bamma or the character Piko. At times the narrative seems chaotic, even preposterous.

Melville, however, stands as *Mardi*'s first critic. Projected through the questers' discussion of Lombardo's epic *Koztanza*, Melville furnishes a self-reflexive critique. When Abrazza remarks that "the Koztanza lacks cohesion; it is wild, unconnected, all episode," Babbalanja lauds Lombardo for his powers of mimesis: "And so is Mardi itself:—nothing but episodes; valleys and hills; rivers, digressing from plains; vines, roving all over; boulders and diamonds; flowers and thistles; forests and thickets; and, here and there, fens and moors. And so, the world in the Koztanza" (597).

While thrashing among unpruned thickets, Melville translates his intellectual and metaphysical concerns in three basic ways. First, in the wake of Media's decree supporting conversational candor, Melville adapts the Platonic dialogue and presents a host of issues from multiples perspectives, no one of which is privileged.[1] The dialogue extends, and complicates, the divided consciousness of the earlier narrator. Second, in depicting the journey, Melville uses places and characters to represent fixed ideational complexes. These fables of identity harken back to Plato's evocation of myths and figures that dramatize the more ethereal aspects of his doctrines. Third, an abiding concern involves the questers' unfulfilled search for an informing standard. Throughout *Mardi*, social, experiential, or textual authorities offer tenuous, problematic correctives to the self-exhausting excesses of philosophical speculation. The search for narrative authority challenges the efficacy of this seemingly interminable enterprise.

THE DIALOGUE

Melville's first book of talk, *Mardi*, prefigures the conversational expansiveness of *The Confidence-Man* and *Clarel*. The quest for Yillah very quickly becomes, in Richard H. Brodhead's words, a "freewheeling island-hopping symposium," a rambling, discursive, unintegrated series of conversations ("Melville's *Mardi*" 36). The philosophical dialogue is congenial to Melville's loose episodic structure, with the questers wrangling indefatigably over such issues as the soul's immortality, art, inspiration, Oro (God), right reason, preexistence, atavism, and practical ethics. A dialogue often generates from a contrived incident or setting that offers a quickly displaced point of departure. For example, Vee-Vee, one of Media's attendants, impulsively rises to the canoe's crow's nest, blows some notes on his conch shell, loses balance, and falls. Always on the lookout for hidden significance, Babbalanja questions Vee-Vee about whether he fell on purpose (424), thus prompting a rambling discussion of fate and "Philosophical Necessity" (425). Though in this chapter, titled "Babbalanja discourses in the Dark," the conversation ranges from fate, to necessity, to predestination, to Oro's potential complicity in the "evil [that] abounds" (427); the discussion resolves nothing, largely because the focus keeps shifting. Merton M. Sealts, Jr., makes the useful distinction that, though in *Mardi* Melville entertained philosophical ideas, he had not as yet become a "full-fledged philosophical novelist" ("Platonic Tradition" 316)—someone who reveals what "it is like to experience the world as the [philosophical] system represents it" (Levin 61). Each quester propounds his particular angle of vision; when tired of a subject, they move to the next issue.

Melville delights in staging the intellectual gyrations of Babbalanja, who is most protean, and most energetic, in exploring the "mystery of mysteries" (389). Along with his demon-self, Azzageddi, Babbalanja seems a frantic, comic reincarnation of Socrates. Even when most dismissive of Platonic idealism, Melville never relinquishes his praise for Socrates the man, who remains to Melville a figure of heroic self-possession and profound wisdom.[2] Melville's sympathy for Babbalanja is similarly divided. However unsystematic and, at times, silly his views, Babbalanja is most heroic in his obsessive search for the essential truth underlying appearances. But while his incessant questioning becomes comically self-defeating and neurotically self-lacerating, and while he lacks the firm faith that characterizes Plato's mentor, Babbalanja nevertheless represents Melville's first relativistic philosopher, whose descendants include Ishmael, Clarel, and Rolfe.

Plato's dialogues are headlong immersions into the stream of intellectual crosscurrents. The process of engagement is not only dramatic in execution but also exploratory, provisional, experimental; though it must be remembered when considering the latter qualities that Plato's dialogues are primarily contrivances that leave no question concerning the dialectical powers of Socrates or the ultimate efficacy of the True and the Good. In *Mardi*, on the contrary, dialogues are dramatic excursions into the unknown. Without either Platonic formalism or a master dialectician, *Mardi* depicts disputations among competing speakers. Driven by the thinking process itself, Melville need not conform the words on the page to any standard other than the speaker's next turn of thought. Discussions can either be utterly fractured or momentarily resolved. Babbalanja, at times, becomes so frantic that he forgets what he says or falls into a fit. At one point the philosopher chides Yoomy because his songs have no deep meanings. Later, Babbalanja celebrates their affinity: "Yoomy: poets both, we differ but in the seeming; thy airiest conceits are as the shadows of my deepest ponderings; though Yoomy soars, and Babbalanja dives, both meet at last. Not a song you sing, but I have thought its thought" (438). This resolution has contextual rather than encompassing validity.

Given Melville's concern with the process of intellection, it is no wonder that *Mardi* is a mayhem of conflicting positions. Not only does the dialogue form release Melville's "play of freedom & invention" (*Correspondence* 106), but it most often demonstrates the indeterminacy of the quest for truth. Media, for example, loses patience with Babbalanja: "And to what end your eternal inquisitions? You have nothing to substitute. You say all is a lie; then out with the truth" (428). The presiding spirit of *Mardi* would suggest that the "end" of "eternal inquisitions" is nothing less paradoxical than the next question. At this point, Media seems to demand that language provide an absolute explanation. Earlier, though, he is closer to the roots of Melville's preoccupation with dialogue and dialectic:

Furthermore, Babbalanja . . . final, last thoughts you mortals have none; nor can have; and, at bottom, your own fleeting fancies are too often secrets to yourselves; and sooner may you get another's secret, than your own. Thus with the wisest of you all; you are ever unfixed. Do you show a tropical calm without? then, be sure a thousand contrary currents whirl and eddy within. The free, airy robe of your philosophy is but a dream, which seems true while it lasts. . . . Babbalanja, you mortals dwell in Mardi, and it is impossible to get elsewhere. (370)

Media's cautionary promulgation seems climactic, but it is delivered halfway through the book. The "unfixed" quality of thought fuels and frustrates the reader for the next 300 pages. We get nowhere but the very human world of Mardi. Crucially, then, the dialogue depicts an eminently social enterprise. As Babbalanja suggests, "[A]nd no need have the great gods to discourse of things perfectly comprehended by them, and by themselves ordained. But you and I, Yoomy, are men, and not gods; hence is it for us, and not for them, to take these things for our themes. Nor is there any impiety in the right use of our reason, whatever the issue" (426). This affirmation of discourse accentuates the abiding dissociation between earthly and heavenly spheres, between relative and absolute frames of reference. The human being speaks, but the gods—or God—remain aloof, wrapped in what the narrator of *Pierre* calls the "Voice" of "Silence" (204).

Nevertheless, the dialogue in *Mardi* allows one to extend mediate knowledge toward the Absolute; analogy aids the attempt to link the seen and the unseen. For Plato, the phenomenal world is an imperfect copy of the noumenal domain; earthly shadows replicate transcendent forms. In *Mardi*, however, analogical correspondence creates more questions than it answers. For example, early in the quest, Babbalanja finds himself pondering the condition of the "illustrious dead." Like Socrates in the *Phaedo*, Babbalanja considers the prospects for the soul's survival of death. Unlike Socrates, whose faith in the soul's immortality is unshakable, Babbalanja has an open-ended view of the matter: analogy identifies the nature of the problem, but its failure to forge absolute explanations reinforces the uncertain status of the human subject. In speaking of the dead, Babbalanja says,

> But whether they ever lived or not, it is all the same with them now. Yet, grant that they lived; then, if death be a deaf-and-dumb death, a triumphal procession over their graves would concern them not. If a birth into brightness, then Mardi must seem to them the most trivial of reminiscences. Or, perhaps, theirs may be an utter lapse of memory concerning sublunary things; and they themselves be not themselves, as the butterfly is not the larva. (209–10)

In the *Phaedrus,* Socrates employs the bird in flight to figure the soul's ascension (3:404). Once again Platonic certainties do not apply to *Mardi*'s dialectical pursuits. Through Yoomy's gentle prodding, Babbalanja admits the fallaciousness of his own analogy:

> No; for the analogy has an unsatisfactory end. From its chrysalis state the silkworm but becomes a moth, that very quickly expires. Its longest existence is as a worm. All vanity, vanity, Yoomy, to seek in nature for a positive warranty to these aspirations of ours. Through all her provinces, nature seems to promise immortality to life, but destruction to beings. Or, as old Bardianna has it, if not against us, nature is not for us. (210)

As Melville suggests in *Pierre,* nature supplies "that cunning alphabet, whereby selecting and combining as he pleases, each man reads his own peculiar lesson according to his own peculiar mind and mood" (342). Like the dialogue, the analogy fails to extend human knowledge from the phenomenal to the noumenal realm. Dialogue and analogy both evoke possibilities for synthesis, though further reflection dismantles them.

Within the encompassing structure of the travelogue as dialogue, one finds the questers occasionally making set speeches: Yoomy recites poems; Mohi narrates legends; Babbalanja delivers lectures.

These excursions differ from Taji's digressive, solipsistic monologues in that the questers engage in performative activities designed to edify a proximate audience within the narrative itself. Babbalanja's speeches, especially "Babbalanja Solus" (Chapter 78), should be seen in the context of Melville's adaptation of the philosophical dialogue. Placed in the midst of the Donjalolo episodes and inspired by a visit to the funereal pavements of the House of the Afternoon, Babbalanja's speech questions the soul's immortality. This meditation has a distinct dramatic focus created by the speaker's use of apostrophe: "Donjalolo, come forth and ponder on thy sires" (236). Babbalanja goes on to pose rhetorical questions both to the deceased kings—"What, no reply? Are not these bones thine?"—and to himself—"But will a longing bring the thing desired? Doth dread avert its object?" (237). His meditation, as Sealts suggests, harkens back to Melville's reading of Thomas Browne's *Urn-Burial* ("Platonic Tradition" 282). In the context of Melville's later work, however, the meditation prefigures dramatic soliloquies that take place before an unresponsive, "dumb" object: Ahab's speech to the whale's head in "The Sphynx" chapter of *Moby-Dick* (310–12), for example, and Pierre's defiant, preposterous invocation to the Memnon Stone (132–34). Indeed, in his soliloquy Babbalanja is a harbinger of later seekers who find themselves face to face with a vexing object, person, or circumstance that focuses a whole range of unanswerable questions. This situational crux appears as early as Tommo's examination of ruined monuments in *Typee*, an examination which anticipates Ishmael's perusal of the painting in the Spouter-Inn. In even more powerful moments, Ishmael ponders the "palsied universe" in "The Whiteness of the Whale" (*Moby-Dick* 195); Pierre studies the portraits of his father (*Pierre* 196–99); the lawyer confronts Bartleby; and Melville himself engages the mute massiveness of the Pyramids (*Journal* 75–79).

While in *Mardi* the actual dramatic context is contrived and the words stilted, Babbalanja's disquisition in "Solus" provides an inchoate rendering of Melville's paradigmatic epistemological quandary: the human seeker, trying to interpret a vexing sign, is driven to conjecture. Just as analogy seeks to extend knowledge from the visible sphere into some invisible—though potentially corresponding—counterpart, so too does the ruminative play of voice attempt to extend knowledge along a line of diminishing probability. In speaking, the inquiring self formulates contextual, and disposable, responses to lurking mysteries. Usually these meditations are self-reflexive: they illuminate the nature of the mind in motion far more than the issues that excite it. "Babbalanja Solus" culminates with a remarkable complex: the recognition of unstable subjectivity amid the encompassing flux of natural forms. In trying to determine the place of the perceiving "I" amid the "stir" and bustle of universal flux, especially the apparent indifference of brute natural forces, Babbalanja wonders if he can have any confidence in the soul's survival of death:

> What ho, hot heart of mine: to beat thus lustily awhile, to feel in the red rushing blood, and then be ashes,—can this be so? But peace, peace, thou liar in me, telling me I am immortal—shall I not be as these bones? To come to this! But the balsam-dropping palms, whose boles run milk, whose plumes wave boastful in the air, they perish in their prime, and bow their blasted trunks. Nothing abideth; the river of yesterday floweth not to-day; the sun's rising is a setting; living is dying; the very mountains melt; and all revolve:—systems and asteroids; the sun wheels through the zodiac, and the zodiac is a revolution. Ah gods! in all this universal stir, am *I* to prove one stable thing? (237–38, Melville's emphasis)

This passage reflects the syncretic quality of Melville's imagination, and though the speech as a whole echoes the essence of Heraclitean thought—all things flow and are in flux—this skeptical, pyrrhonic passage also resonates in Ecclesiastes, Seneca, Montaigne, and Thomas Browne. Babbalanja, however, does not, as Melville himself once admitted to Hawthorne, "pretty much [make] up his mind to be annihilated" (Leyda 529).[3] This meditation offers but one configuration among the many wherein Melville dramatizes the human voice speaking in the face of cosmic silence.

Relative and dialectical possibilities, however bleak any one formulation might be, momentarily displace the vacuum.

"Time, Strength, Cash, and Patience" (*Moby-Dick* 145) prohibit one from charting and explicating the numerous situations and *topoi* in *Mardi*. The attempt to include discussion of Melville's numerous dialogues would be more exhausting than illuminating. Thus *Mardi's* paradigmatic Chapter 143, "Wherein Babbalanja discourses of himself," exemplifies the protean, if not manic, intensity with which Melville adapts the philosophical dialogue to storytelling. The chapter begins in a customarily arbitrary manner. Babbalanja starts from silence, points to the setting sun, and observes, "As old Bardianna says—shut your eyes, and believe" (455). Then Babbalanja ponders the credulousness of Mardians, who are equally ready to believe that the sun revolves around Mardi as they are to affirm that Mardi encircles the sun. No more capable of proving or refuting either theory, "the mass of Mardians do not believe because they know," the philosopher suggests, "but because they know *not*" (455, Melville's emphasis). The problem of epistemological uncertainty leads Babbalanja not outward, toward a consideration of empiricism, but inward, toward his most teasing, least knowable subject—himself: "[T]hough I have now been upon terms of close companionship with myself for nigh five hundred moons, I have not yet been able to decide who or what I am" (456). It is because consciousness is inherently unstable, Babbalanja avers, that one's knowledge of the physical world is so problematic. What specifically troubles him is how psychological volition exists independent of conscious control: "To you, perhaps, I seem Babbalanja; but to myself, I seem not myself. . . . For aught I know, I may be somebody else. . . . There is something going on in me, that is independent of me. Many a time, have I willed to do one thing, and another has been done" (456).

Joining Azzageddi within the philosopher's crowded constitution is the "mysterious indweller," or "inscrutable stranger" (457), who delivers to the conscious mind "unsought, spontaneous" intuitions and inspirations (456). Whether this "mysterious indweller" is a Platonic daemon, creative muse, Christian devil, or proto-Freudian Id, one conclusion seems clear: animating the self is neither unity nor coherence but a collision of duplicitous forces. The conscious "I" wrestles with internal agitation. Indeed, Melville's philosophical assays frequently possess psychological implications.[4]

Characteristically, Media harasses Babbalanja about the subversive moral and legal implications of such diverse complexes finding expression in one's behavior. For example, Media warns the philosopher to "take not the leap" into affirming the primacy of instinct over ethical precept. The play of Babbalanja's speculations, surely, has little in common with the demands of Media's political conservatism. Instead, Babbalanja considers how "in one life-time we live a hundred lives" (457). Since identity reflects the interplay of conscious and unconscious forces, Babbalanja cannot offer an intelligible conclusion, prompting Mohi and Media to twit him for trying to square the circle. Exaggerating the chaotic indeterminacy of Babbalanja's colloquy is the fact that he loses his train of thought: "To exist, is to be; to be, is to be something; to be something, is—" (458). In response to the rational, pragmatic Media, who chides the philosopher for being "inconsistent," Babbalanja points to the intrinsic flux within self and world: "And for that very reason, my lord, *not* inconsistent; for the sum of my inconsistencies makes up my consistency. And to be consistent to one's self, is often to be inconsistent to Mardi. Common consistency implies unchangeableness; but much of the wisdom here below lives in a state of transition" (459, Melville's emphasis).

The dialogue charts the ebb and flow of the philosopher's transitory and transitional progress. At the end of the chapter, Babbalanja's response to Media's assertion that "the wisest Mardians make the most consummate fools" (460) points directly to an underlying paradox: any proposed fixity is but the prelude to its necessary displacement; any statement gives way to the next. Babbalanja quotes Bardianna in "his roundabout chapter on Cycles and Epicycles. . . 'All things revolve upon some center, to them, fixed: for the centripetal is ever too much for the centrifugal. Wherefore, it is a perpetual cycling with us, without progression; and we fly round, whether we will or no. To stop, were to sink into space'" (460). In a roundabout chapter that ranges from the macroscopic to the microscopic, the astronomical to the ontological, Melville celebrates the ongoing motion of the mind.

FABLES OF IDENTITY

In Plato, figures and myths dramatize the essential content of a particular philosophical position, and interpolated tales exemplify and relieve the rigors of Socratic dialectic. In *The Republic,* it is one thing for Socrates to argue for the un-Reality of the phenomenal world; it is quite another for the Allegory of the Cave (Book VII) to translate the terms of Platonic idealism into a dramatic scenario. Similarly, the Myth of Er (Book X) uses story to depict Plato's conceptions of a harmonious cosmological order. The human soul, guided by an attending spirit, passes the three sisters of Fate before proceeding to the Lethean waters and then to birth. Such figures and myths do not merely serve as heuristics; rather, they testify to the integral power of images and story to dramatize the quest for wisdom.

As a reader of the *Phaedrus, Phaedo,* and *The Republic,* and as a student of Rabelais and his madcap proliferation of ideas masquerading as characters, Melville responded to the self-imposed challenge of liberating his art from the perceived confinements of his own lived experience. In *Mardi,* the Platonic figure or myth marries the Rabelaisian comic escapade. Rabelais taught Melville that the limits of fiction were no less than the limits of imagination. Melville was drawn to Rabelais's practice of making distinct ideas the source of characters, and the travelogue allowed Melville to vary his ideas from island to island. Just as the philosophical dialogue can embrace or dispose of any topic, so too can the travelogue provide an inexhaustible series of new worlds to be explored, discussed, and then left behind. As a metaphysical improvisation, *Mardi* is not merely a book of talk; it tirelessly locates the roots of behavior in ideas. Thus *Mardi* contains a gallery of eccentric character studies. These fables of identity give a habitation and name to specific concepts. Melville translates intellectual problems into representational types—flat allegorized abstractions representing a single ruling behavioral attribute.

In the most simple instances, Melville's intention is usually satirical. The questers arrive at one island where they confront an individual's (or an entire community's) behavioral fixation. For example, Oh-Oh is a harmless antiquarian who collects such metaphysical tracts as "Necessitarians not Predestinarians," "Philosophical Necessity and Predestination One Thing and The Same," "Whatever is not, is," and "Whatever is, is not" (383). On the island of Quelco, Mohi relates how the residents blame all problems, however trivial or profound, on invisible demons called Plujii (262–64). On the island of Pimminee, the Tapparians legalistically prescribe the minutest affairs of life, thereby maintaining their ridiculous aristocratic affectations (398–413). On Diranda, the Lords Piko and Hello do nothing but wage deadly war games, partly for their sadistic amusement, partly for population control (443–54). Elsewhere, when vexed by a countryman, a Mindarian solicits a sorcerer and the prospective victim counteracts the spell by hiring his own sorcerer. A stalemate ensues: sorcerer fights sorcerer. As parodic versions of lawyers, these Mindarian sorcerers "affected even more mystery than belonged to them. . .[and] would confound the inquirer by answers couched in an extraordinary jargon, employing words almost as long as anacondas" (463). The false sage Doxodox does not instruct Babbalanja in his beloved "dialectics" (563). Instead, as Sealts indicates, Doxodox spews absurdly recondite terminology, which Melville gleaned from Proclus ("Neoplatonic Originals"). Like Mark Winsome, who is fond of using "some unknown word" (*The Confidence-Man* 193), Doxodox, the "shallow phraseman," revels in the use of "preposterous gibberish" (564).

However whimsical or tedious, this gallery of straw men offers telling prefigurations. For example, Oh-Oh anticipates Melville's attraction to philosophical play that will be most evident in *Moby-Dick* and *The Confidence-Man*. The islands of Quelco, Pimminee, Diranda, and Minda, respectively, point to such abiding concerns as the source of evil, the absurdity of arbitrary codes, the instinct for war, and the perversion of rhetoric. Indeed, while the residents of Quelco reveal the human propensity to blame adverse contingencies on malicious supernatural agents, they also foreshadow Ahab's obsession with those inscrutable forces animating material forms.

In trying-out his capacity for invention, Melville frequently projects the problematic interrelation between freedom and necessity into contrasting character studies. Philosophical dialectic merges with his exploration of identity. For example, with King Uhia on the island of Ohonoo, Borabolla on Mondoldo, Peepi on Valapee, the escapists on Nora-Bamma, Donjalolo on Juam, and the republicans on Vivenza; physical, psychological, or political freedoms are seriously qualified by potentially self-destructive forms of restriction.[5] In exploring the nuances of this complex, Melville juxtaposes a series of behavioral opposites, anticipating such diptychs as "The Paradise of Bachelors and the Tartarus of Maids," "The Two Temples," and "Poor Man's Pudding and Rich Man's Crumbs." For example, Uhia is jealous and misanthropic, while Borabolla is fraternal and trusting; Peepi has conflicting identities and various souls, while the lotus eaters on Nora-Bamma have no consciousness of self. Donjalolo is schizophrenic, thus divided against himself. And in Vivenza, boasted freedoms conflict with the hypocritical usurpation of liberty.

As he shifts his dramatization of ideas from island to island, Melville varies the narrative forms he uses to exploit his materials. Peepi, Uhia, and Borabolla provide very simple comic portraits of imbalance; they are nothing more than one dimensional figurines. Melville's fables of identity have their most complex realization when articulated *within* individual or collective character. Donjalolo's predicament in Willamilla and the divided nature of the republicans on Vivenza constitute *Mardi*'s most fully realized fables of identity. Donjalolo's story, for example, is a highly refined, intense psychological study of the dangers of repression. The Vivenza episodes reflect a polemical projection of Donjalolo's schizophrenia. Continuing his earlier assaults in *Typee* and *Omoo* on the evils of western expansionism, Melville specifically exposes the self-destructive dimensions of American millennialism.[6] In the anonymous diatribe the "Voice from the Gods," he summarizes the conservative implications of his political philosophy.

In exploring paradoxical imbalances between freedom and necessity, Melville fuses philosophical, psychological, and political contexts. Donjalolo's intense self-loathing generates from his status as king and slave. He is imprisoned by the very conditions that empower him. In Vivenza, doctrines of self-righteous millennialism mask the insidious repression of slaves and dissenters.

A world of heightened splendor, beautiful sights, and lush verdure, Willamilla is nevertheless hemmed in by mountain walls. The glen's fortress-like perimeters are complemented by a jungle of labyrinthine corridors. Before becoming king, Donjalolo had the option of choosing either political sovereignty and lifelong immurement or free movement and no political power. He took the course of action most destructive to his spirit. Now trapped forever in an insular world of dualities, he follows a carefully regimented passage from the House of the Morning to the House of the Afternoon and wishes he could dodge "day's luminary through life" (235). His entire life oscillates between pattern and license. His weakness of character, his inexperience, and his frustrated longing coalesce and mangle him in this vise of opposites. One of Melville's lost souls, Donjalolo is doomed by one mistake to live within the dictates of iron necessity. Rebelling against these restrictions, he directs his rebellion against himself and plunges into debauchery, dissipating powers of mind and body:

> His generous spirit thirsting after some energetic career, found itself narrowed down within the little glen of Willamilla, where ardent impulses seemed idle. But these are hard to die; and repulsed all round, recoil upon themselves. . . .
>
> At times, loathing his vicious pursuits, which brought him no solid satisfaction, but ever filled him with final disgust, he would resolve to amend his ways; solacing himself for his bitter captivity, by the society of the wise and discreet. But brief the interval of

repentance. Anew, he burst into excesses, a hundred fold more insane than ever.

Thus vacillating between virtue and vice; to neither constant, and upbraided by both; his mind, like his person in the glen, was continually passing and repassing between opposite extremes. (223–24)

In compensation, Donjalolo sends agents to gather reliable information about Mardi. He wishes to "avail himself of the researches of others, and see with their eyes" (248). Here, Melville offers a case study in epistemology, pointing out that knowledge of phenomena is dependent on the perceiver. Donjalolo recognizes "how hard is truth to be come at by proxy! Fifty accounts have I had of Rafona; none of which wholly agreed. . . . Are the lenses in their eyes diverse-hued, that objects seem different to both" (249). Anticipating the story of Narcissus in *Moby-Dick*, Donjalolo recognizes, "Truth dwells in her fountains; where every one must drink for himself" (250).

Indeed, the figure of Donjalolo is germinal. He evokes the effeminate qualities of *Redburn's* Harry Bolton and the suicidal self-destruction of Pierre, Bartleby, and Mortmain. This story of an effeminate, enslaved king constitutes, perhaps, an early version of the psychology of place later depicted in Melville's story of Wall Street. Donjalolo's ironic entrapment anticipates the enervated, and morally culpable, captain-prisoner Benito Cereno, and Donjalolo's peculiar "monomania" offers an inviting contrast to Melville's greatest absolutist (227), Captain Ahab. Unlike Ahab, however, Donjalolo cannot alleviate his vexed condition through some grand action. The cure, as it were, would demand Donjalolo's death, for he would be executed upon leaving the glen. While Ahab focuses his frustration and rage on one object, Donjalolo pursues no White Whale. Instead, he is heaped and tasked by his own being. With trapped body and questing mind, Donjalolo languishes as a pathetic, burned-out neurotic—a man victimized by whim, taunted by unlived possibilities, and haunted by specters of an undiscovered self.

Donjalolo's self-destructiveness derives exclusively from his inability to balance the personal, psychological, and historical contingencies of freedom and necessity. In a tour de force of description, Melville evokes oxymoron and hyperbolic images of immurement:

> And here, in this impenetrable retreat, centrally slumbered the universe-rounded, zodiac-belted, horizon-zoned, sea-girt, reef-sashed, mountain-locked, arbor-nested, royalty-girdled, arm-clasped, self-hugged, indivisible Donjalolo, absolute monarch of Juam:—the husk-inhusked meat in a nut; the innermost spark in a ruby; the juice-nested seed in a golden-rinded orange; the red royal stone in an effeminate peach; the insphered sphere of spheres. (240)

Combining expansiveness and enclosure, these images proceed in constricting sequential order. The imagistic vista extends from universal spaciousness to microscopic minuteness. The prose rhythms reflect a continuing compression of space, which points to an analogous diminution in Donjalolo's being. Expansive images are matched by qualifying reductive images. Paradoxically, the universe is "rounded"; the horizon is "zoned"; the sea is "girt." Finally, Donjalolo is nestled—both womblike and tomblike—within an "insphered sphere of spheres."

Just as the portrait of Donjalolo constitutes Melville's most fully developed fable of individual identity, the Vivenza episodes render Melville's climactic treatment of collective identity. Again Melville draws upon the seminal conflict between freedom and necessity. Belligerently intolerant, the men of Vivenza pride themselves on their justice and equality; glib assertions of political freedom counterpoint their all-consuming pride and willfulness. Vivenza is a nation in which "freedom is the name for a thing that is *not* freedom" (528, Melville's emphasis). The promulgation of cultural, theological, and political supremacy has its sublimated corollary in the brutality of a fascistic repression. Melville exploits the disparity between rhetorical pieties of universal liberties, on the one hand, and the pernicious actions of the republican citizens, on the other. As the questers enter Vivenza, for example, they gaze on the arch of freedom and its inscription promising liberty to all (512). On closer inspection, Mohi deciphers some hieroglyphic fine print: "Except-the-tribe-of-Hamo" (513). Arriving at the Great Temple of Freedom, "the handiwork of slaves," the five questers encounter a black man, a member of Hamo's tribe. This man has a "collar round his neck" and bears "the red marks of stripes upon his back" (515). He is raising the flag of Vivenza. Melville associates Vivenza with not only slavery but violence. In celebrating the revolutions in Porpheero (Europe), the republican crowd cries, "Hurrah! another kingdom is burnt down to the earth's edge; another demigod is unhelmed; another republic is dawning. . . . The times tell terrible tales to tyrants! Ere we die, freemen, all Mardi will be free" (524).

History looms as the corrective for the rampant willfulness of the slave-ridden free society. While Babbalanja vaguely claims that "all-healing Time" will alleviate Vivenza's imbalances (535), the "Voice from the Gods" specifically proclaims that the republicans must recognize their own evil. The "grand error" of Vivenza is the conceit of naive providentialism, the romantic assumption that finds Mardi "now in the last scene of the last act of her drama; and that all preceding events were ordained, to bring about the catastrophe you believe to be at hand,—a universal and permanent Republic" (525). Ironically, Vivenza must internalize the virtues of a monarchy, thus curbing its expansive, all-consuming urge: "For, mostly, monarchs are as gemmed bridles upon the world, checking the plungings of a steed from the Pampas. And republics are as vast reservoirs, draining down all streams to one level; and so, breeding a fullness which can not remain full, without overflowing" (525). For Melville's Voice, freedom provides no end in itself but is the noblest means to enlightened rule. A just authority, then, might restrain the nation from murderous anarchy like that in Franco (France), where the recent revolution has brought "the executioner's ax [to] every corner" (527). The Voice affirms the supremacy of God: "A born thrall to the last, yelping out his liberty, he still remains a slave unto Oro; well is it for the universe, that Oro's scepter is absolute" (528).

After hearing the contents of the scroll, the men of Vivenza tear it up; the reader turns the page; the questers move on. This convenient disposal of narrative materials drives Melville's aesthetic liberation in the same way that it assures *Mardi*'s patchwork quality. The philosophical dialogue can be ended as arbitrarily as it can be extended; any fable of identity becomes expendable as soon as its animating idea is played out.

THE QUESTION OF AUTHORITY

Melville's pursuit of ultimate Truth presupposes its intrinsic futility. Rather than reflecting a static paradox, this position manifests a dialectical concomitant to the philosophical dialogues and fables of identity. Given the fact that Yillah is not to be found, the questers, especially Babbalanja, need to reconcile themselves to what Ishmael calls a lowered "conceit of attainable felicity" (*Moby-Dick* 416). Throughout *Mardi,* Melville presents putative correctives to philosophical excess. These correctives emerge as invocations of textual or political authorities. *Mardi* contains, for instance, a series of texts within the text, verbal icons that purport to instruct the readers how to achieve balance. One among them, the "Voice from the Gods," offers a political text designed to curb national chauvinism. Another, Babbalanja's discovery of "A Happy Life," excites the philosopher, especially with its steady, stoical common sense. Taken verbatim from Seneca's *Morals By Way of Abstract,* "A Happy Life" offers such easily digestible maxims as "True joy is a serene and sober motion" (388). Babbalanja, for one, credits this text with an extrinsic authority far superior to his own improvisational metaphysics: "And mark me, my lord, this time I improvise nothing. What I have recited, is here. Mohi, this book is more marvelous than the prophecies." In the same reverent spirit, Babbalanja cites Bardianna's "Ponderings."

These texts share claims to authority, claims that ironically dissolve as soon as they impinge on the world of practical affairs. For example, the mob tears up the scroll; or the precepts offered by "A Happy Life" merely lead Babbalanja to the next series of questions.

For example, Media asks, "Have you that, then, of which you speak, Babbalanja? Are you content, there where you stand?" (389). Babbalanja responds, "I am not content. The mystery of mysteries is still a mystery. How this author came to be so wise, perplexes me." Babbalanja longs to comprehend not the *content* of the author's thought but the process that impels the author's search. "A Happy Life," however excellent a book, remains inadequate: "The rays that come to me are but faint cross lights, mazing the obscurity wherein I live. And after all, excellent as it is, I can be no gainer by this book" (389). Babbalanja's search for textual authority, therefore, is undermined by the flux of consciousness itself. Texts lose their privileged position as soon as the reader assimilates and inevitably transfigures the information. Paradoxically, the acquisition of knowledge is not an incremental expansion but a "substitution": "For the more we learn," Babbalanja observes, "the more we unlearn; we accumulate not, but substitute; and take away, more than we add" (389). Evoking Bardianna—an "older and better authority than myself" (503)—Babbalanja renders the "answer" useless:

> Yes, yes, Bardianna, all is in a nut, as thou sayest; but all my back teeth can not crack it. . . . All round me, my fellow men are new-grafting their vines, and dwelling in flourishing arbors; while I am forever pruning mine, till it is become but a stump. Yet in this pruning will I persist; I will not add, I will diminish; I will train myself down to the standard of what is unchangeably true. (389–90)

The central philosophical action of *Mardi*—the pursuit of the "unchangeably true"—is expressed in a series of repetitions culminating in exhaustion. As in *The Confidence-Man* and *Clarel*, *Mardi* depicts an ostensible movement to both old and new points of reference and departure where the questers do little more than reformulate their basic positions. The very activity that impels the characters exhausts them.

Texts within the text do not resolve "the mystery of mysteries." In the person of Media, however, Melville resorts to another kind of putative authority. Media repeatedly asserts the utter worthlessness of philosophical discourse. In playing the role of demigod, he takes a stand above the swirl of Babbalanja's incessant pondering and frequently advises him to give up such runaway speculations. Like the texts within the text, Media's pronouncements seek to correct potentially self-exhausting excesses. One should, Media asserts, "[l]ay down the great maxims of things, but let inferences take care of themselves. Never be special; never, a partisan. . . . And if doubts distract you, in vain will you seek sympathy from your fellow men" (369). One merely encounters formulas, lies, indifference, hypocrisy, flunkyism, or

> a brutality of indiscriminate skepticism. Furthermore, Babbalanja, on this head, final, last thoughts you mortals have none; nor can have; and, at bottom, your own fleeting fancies are too often secrets to yourselves; and sooner may you get another's secret, than your own. Thus with the wisest of you all; you are ever unfixed. . . . The free airy robe of your philosophy is but a dream, which seems true while it lasts. . . . Babbalanja, you mortals dwell in Mardi, and it is impossible to get elsewhere. (369–70)

In this formulation, philosophy seems an evasion, a nuisance, a self-delusion. Inevitably, the "unfixed" character of the thinking mind restrains one from transcending the quotidian world of Mardi.

In the act of repudiating the philosophical quest, Media describes the "flux and reflux" that characterizes the limited world of social and natural contexts. There are moments, appearing with greater frequency as the narrative unfolds, when the philosopher agrees with the king. Babbalanja says that Mardians need to "quit this insanity. Let us be content with the theology in the grass and the flowers. . . . My Lord, my lord! sick with the spectacle of the madness of men, and broken with spontaneous doubts, I sometimes see but two things in all Mardi to believe:—that I myself exist, and that I can most happily, or least miserably exist, by the practice of righteousness" (428). Though Babbalanja "too often. . . . [swings] from these moorings," he finally abandons the dictum, *Dubito ergo sum,* in favor of the Christianized haven of Serenia. He evades rather than resolves the still lingering mysteries.[7]

Behind Media's petulance hides a human being whose empathy is often at odds with his autocratic self-image. All certainties—including Media's role of demigod—dissolve before the self-generated abyss of human subjectivity, the very nature that the king shares with his subjects. Media will eventually return to the historical condition—the "madding mobs" on his isle of Odo (566)—to face a popular insurrection, equipped perhaps, as Milton R. Stern argues, with a tempered wisdom (*Fine Hammered Steel* 146). Not merely a mocker, Media cares deeply about mortals in general and Babbalanja in particular. In Chapter 172, "King Media Dreams," Media summarizes the philosopher's vexed condition. In rejecting the conventional wisdom, Babbalanja wanders through an "endless vestibule":

> Brother gods, and demi-gods, it is not well. These mortals should have less or more. Among my subjects is a man, whose genius scorns the common theories of things; but whose still mortal mind cannot fathom the ocean at his feet. His soul's a hollow, wherein he raves. . . . Like lost children groping in the woods, they falter through their tangled paths; and at a thousand angles, baffled, start upon each other. And even when they make an onward move, 'tis but an endless vestibule, that leads to naught. (565–66)

Media's dream summarizes the complex forces assailing Melville's attempt to write philosophy in the form of fiction and fiction in the form of philosophy. The dream identifies the human being's tenuous position between phenomenal and noumenal realms. After repudiating orthodoxy, the philosopher is enmeshed and defeated by the very element—the dialectical nature of consciousness—that first opened the way to "tangled paths; and . . . a thousand angles."

PART TWO

"*The Absolute Condition of Present Things*"

4

Redburn and *White-Jacket:*
"Concocting Information into Wisdom"

But all events are mixed in a fusion indistinguishable.

—White-Jacket

ON 28 JANUARY 1849 Melville mailed the page proofs of *Mardi* to John Murray with the heady, nonnegotiable demand for a 200 guinea advance. Once again, Melville was dictating terms. Murray had had months to mull over the implications of the author's "blunt" embrace of romance. The publisher's resulting reply—in an "Antarctic tenor"—did little to deter Melville's self-promotion (*Correspondence* 109). Demanding that he not be identified as " 'the author of Typee & Omoo,' " Melville flatly stated, "I wish to separate '*Mardi*' as much as possible from those books" (*Correspondence* 114–15). Melville seemed to be courting Murray's rejection as a kind of inverted imprimatur of exalted literary achievement.

In this state of postcompositional confidence, Melville went to Boston to await the birth of his first child. On 5 February 1849 Melville turned out to hear a speaker in Boston's Freeman Place Chapel; it was Ralph Waldo Emerson, lecturing on "Mind and Manners in the Nineteenth Century."[1] Since this first sustained encounter with Emerson occurred during a period when Melville was immersing himself in Shakespeare's plays, it is no surprise that he was thinking at the time about the meaning of literary greatness. As his letters to Duyckinck attest, Melville included Emerson and Shakespeare in "the whole corps of thought-divers, that have been diving & coming up again with blood-shot eyes since the world began" (121). While praising Shakespeare to the heavens, Melville qualified his assessment of Emerson, taking care to distinguish between his "merit" and his "gaping flaw." Part of Melville's energy was directed toward asserting his independence from Emerson's reputed "transcendentalisms, myths & oracular gibberish." When he proclaimed, "I do not oscillate in Emerson's rainbow, but prefer rather to hang myself in mine own halter," Melville was not chaffing under the anxiety of influence (121).[2] It was a matter of priority. Melville had imbibed his own decoction of "transcendentalisms" from Plato, a point that cannot be too strongly reinforced. And Melville cared little for parochial disputes over the aging transcendental newness. He even defended the "brilliant" Emerson against Duyckinck's apparent imputation that Emerson's work was derivative:

> Be his stuff begged, borrowed, or stolen, or of his own domestic manufacture he is an uncommon man. . . . Lay it down that had not Sir Thomas Browne lived, Emerson would not have mystified— I will answer, that had not Old Zack's father begot him, Old Zack would never have been the hero of Palo Alto. The truth is that we are all sons, grandsons, or nephews or great-nephews of those who go before us. No one is his own sire. (121)

Couched in a simulated dialogue—"Lay it down . . . I will answer"— Melville's allusion to Browne suggests that Melville's attraction to Emerson had less to do with the content of Emersonian thought than with the process of intellection and his own relation to earlier traditions. Though Melville probably went on to read some or all of Emerson's *Essays: First Series,* his primary response was to defend Emerson's practice in light of his own developing aesthetic. Melville's notion that we are "all sons. . . . No one is his own sire" paradoxically liberated him from being anyone's disciple. In February 1849 Emerson appealed to Melville as one more thought-diver recasting the wisdom of the ages in the language of the day (*Correspondence* 121–22). At the very least, Melville's encounter with Emerson as lecturer and author would have reinforced Melville's penchant for the dialectical possibilities of literary art, while the

plays of Shakespeare would have encouraged his desire to dramatize great ideas through tragic action.

Melville's encounters with Plato and Browne in 1848 and Emerson
and Shakespeare in 1849 provided stimulating contexts for dramatizing ideas. In his purchase of Pierre Bayle's *An Historical and Critical Dictionary,* Melville recognized an opportunity to extend his
researches: indeed, he imagined himself peacefully presiding over a
three-way textual interchange. In a 5 April 1849 letter to Duyckinck,
Melville mentioned that he "bought a set of Bayle's Dictionary the
other day, & on my return to New York intend to lay the great old
folios side by side & go to sleep on them thro' the summer, with the
Phaedon in one hand & Tom Brown in the other" (128–29).[3] Melville
had evolved a fantasy of the good life: he would lull himself to sleep
while absorbing ancient and modern wisdom. This act of self-dramatization exposes his tendency to view reading as a procreant fusion of multiple resources. The principle of fusion, as it were, is
nothing other than the reader's focusing eye and inquiring mind.

In the *Dictionary,* Bayle seeks to explain and critique *all* thinkers, movements, and systems. Obviously his obsessive pursuit of
argumentative totality is doomed. Books can only fail attempting
to contain an entire world. But like Plato's dialogues and Burton's
Anatomy, Bayle's ten-volume tome offers a model of artistic and
philosophical self-cultivation; it may be the world's ultimate book
for serendipitous browsing. In his reading Melville may have confronted Bayle's tirade against Spinoza's pantheism, his refutation
of Gnostic heresies, his exploration of Chrysippus' stoicism, and
his discussion of Zoroaster's interest in magic.[4] To open any volume to any page is to find the sort of intellectual feast Melville
appreciated. The very layout of the pages overwhelms one with the
dialectical interstices of argument. In large print Bayle covers the
contours of historical narrative—the general matters of biography
and thought. In small print the footnotes contain gnarled, often
vituperative, commentary replete with etymologies, extracts, and
reading lists. In forging one text from many, Bayle locates the principle of cohesion in his own adjudication. Melville's very desire to

pursue Bayle in the company of Plato and Browne reflected a habit of mind in which any direct statement is a prelude to a tangled interplay of competing positions—a quality already exhibited in *Mardi* and which would find muted issue in *Redburn,* a polemical cast in *White-Jacket,* and quintessential expression in *Moby-Dick,* especially in such chapters as "The Chapel," "Moby Dick," and "The Whiteness of the Whale." Bayle's example confirmed that all argument has roots in historical and literary contexts. Such a condition pertains directly to two of Melville's informing beliefs: first, that there are very few thoughts per se; for the few true thoughts have been abroad throughout the ages; and second, that once ascertained through study or inspiration, these ideas are the materials that true genius reinvents.

Murray rejected *Mardi.* Through his agent, John R. Brodhead, Melville made arrangements to get the page proofs to Richard Bentley, a publisher who had courted Melville and now paid handsomely—a 200 guinea advance—for the rights to publish *Mardi.* The book made its British appearance on 15 March 1849, and soon thereafter negative reviews and slow sales revealed that it would be neither a critical nor a financial success.[5] It is not clear how surprised or disappointed Melville was. He had already claimed to have detached himself from the book and was looking ahead to new work, new vistas. In the same letter in which he outlined his summer plans for Bayle and company, he commented on his chronic incapacity to rest with the fiction of closure:

> I am glad you like that affair of mine. But it seems so long now since I wrote it, & my mood has so changed, that I dread to look into it, & have purposely abstained from doing so since I thanked God it was off my hands.—Would that a man could do something & then say—It is finished.—Not that one thing only, but all others—that he has reached his uttermost, & can never exceed it. But live & push—tho' we put one leg forward ten miles—its no reason the other must lag behind—no, *that* must again distance the other—& so we go till we get the cramp & die. (128, Melville's emphasis)

Although Melville, when writing to Judge Lemuel Shaw, seemed irked that *Mardi* was "cut into by the London Atheneum, and also burnt by the common hangman in the Boston Post," with this letter to his father-in-law, Melville adopted a pose of stoical forbearance: "These attacks . . . are essential to the building up of any permanent reputation. . . . But Time, which is the solver of all riddles, will solve 'Mardi'" (130).

Melville now dismissed any notion of treating himself to a lazy summer. Unable to enjoy what he later would call "the silent grass-growing mood in which a man *ought* always to compose," Melville felt pressed by the dunning devils of economic necessity (*Correspondence* 191, Melville's emphasis). By the end of April 1849 Melville had begun *Redburn,* and by the end of August he had completed *White-Jacket.*[6] He pushed himself along but did not view these works as a forward march. In reluctantly eschewing *Mardi's* mindscape, Melville returned to an art predicated on, but by no means contained by, the contours of direct personal experience. In *Redburn,* Melville fictionalizes his 1839 voyage as a twenty-year-old green hand sailing round-trip between New York and Liverpool; in *White-Jacket* he bases his anatomy of the world aboard a man-of-war on his 1843–44 experiences as a sailor homeward bound from Hawaii to Boston on the frigate *United States.* With improvisational romance ostensibly giving way to mimetic representation, Melville felt resentment for these "two *jobs,* which I have done for money—being forced to it, as other men are to sawing wood" (*Correspondence* 138). Now a day laborer, or worse, a tramp, Melville was particularly hard on *Redburn,* finding its laudatory reviews "laughable" (*Journals* 14). While in London to peddle *White-Jacket,* Melville happened to glean—without purchasing—*Blackwood's Magazine's* "long story about a short book." Melville remarks, "It's very comical—seemed so, at least, as I had to hurry over it—in treating the thing as real. But the wonder is that the old Tory should waste so many pages upon a thing, which I, the author, know to be trash, & wrote it to buy some tobacco with" (*Journal* 13).

Melville's deepest artistic desires had been compromised by economic constraints. His predilection was for writing "those sort of

books which are said to 'fail' "—books like *Mardi* that gave vent to
the free play of intellectual curiosity (*Correspondence* 139). These
inclusive narratives not only lacked form but flaunted it, making
prodigious demands on readers. On 5 June 1849, in a letter to
Bentley, who absorbed the brunt of *Mardi's* economic failure,
Melville summed up the problem: "the metaphysical ingredients
(for want of a better term) of the book, must of course repel some
of those who read simply for amusement"(131). Echoing Babbalanja,
Melville explains that some literary artists do not *control* the processes of invention: "But some of us scribblers . . . always have a
certain something unmanageable in us, that bids us do this or that,
and be done it must—hit or miss" (132). For purposes of prudence,
Melville describes the nearly completed *Redburn* as being com-
pletely manageable, "a plain, straightforward, amusing narrative
of personal experience," an entertaining story with "no metaphysics, no conic-sections, nothing but cakes & ale." If in *Mardi*
Melville attempted to include the broad range of his accumulated
learning, in *Redburn* he professedly tried to exclude or repress it.
While never openly deprecatory toward *White-Jacket*, Melville still
branded it with the stamp of mere labor.

When all is said about dunning devils and conscripted labor,
and the grousing and juggling that informs the biographical
record, one must confront the vexing (and liberating) critical fact:
Melville's reductive descriptions of these literary *"jobs"* do not
describe his achievement. As he admits in one disjunctive and telling remark, he had "not repressed myself much—so far as *they* are
concerned; but have spoken pretty much as I feel" (*Correspondence* 139). Indeed, in both *Redburn* and *White-Jacket*, "straightforward, amusing" narrative stands in uneasy tension with
"metaphysical ingredients" that rupture *Redburn* and permeate
White-Jacket. These elements appear in three primary forms: first,
Melville exercises his allusive reflex, sporadically in *Redburn* and
aboundingly in *White-Jacket*; second, he fashions scenes of reading, in *Redburn* especially, in which the narrator initiates and arrests the story's progress in order to interpret texts and objects,
revealing the mind's activity as it plays on meanings; third,

Melville offers essayistic excursions, extended meditations on issues both integral and tangential to each narrative's informing purpose. In adapting these forms, Melville moves toward controlling *Mardi*'s scattershot discharges. Through his allusions, scenes of reading, and essayistic excursions, Melville avoids artistic repression and dramatizes the interaction of multiple voices. In *Redburn* and *White-Jacket* the inclusion of "metaphysical ingredients (for want of a better term)" becomes Melville's chief means of "concocting information into wisdom" (*White-Jacket* 322), linking the narrator's story with what White-Jacket himself describes as "philosophy—that is, the best wisdom that has ever in any way been revealed to our man-of-war world." Rather than propounding fixed precepts, this "best wisdom" leads one into "a slough and a mire, with a few tufts of good footing here and there" (186).

THE PLAY OF ALLUSION

Allusion, by its very nature, is dialectical. It incorporates material from other contexts—personal, literary, historical—and transforms it within the host text. Whether consciously or unconsciously forged, an allusion appears as a selective appropriation, functioning locally and intertextually. By its very importation, the "revisionary power" of allusion "generates new figuration" (Hollander ix). As Bloom notes in *The Anxiety of Influence,* "[P]oetic influence need not make poets less original; as often it makes them more original, though not necessarily better" (7).[7]

Allusion inevitably complicates the experience of writing and reading. An overt allusion creates a nexus between two literary works. The original source is directly identified, and its pertinence enriches the new context by extending the range of association. A buried allusion or echo, on the contrary, makes no pronounced claim to be intertextual resonance. Though purporting to be a narrator's creation, these vestigial phrases, words, or echoes may reflect the narrator's unconscious transumption of his reading.[8] In Melville's work, it is not always possible to distinguish between conscious and unconscious allusions. Sir Thomas Browne had such an impact that Melville at times subsumes Browne's voice, style, and tropes. In *Religio Medici,* for example, Browne attacks intellectual pride: "for indeed heads of capacity . . . thinke they know nothing, till they know all; which being impossible, they fall upon the opinion of *Socrates,* and only know they know not any thing" (78). When discussing the sailor as a jack-of-all-trades, Melville gives Redburn some of Browne's words, without attribution. The multitalented sailor exemplifies how knowledge leads one to ignorance: "And this, perhaps, in a greater or less degree, is pretty much the case with all things else; for you know nothing till you know all; which is the reason we never know any thing" (121). If Melville borrows without remembering, then Browne's words undergo a kind of transmigration. If Melville remembers the source, then he consciously excludes overt reference, perhaps to maintain the appearance that *Redburn* is "plain" and "straightforward."

In another instance, Redburn, on leaving home, makes an indirect allusion to Adam and Eve's expulsion from the garden in *Paradise Lost* by remarking, "[T]he world was before me" (11) while he himself stands on the threshold of a stark and horrifying newness.[9] The allusion reinforces his imminent separation from the preexperiential idyll. Two paragraphs later, Redburn makes explicit the postlapsarian nature of his figure: the "blights" of experience "leave such a scar that the air of Paradise might not erase it." For the receptive reader, the allusion creates a dialectical relationship between Melville's language and Milton's poem. In one view, the reference to the archetypal Fall might seem ironic, a case of Redburn bloating his own self-importance. It may even involve his misreading of his own experience, since his paradise had ended much earlier with the death of the father. In any event, the circumstance of the boy forced by necessity to become a man is not only archetypal—hence the allusion to our first parents—but this initiation is also personal and terrifying—hence Redburn's anticipation of his impending immersion into the brutal world of work. At the very least, narrator and reader must contend with the teasing limits of an allusion's application.

Frequently, in Melville's conscious use of allusion he restricts his application of the figure. In *Redburn* direct allusions to learned traditions infrequently appear. When they do, they often function as synoptic metaphors—distilled, concise evocations of complex systems of thought that resonate with associational possibilities. For example, Redburn discusses the boredom of ship life: "However, I endeavored to bear it all like a young philosopher, and whiled away the tedious hours by gazing through a port-hole. . . . Yes, I got used to all these matters, and took most things coolly, in the spirit of Seneca and the stoics" (122). The narrator links himself with the school of patient suffering, as Ishmael later does with his own "strong decoction of Seneca and the Stoics" (*Moby-Dick* 6). Consistently, Melville associates Seneca with a humorous, if rueful, capacity for high-minded endurance. In trying to restrict learned discourse, Melville avoids the kind of allusive catalog so prevalent in *Mardi*. At one point, in an uncharacteristic spree, Redburn makes three references in the space of a sentence. In discussing Captain Riga's paternal qualities, the narrator exploits the disparity between ignorant idealization and deflating actuality:

> Indeed, I had made no doubt that he would in some special manner take me under his protection . . . as I had heard that some sea-captains are fathers to their crew; and so they are; but such fathers as Solomon's precepts tend to make—severe and chastising fathers . . . who . . . play the part of Brutus, who ordered his son away to execution, as I have read in our old family Plutarch. (67)

Multiple allusions explicitly signal the displacement of the tyro actor; an older retrospective voice levies judgments in the present-tense compositional moment. As in *Mardi*, Melville develops dichotomous voices within a single narrator. Indeed, the older retrospective narrator, speaking in the present tense, betrays a bitter impatience with the implications of recounting his own tale. At one point he must stifle his memories of those "delightful days" before his father died bankrupt: "[W]hen I think of those days, something rises up in my throat and almost strangles me" (36). Like the evocation of the narrator's present moment, allusion disrupts the past-tense account of his initiation: it jars the surface of mimetic representation with imported materials. Just as the retrospective narrator calls attention to the activity, or process, of interpretation, so too does allusion imbue the narrative with dialectical possibilities that no naive account could contain. Learned allusion becomes the province of an experienced narrator rather than the tyro actor.

While in *Redburn* allusions tend to appear as incidental irruptions that suggest the intensity of Melville's repression, in *White-Jacket* allusions abound. White-Jacket constructs an intertextual matrix, appropriating materials from multiple sources and applying them to his present narrative moment. The narrator insistently links his story with a learned tradition, and his extensive experience with books informs and shapes his anatomy of the world. *White-Jacket* contains numerous classical allusions—to Ovid, Jupiter, Virgil, Ulysses, Plutarch, Sophocles—as well as literary allusions—to Chaucer, Marlowe, Don Quixote, Shakespeare, Jonson, Spenser, Beaumont and Fletcher, Milton, Shelley, Byron—and philosophical and religious allusions—to Plato, Seneca, Heraclitus, Aristotle, Tertullian, and the Gnostics. As these selective listings suggest, the narrator's experience of books informs his characterization. In one such instance Ushant, a humble sailor, assumes the status of a high-minded wisdom seeker and is celebrated by White-Jacket as a reflective, stoic philosopher:

> [Y]et when his duty did not call for exertion, he was a remarkably staid, reserved, silent, and majestic old man, holding himself aloof from noisy revelry. . . . He resolutely set his beard against their boyish frolickings, and often held forth like an oracle concerning the vanity thereof. Indeed, at times he was wont to talk philosophy to his ancient companions. . . . Nor was his philosophy to be despised; it abounded in wisdom. For this Ushant was an old man, of strong natural sense, who had seen nearly the whole terraqueous

globe, and could reason of civilized and savage, of Gentle and Jew, of Christian and Moslem. (353)

Melville's portrait of the aged philosopher focuses on Ushant's common station and his commonsense apprehension. Philosophy is married to the quotidian: it finds expression as a habit of mind, an engagement of "the reflective faculties of any serious-minded man, however humble or uneducated." To be a philosopher, then, one does not have to study any particular school. One must simply seek wisdom. Linking Ushant to Socrates, and evoking Spenser and Persius, White-Jacket fuses the common life and the world of mind: "[Ushant] was a sort of sea-Socrates, in his old age 'pouring out his last philosophy and life,' as sweet Spenser has it; and I never could look at him, and survey his right reverend beard, without bestowing upon him that title which, in one of his satires, Persius gives to the immortal quaffer of the hemlock—*Magister Barbatus*— the bearded master" (353). The allusion to Socrates evokes not only wisdom but also heroic self-possession and absolute integrity.

If in *Redburn* allusion tends to displace the tyro actor's limited knowledge in favor of the older narrator's intellectual apprehension, then in *White-Jacket* allusion tends to accentuate the sailor-narrator's judgmental authority. As I demonstrate below, White-Jacket's bookishness is a tactical complement to his intermittent polemical purposes, whether his target be inept tyrannical captains, the Articles of War, or the hypocrisy of Christian preachment on a ship of war. At one point White-Jacket makes murder and suicide sound like reasonable applications of Natural Law. Essentially, in *White-Jacket* Melville finds a way to adapt the allusive reflex to support his narrator's credibility. The learned narrator applies his intellectual elevation to advance the cause of the much-abused "people." Melville's erudition, as it later does in *Moby-Dick*, comes to serve populist, or democratic, purposes.

Scenes of Reading

Throughout his first three books, Melville insistently dramatizes the attempt to interpret strange places, objects, surfaces, or signs:

for example, Tommo confronts the indecipherable jungle ruins; Taji wants to translate Yillah's alien language; and Babbalanja wrestles with the meanings of stories, songs, stones, islands. To Melville's most inquisitive metaphysical questers—Ishmael, Ahab, Pierre, Celio, Mortmain—the world offers multiple texts.

The narrator of *Redburn* shares this sensibility, repeatedly enacting scenes of reading, self-consciously interpreting some arresting surface. In keeping with *Redburn*'s scaled-down concerns, the surfaces in question tend to be pedestrian, if not trivial. Early on, for example, Redburn examines a shipping advertisement and considers the meaning of the family's glass ship. These objects have their experiential counterpoints later in the book: the romanticized advertisement anticipates Redburn's attempt to read contemporary Liverpool through his father's guidebook, and the glass ship offers an iconic encapsulation of the tyro's degrading initiation into ship life. For the older Redburn, writing the story re-creates young Redburn's involvement with the making of meaning. For Melville, writing *Redburn* allows him to dispose of *Mardi*'s overtly metaphysical purpose while retaining its epistemological underpinnings.

While reading, Redburn invents the stuff of fiction. His transformation of an advertisement reflects the paradigmatic act of Melville's philosophical voyager. Perception *is* the adventure. By interpreting signs, one creates a world. In *Mardi* the narrator's vision on the masthead generates his successive fictional domain. On a more pedestrian plane, Redburn fashions his idealized world from the newspaper. In a phrase-by-phrase exegesis, he "devoured such announcements" (3), reading as if "every word . . . suggested volumes of thought" (4). He shapes the contours of desire: "Indeed, during my early life, most of my thoughts of the sea were connected with land; but with fine old lands. . . . As I grew older my thoughts took a larger flight." And he imagines "remote and barbarous countries. . . . how dark and romantic my sunburnt cheeks would look" (5).

These idealizations are as fragile as his parents' bottled glass ship, yet his youthful examination of this ship recasts his reading of the advertisement. The icon, like the text, provides an open, imaginative space: "[A]mong . . . mazes of spun-glass I used to rove in imagination, till I grew dizzy at the main-truck" (8). However beautiful, this memory is no more applicable to his actual voyage than the glass ship would be to the business of sailing. Nor can the recollected image of the intact glass ship be separated from its current decrepitude. Indeed, its dilapidation reflects the older narrator's fractured condition. Speaking of the broken sailor, the narrator remarks, "I will not have him put on his legs again, till I get on my own" (9). For both Redburn and Melville, the process of reading forges a self-reflexive world.

Older Redburn's reconstruction not only describes the folly of youth but also situates him in the compositional present. Nothing in the text reveals the dissociation between the older narrator and the tyro actor better than the two radically distinct renderings of his father's "outlandish" guidebook. Chapters 30 and 31 offer two scenes of reading. In the first the older narrator, while writing, takes the book from the shelf and pages through it. In the following chapter the narrator depicts Redburn's attempt to use the anachronistic guidebook. The first scene describes the older narrator engaging a text; the second dramatizes the tyro's discovering how the "moving world" cannot be circumscribed by an iconic text.

The older narrator wishes to bring the guidebook before the reader's eye: "But let me get it down from its shrine and paint it, if I may, from the life" (143). When he says, "But let us open the volume," he initiates a mental journey. The enshrined icon becomes subsumed in the narrator's mental process; the old fuses with the new. This scene situates the narrator—not the book—as guide. His experience of reading cannot be separated from the activity of writing: "Turning over that leaf, I come upon some half-effaced miscellaneous memoranda in pencil" (144). His father's pencil marks, "from the numerous effacements," are a strain to see. Remarkably, Redburn prefigures Ishmael before the painting in the Spouter-Inn: "[I]t is much like cross-reading to make them out" (*Redburn* 144). He then retraces his father's path through a city map, scrutinizing various plates, illustrations, insignias. As he fondly "linger[s] over this circumstantial paragraph," he laments that the anonymous author did not mark "the precise hour of the day." Nor did he mention "his age, occupation, and name."

Seeking to quantify and thereby delineate the diachronic distance between himself and the author, the narrator plays futilely on the possibility of filling in the text's lacunae: "But all is now lost; I know not who he was; and this estimable author must needs share the oblivious fate of all literary incognitoes" (146). Like Babbalanja in *Mardi,* the narrator reflects on the meaning of personal absence. The act of reading depicts, as it were, the mind creating meaning as it plays over a recalcitrant text. This activity leads to the kind of essayistic or metaphysical excursion most characteristic of *White-Jacket* but manifest infrequently in *Redburn.* In considering the antiquarian inapplicability of the guidebook, the narrator decries the vanity of human wishes. He evokes the strains of Heraclitus and Ecclesiastes that resonate in Babbalanja's meditation on the "flux and reflux" of experience. He also echoes Taji's meditation in the "Time and Temples" chapter on the way in which architectural constructs are built over ruins. Such ruins, of course, in Melville's aesthetic, are analogs of old texts:

As I now fix my gaze upon the faded and dilapidated old guidebook. . . . I am forcibly reminded that the world is indeed growing old. And when I . . . skim over page after page throughout the volume, all filled with allusions to the immense grandeur of a place, which, since then, has more than quadrupled in population, opulence, and splendor, and whose present inhabitants must look back upon the period here spoken of with a swelling feeling of immeasurable superiority and pride, I am filled with a comical sadness at the vanity of all human exaltation. For the cope-stone of to-day is the corner-stone of to-morrow; and as St. Peter's church was built in great part of the ruins of old Rome, so in all our erections, however imposing, we but form quarries and supply ignoble materials for the grander domes of posterity. (148–49)

In the following chapter, the narrator recounts his youthful attempt to use the old guidebook on the contemporary city. The guidebook's failure has already been interpretively determined, both in the preceding scene of reading and in Redburn's foreboding about the incongruity between his romantic idealizations and the experiential actuality:

> As I stood leaning over the side, and trying to summon up some image of Liverpool, to see how the reality would answer to my conceit . . . I was startled by the doleful, dismal sound of a great bell, whose slow intermitting tolling seemed in unison with the solemn roll of the billows. I thought I had never heard so boding a sound; a sound that seemed to speak of judgment and the resurrection, like belfrey-mouthed Paul of Tarsus. (126–27)

Indeed, by the time Redburn marches through Liverpool, the guidebook has been discredited. Clearly, the "reality" has no chance of "answer[ing] my conceit." By predetermining the outcome, Melville accentuates the failure of Redburn's reading even to the point of undercutting the scene's dramatic power. Redburn seeks to make an outmoded icon serve the rushing movement of his day. In the preceding chapter the older narrator's activity of reading contrasts with young Redburn's naive attempt to make a static textual product express the ongoing flux of life. Redburn's epiphany is a stale redaction of the aesthetic principle already demonstrated: "Yes, the thing that had guided the father, could not guide the son." Redburn meditates on the "moving world" in which "Guide-books . . . are the least reliable books in all literature; and nearly all literature, in one sense, is made up of guide-books. . . . Every age makes its own guide-books" (157). However tired the writing, this passage focuses on the relationship between a text and the world. The loosely Emersonian dictum—"Every age makes its own guide-books"— does not affirm an ahistorical relativism but the need to make new books out of the old. The object, monument, or iconic text must inform the reader's imaginative reconstruction of new forms.

The presentation of the Liverpool docks adapts to the tyro's experience the narrative process manifest in the older Redburn's scene of reading. This climatic scene, which displaces the guidebook in favor of an object from everyday experience—the docks—contrasts these docks with the glass ship and guidebook. For example, Redburn eschews the construction of "cenotaphs" and contends that a hero's name should be linked with the "living interests of the race." The docks should be named after such heroes as Nelson and Rodney:

> And how much better would such stirring monuments be; full of life and commotion; than hermit obelisks of Luxor, and idle towers of stone; which, useless to the world in themselves, vainly hope to eternize a name, by having it carved, solitary and alone, in their granite. Such monuments are cenotaphs indeed; founded far away from the true body of the fame of the hero; who, if he be truly a hero, must still be linked with the living interests of his race; for the true fame is something free, easy, social, and companionable. They are but tomb-stones, that commemorate his death, but celebrate not his life. (162)

Forging an aesthetic distinction between "stirring monuments" and "tomb-stones," the older narrator fuses a hero's reputation with everyday "commotion." As a text, the guidebook must soon lose its applicability. Like the docks, literature provides the greatest tribute: "And more enduring monuments are built in the closet with the letters of the alphabet, than even Cheops himself could have founded, with all Egypt and Nubia for his quarry." As in *Mardi*'s "Time and Temples" chapter, Melville projects the literary artist as a builder who takes existing, even ruined, structures and transforms them into literary artifacts containing the "flux and reflux" of experience. The artist-builder expresses the process of thinking on the printed page.

ESSAYISTIC EXCURSIONS

Scenes of reading are the phenomenological basis for Melville's essayistic excursions. These flights of mind exemplify his attempt to blend fiction and philosophy.[10] Whereas in *Redburn* Melville tries to avoid "metaphysical ingredients," in *White-Jacket* they constitute an integral part of the narrator's anatomical and polemical designs. Here the essayistic excursion replaces *Mardi*'s philosophical dialogue as Melville's primary technique for elaborating on critical issues. As noted earlier, White-Jacket's own allusive reflex imbues him with intellectual authority—an authority that supports him in his metaphysical and polemical enterprises. He not only describes the world; he *judges* the world in tones of both jest and earnest. For example, in discoursing on the philosophy of the maintop, White-Jacket presents a playful parody of transcendental clichés; at the same time combining Platonism, transcendental idealism, stoical acceptance, cultural relativity, indeterminacy, and providentialism:

> We perceived how that evil was but good disguised, and a knave a saint in his way; how that in other planets, perhaps, what we deem wrong, may there be deemed right; even as some substances, without undergoing any mutations in themselves, utterly change their color, according to the light thrown upon them. . . . And we fancied that though some of us . . . were at times condemned to sufferings and slights, and all manner of tribulation and anguish, yet, no doubt, it was only our misapprehension of these things that made us take them for woeful pains instead of the most agreeable pleasures. (186)

This passage reflects White-Jacket's expansive temperament. At one point he physically reclines, "serenely concocting information into wisdom" (322). For White-Jacket the philosophical act is not an attempt to discover a priori truths but to engage the complexities of lived experience: "For after all, philosophy—that is, the best wisdom that has ever in any way been revealed to our man-of-war world—is but a slough and a mire, with a few tufts of good footing here and there" (186).

Given this sensibility, White-Jacket understandably satirizes the ship's chaplain for his failure to critique the "castle of war" (157).

The chaplain never considers the ironic disparity between the Sermon on the Mount and the Articles of War. Instead he flutters in rapture, his positions mere platitudes. White-Jacket's critique mocks the chaplain, especially his failure to act upon his precepts:

> He had drank at the mystic fountain of Plato; his head had been turned by the Germans . . . White-Jacket himself saw him with Coleridge's Biographia Literaria in his hand.
>
> Fancy, now, this transcendental divine standing behind a gun-carriage on the main-deck, and addressing five hundred salt-sea sinners upon the psychological phenomena of the soul, and the ontological necessity of every sailor's saving it at all hazards. He enlarged upon the follies of the ancient philosophers; learnedly alluded to the Phædon of Plato; exposed the follies of Simplicius's Commentary on Aristotle's "DeCœlo". . . . He was particularly hard upon the Gnostics and Marcionites . . . but he never, in the remotest manner, attacked the every-day vices of the nineteenth century. (155–56)

Mardi's preoccupation with the ideational relationship between phenomenal and noumenal realms becomes adapted in *White-Jacket* to a consideration of practical political problems.[11] Either a learned hypocrite or an effete apologist, the chaplain professes to believe in Christian fellowship while supporting the bloody realpolitik of war. Given his sanitized philosophy, this separation between ideas and action is irrelevant, for in his world, absolute precepts or ideals become so many pretty, but inaccessible, lights twinkling in the empyrean.

White-Jacket finds such a dissociation disturbing and later summarizes what happens when realpolitik is divorced from moral imperatives. In this excursion, the present tense functions as a ground-clearing act. Displacing the recollecting voice and releasing himself into direct address, he breaks forth in lamentation:

> Ah! the best righteousness of our man-of-war world seems but an unrealized ideal, after all; and those maxims which, in the hope of bringing about a Millennium, we busily teach to the heathen, we

Christians ourselves disregard. In view of the whole present social frame-work of our world, so ill adapted to the practical adoption of the meekness of Christianity, there seems almost some ground for the thought, that although our blessed Savior was full of the wisdom of heaven, yet his gospel seems lacking in the practical wisdom of earth.[12] (324)

In maintaining a stark polarization between ideal and practical affairs, the chaplain preempts the dangers and rewards of plunging into the "slough and . . . mire" of dialectic. Conversely, Melville's narrator pursues the "best wisdom" within a provisional and open-ended forum.

Just as an inquiring mind is compelled to engage the impenetrable mystery at the heart of things, in *White-Jacket* the mystery of the world cannot be dissociated from the mystery of the self. Toward the end of this narrative wherein human ontology opens the way to soundless depths, White-Jacket unifies the images of sailing and self-scrutiny: "Thus sailing with sealed orders, we ourselves are the repositories of the secret packet, whose mysterious contents we long to learn. There are no mysteries out of ourselves" (398). In a remarkable passage that anticipates Ishmael's meditation in "The Mat-Maker" chapter of *Moby-Dick,* White-Jacket offers his most profound excursion, speculating on the intersection between things as they are—here identified as Fate—and the inscrutable powers of self-making. Here, Fate provides the encompassing context within which one molds one's being. This meditation evolves from White-Jacket's consideration of the difficulties involved in interpreting victory or defeat in war as a sign of divine will. The simple fact is that Christian and Pagan have always fallen at one another's hands: "But all events are mixed in a fusion indistinguishable. What we call Fate is even, heartless, and impartial; not a fiend to kindle bigot flames, nor a philanthropist to espouse the cause of Greece. We may fret, fume, and fight; but the thing called Fate everlastingly sustains an armed neutrality" (320).[13]

White-Jacket anticipates both Ahab's fear that there may be "naught beyond" the pasteboard masks of material forms (*Moby-Dick* 164) and the body of naturalistic and existential thought that depicts the universe of physical force as a dumb, indifferent domain of chemical process.[14] For White-Jacket, however, the notion of Fate's "armed neutrality" offers no invitation to nihilistic despair. Rather, the blank, neutral mask of Fate establishes the perimeters wherein one fashions a private vision of universal ordinance, a kind of personal fiction to be inscribed on the blank surfaces of passing phenomena. It is no wonder, then, that he goes on to echo the Heraclitean notion that character is Fate:

> Yet though all this be so, nevertheless, in our own hearts, we mold the whole world's hereafters; and in our own hearts we fashion our own gods. Each mortal casts his vote for whom he will to rule the worlds; I have a voice that helps to shape eternity; and my volitions stir the orbits of the furthest suns. In two senses, we are precisely what we worship. Ourselves are Fate. (320–21)

In these remarkable passages, Melville construes cosmology as Fate but suggests that one's will can alter Fate. Within the "fusion indistinguishable," one constructs an interpretive paradigm which in turn informs action and re-forms character. White-Jacket is not merely saying that transcendent or absolute realms are compensatory fabrications. Rather, individual consciousness shapes, or "casts a vote," for what will constitute the supreme fiction.

White-Jacket's essayistic excursions manifest his commitment to examining abstract metaphysical concepts in relation to the "slough and . . . mire" of life. They offer versions of what Melville meant when he later wrote of his attempts to extract poetry from blubber (*Correspondence* 162). Indeed, the preceding passages suggest the ideational substratum of Melville's greatest works. In considering Taji and Yillah, Ishmael, Ahab and the whale, Pierre and Isabel, the Confidence Man and his dupes, and Captain Vere and Billy Budd, one must recognize how their stories all turn on the opposition between absolute and quotidian complexes, especially the problem of translating the dictates of ideal existence into the sordid contexts of the everyday. In a letter to Hawthorne, Melville insists that the greatest heroes confront "the absolute condition of present things" (186).[15] In *Redburn* and *White-Jacket,* Melville does not surrender his metaphysical purpose. Rather, he depicts his narrators' informing intellectual imperatives through the allusive reflex, which betrays their debts to earlier thinkers; scenes of reading, which dramatize the hermeneutical process; and essayistic, or metaphysical, excursions, which engage the "mystery of mysteries." Melville's insistence on seeding these narratives with philosophical materials is neither pedantic nor effete but an integral part of his creative life, a life in which the interpolation of "metaphysical ingredients" informs his evolving poetics.

Moby-Dick and the Impress of Melville's Learning

Oh, busy weaver! . . . the shuttle flies—the figures float from forth
the loom.

—*Moby-Dick*

IN A 1 May 1850 letter to Richard Henry Dana, Jr., perhaps three
months into the composition of his sixth book, Melville discussed
his ongoing attempt to extract poetic truth from unlikely elements:

> About the 'whaling voyage'—I am half way in the work. . . . It will be
> a strange sort of a book, tho', I fear; blubber is blubber you know; tho'
> you may get oil out of it, the poetry runs as hard as sap from a frozen
> maple tree;—& to cook the thing up, one must needs throw in a little
> fancy, which from the nature of the thing, must be ungainly as the gam-
> bols of the whales themselves. Yet I mean to give the truth of the thing,
> spite of this. (162)

Almost two months later, on 27 June 1850, Melville informed his
English publisher, Richard Bentley, that this "romance of adventure, founded upon certain wild legends in the Southern Sperm
Whale Fisheries" would be ready in autumn (*Correspondence* 163).
A little more than a month later, on 7 August 1850, Evert Duyckinck
wrote to his brother George, echoing the substance and tenor of
Melville's letter to Bentley. While Melville may have been trying to
entice a hefty advance from his publisher, he would have had no
reason to tell his friend about "a new book mostly done—a romantic, fanciful & literal & most enjoyable presentment of the
Whale Fishery—something quite new" (Leyda 385). Duyckinck

might even have read, or have listened to Melville read, part of the narrative. Since the narrative we know as *Moby-Dick* was not completed until July 1851, Melville must have radically altered his intentions. He probably began recasting the book not long after the Duyckinck letter.[1]

In "Unnecessary Duplicates: A Key to the Writing of *Moby-Dick*" Harrison Hayford proposes the landmark hypothesis that the presence of duplicated elements—"two narrative starts, two whaling ports, two inns . . . two innkeepers, two beds and goings-to-bed, two comrades . . . two signings-aboard, two Quaker captain-owners and a third Quaker captain-in-command," among other replications—indicates the textual fusion of a vestigial narrative with its redesigned complement and extension (134). According to Hayford, the original "whaling voyage" focused on a veteran-narrator and his companion (Bulkington) as they went to sea under a crusty, possibly peg-legged captain (Peleg). This narrative would probably have had close affinities to Melville's anatomical treatment of the man-of-war world in *White-Jacket*. The marvelous events of the sperm whale fishery, especially the expository materials and action scenes associated with *Moby-Dick*'s cetological sections, would have supplied the context wherein Melville could have presented the relationship between the questing Bulkington and the veteran-narrator—a replay, as it were, of the friendship between White-Jacket and Jack Chase. When Melville changed his book, "Four central characters . . . were involved . . . in a multiple reassignment of roles, which also redefined a fifth, the narrator. . . . In the process of reassignment, each of the four became in certain ways a duplicate; but while [Queequeg and Ahab] gained and consequently became major characters, [Peleg and Bulkington] lost and became to a degree vestigial—'unnecessary duplicates'" (145).

Hayford's hypothesis is compelling and provocative. In the process of composing this "strange sort of a book," Melville aspired to tell "the truth of the thing" and succeeded in making a book "broiled" in "hell-fire" (*Correspondence* 162, 196). The invention of Ahab alone would have shifted the aesthetic antecedent away from Melville's practices in *White-Jacket* and toward the metaphysical pursuits of *Mardi*. The figures of Promethean Ahab and, perforce, the White Whale probably loomed with Melville's decision to shift the dour, alienated, self-absorbed narrative voice of "The Carpet-Bag"—the probable vestigial opening chapter—to the genial, all-embracing, and accommodating narrative voice of "Loomings." In fact, the development of the absolutistic Ahab and the democratic Ishmael distinctively personalizes the intermittently solipsistic and genial voices evident in *Mardi*'s narrator during the pre-Yillah chapters. After Yillah's disappearance, Melville prefigures his great discovery of Ahab and Ishmael by isolating the absolutist in the demigod Taji and exploring the humane and social possibilities of dialectic and comic play in the representational voices of Philosophy, Poetry, History, and Authority. In *Moby-Dick* the voices and characters of Ahab and Ishmael focus the philosophical contexts of the whaling voyage.

While it is impossible to ascertain exactly when and how Melville transformed the apparently vestigial narrative, it is possible to examine those elements that appear instrumental in Melville's reformulation, especially those intellectual encounters that derive from Melville's journey to Europe after the composition of *Redburn* and *White-Jacket*, focusing in particular on books acquired in Europe and later at home in 1850 while he was actively composing *Moby-Dick*. Elements from this reading inform the development of Ishmael's voice and Ahab's character and provide sources for *Moby-Dick*'s central symbolic contexts, especially the world as loom and the whale as hieroglyph and Sphinx. The impress of Melville's learning provided hints or materials for his assimilative genius. Indeed, the fecund period between February 1849 and September 1850 culminated in Melville's decision to pursue within the gestating contours of his "whaling voyage" the philosophical implications of an essentially comic voice presenting an essentially tragic tale. One good book ended and a masterpiece began.

In the fall of 1849, Melville left home with the intention of staying away for the better part of a year and extending his travels through Europe and the Middle East.[2] Though grounded in a justifiable economic imperative—the in-person attempt to secure the best terms possible for *White-Jacket*'s publication—Melville's voyage to England derived in great part from his need "to take an airing through the world" (Leyda 528).[3] And in working to place the book himself, Melville sought to acquire the economic means that would secure his family's fiscal well-being and thereby release him to travel. Setting off on his trip with relief and high hopes, he was pleased to be away from the strains of work and domestic life and anticipated the salutary tonic of travel, talk, and literary lionizing. However homesick he might become, Melville had every intention of living with it.

On the voyage Melville had the good luck to encounter the perfect companion. Like Melville, George J. Adler was coming off a strenuous period of intellectual exertion.[4] Melville was fascinated by Adler's imposing scholarly mind: "He is author of a formidable lexicon, (German & English); in compiling which he almost ruined his health. He was almost crazy, he tells me, for a time. He is full of the German metaphysics, & discourses of Kant, Swedenborg, &c. He has been my principal companion thus far" (*Journals* 4). Sanford E. Marovitz examines Adler's epigraphs from Coleridge's *Biographia Literaria*, Plato's *Cratylus,* and Jean Paul Richter's *Levana oder Erziehlehre*, all of which depict "the power of language through literary tradition and through the distinctions that linguistic classification makes possible" (377). While there is no documentary evidence to suggest that Melville ever read Adler's "Preface," it is highly unlikely that Adler would have avoided his most cherished subjects in conversation. Marovitz plausibly speculates that Melville adapted at least some of Adler's methods and intentions in composing *Moby-Dick,* especially Adler's sense—gleaned from Richter—that "every good grammarian must of necessity, be a partial philosopher" (qtd. in Marovitz 380). According to Marovitz, Adler stimulated Melville's interest in the "double value of terminology" (381). In *Moby-Dick,* Melville's multiple uses of the loom and the Sphinx alone suggest the procreant possibilities of seeing objects in a range of associative meanings. Essentially, Adler stimulated Melville's metaphysical predisposition, especially the pursuit of what Melville called "the problem of the universe" (*Correspondence* 180,

185, 186, 452; *Moby-Dick* 158, 293). In one journal entry Melville relates their conversations to an appropriate Miltonic context and evokes the sedate demons of *Paradise Lost* who

> reason'd high
> Of Providence, Foreknowledge, Will and Fate,
> Fixt Fate, Free Will, Foreknowledge absolute
> And found no end, in wand'ring mazes lost.
> (Bk. II, lines 558–61)

Melville's own words—"Walked the deck with the German, Mr Adler, till a late hour, talking of 'Fixed Fate, Free-will, foreknowledge absolute'" (*Journals* 4)—do not associate him with the dour and tedious futility of Milton's damned; instead, Melville seems deft and wry in alluding to the endlessness of human speculation. The allusion indicates Melville's instinct for linking his own endeavors with appropriate textual corollaries. Similarly, not far from land, Melville comments on the rampant seasickness among his fellow passengers, at the same time echoing *Job* and prefiguring his epigraph to *Moby-Dick*'s epilogue: "A gale of wind, & every one sick. . . . & I alone am left to tell the tale of their misery" (*Journals* 6).

Melville's relationship with Adler on a voyage at sea constituted a propitious conflation of many elements in his life and work. The trip to England allowed Melville to reexperience his past as a sailor, though now he had no work to do and could rove in the rigging at will. Forced by circumstance to labor on his first voyage as a green hand, he traveled now as author and intellectual. Melville took note of the transfiguration: "*then* a sailor, *now* H.M. author of 'Peedee' 'Hullabaloo' & 'Pog-Dog'" (*Journals* 12, Melville's emphasis). Removed from wife, children, home, and work, Melville found himself in the experiential position of bachelorhood. He could enjoy the comradeship, the boozing, the intellectual repartee. It must have seemed that Melville was living out the peripatetic life of his questers in *Mardi*. The association of travel and talk was the dynamic, symbiotic force that tirelessly impelled *Mardi*'s action, and it invigorated his mind on the voyage.

Once in England, with the band of boon companions disassembled and plans for extended travel ruptured—*White-Jacket* did not garner a sufficient advance—Melville spent much of his time sightseeing, meeting potential publishers, and buying books. On his book-buying rambles Melville evinced a recurrent inclination for four kinds of narratives: romance, autobiography, biography, and a fictional hybrid that combines personal narrative and biography. The acquisition of William Godwin's *Caleb Williams* (Sealts, *Reading* #225) and William Beckford's *Vathek* (#54) reflected Melville's respective interest in the romantic potboiler and the exotic travelogue, and these books point further ahead to the composition of *Pierre* rather than to *Moby-Dick*. In the genre of autobiography, Melville acquired Thomas De Quincey's *The Confessions of an English Opium-Eater* (#180), Goethe's *Autobiography* (#228), and Rousseau's *Confessions* (#429). And turning to biography, Melville purchased Boswell's *Life of Johnson* (#84). This interest in biography continued through 1850, when he borrowed Carlyle's *On Heroes, Hero-Worship, and the Heroic in History* (#122) and probably read all or part of Emerson's *Representative Men* (#206a).

The hybrid genre of fictionalized autobiography that contains the fictional biography of another person was congenial to Melville's instincts and was reflected in his own writing. At the very least the autobiographically based *Typee, Omoo, Redburn,* and *White-Jacket* all fuse elements of fact and fiction in the cause of synthesizing such disparate generic contexts as travelogue, romance, novel, bildungsroman, satire, anatomy, and essay.[5] Similarly, in the biographically based *Israel Potter* and *Benito Cereno,* Melville looks to personal narrative for the raw materials to inspire his invention. In this regard Mary W. Shelley's *Frankenstein* (#467) was a notable purchase. In *Frankenstein,* Walton's first-person narrative contains the inset narratives of both Frankenstein and the monster. The contours of Shelley's novel find a provocative aesthetic complement in Carlyle's use of multiple narrators in *Sartor Resartus,* which Melville borrowed in June or July of 1850 (#123).

Of these acquisitions, De Quincey's *Confessions,* Shelley's *Frankenstein,* and Carlyle's *Sartor Resartus* offer the greatest range of suggestive possibilities for understanding the impress of Melville's more recent reading in relation to his auspicious reformulation of *Moby-Dick*. These works, whether read in London, as was the case with DeQuincey's *Confessions,* or later, as probably occurred with *Frankenstein* and *Sartor Resartus,* had the cumulative effect of supplying general and particular suggestions and materials for Melville's transformation of the Peleg-Bulkington "whaling voyage" into the Ishmael-Queequeg-Ahab voyage of *Moby-Dick.* It must be noted, however, that this particular cluster cannot be somehow viewed as a force separate from the inscrutable alchemical process of Melville's genius—a process that was also shaped by Melville's five previous books, his fascination with Shakespeare,[6] his August 1850 discovery of Hawthorne as artist and man, his self-reflexive review of Hawthorne's *Mosses from an Old Manse,* and his abiding interest in Emerson's work, among other forces. In viewing the relationship of particular texts to the gestation of *Moby-Dick,* one seeks to identify a symphony of possibilities that has a plausible relation to Melville's finished text. The danger of fixing a single resource as preeminent, as Nina Baym and John B. Williams do with Emerson, is that one cuts the Gordian knot of entangled interrelation. As most scholars would agree, source materials not only emerge in distinct topical contexts, but they also change shape, becoming, through a process of conscious and unconscious adaptation, the author's own. Like Ishmael in "The Whiteness of the Whale," one must proceed inductively by way of accumulation, keeping in mind that the sum of multiple possibilities does not add up to an answer—or a key—but to an articulation of those elements that might best formulate the best questions. Speculative surmises on De Quincey and Shelley, then, will pave the way for an examination of the possible interweaving of elements in *Moby-Dick,* Emerson's "History," and Carlyle's *Sartor Resartus.*

In a 22 December 1849 London journal entry, Melville notes that he "at last got hold of 'The Opium Eater'" (*Journals* 46). He started this "most wondrous book" immediately and finished it the next day (*Journals* 47). Given to "the sleep of endless reverie, and of dreamy abstraction from life and its realities," De Quincey's book provides a narrative analog to Ishmael (24). Both narrators combine meditative voice and orphaned status—traits that also characterize Rousseau in his *Confessions*. A "homeless vagrant upon the earth before I had accomplished my seventeenth year," De Quincey is alienated from a lost world of familial coherence and grandeur (54). Thrust forth into psychological exile, he must construct an order based on the "innumerable acts of choice [that] change countenance and are variously appraised at varying stages of life [and] shift with the shifting hours" (74). The meditative wanderer not only contemplates the flux of experience but also perceives that the act of choice circumscribes one's fate. Not only alive to the confluence of freedom and fate, the narrator often speaks in the self-possessed and proprietary tones that evoke Ishmael's comic voice. De Quincey on opium resembles Ishmael on the whale: "And therefore, worthy doctors, as there seems to be room for further discoveries, stand aside, and allow me to come forward and lecture on this matter" (156). Like Ishmael, De Quincey infuses his observations with humorous and genial assertions of authority: "This is the doctrine of the true church on the subject of opium. . . . I speak from the ground of a large and profound personal experience, whereas most of the unscientific authors who have at all treated of opium . . . make it evident, by the horror they express of it, that their experimental knowledge of its action is none at all" (158).

Bereft of traditional faith in a benevolent cosmos, De Quincey ponders a silent universe that haunts the inquiring mind. Like Emerson, Carlyle, and Melville, De Quincey associates the mysteries of creation with the image of the Sphinx: "If in this world there is one misery having no relief, it is the pressure on the heart from the *Incommunicable*. And, if another Sphinx should arise to propose another enigma to man—saying, What burden is that which only is insupportable by human fortitude? I should answer at once—*It is the burden of the Incommunicable*" (92, De Quincey's emphasis). This "insupportable . . . *burden*" provides a possible analog for Ahab's detestation of whatever force may lurk behind the "pasteboard masks" of material forms. As Ahab exclaims, "That inscrutable thing is chiefly what I hate" (164). De Quincey's

"Incommunicable" may also contain a germ of the narrator's speculation in *Pierre* on how "Silence is the only Voice of our God" (204).

Melville acquired Shelley's *Frankenstein* on 20 December 1849.
Though we have no evidence indicating when he might have read
it, striking affinities between *Frankenstein* and *Moby-Dick* suggest
that Melville read the novel with care. In pertaining to the characters and voices of Ahab and Ishmael, these affinities support the
notion that Shelley's book contributed to Melville's transformation of the "whaling voyage."

Of the most topical nature, Ahab's speech to the carpenter on
how to make a mighty man constitutes a probable adaptation of
Frankenstein's plan for making his monster. Ahab addresses the
carpenter as "manmaker" and the blacksmith as "Prometheus,"
perhaps alluding to Shelley's presentation of the modern
Prometheus, especially the myth of Prometheus *Plasticator*. Ahab
remarks, "I do deem it now a most meaning thing, that that old
Greek, Prometheus, who made men, they say, should have been a
blacksmith, and animated them with fire" (470). As scientist, artist, and creator, Frankenstein is obsessed with "bestowing anima-
tion upon lifeless matter" (52).[7] He usurps the divine power of
creation, desiring "to make the being of a gigantic structure; that
is to say, about eight feet in height, and proportionably large" (54).
In attempting to imagine a warrior gigantic enough to overcome
the vicissitudes of human life, Ahab conflates the myth of
Prometheus *Plasticator* with its associative counterpart: the myth
of the defiant Titan who stole fire from the gods and gave it to man.
Rooted in place, though not chained to a rock, Ahab's man would
presumably be ready to do battle with the gods. Ahab says, "Hold;
while Prometheus is about it, I'll order a complete man after a desirable pattern. Imprimis, fifty feet high in his socks; then, chest
modelled after the Thames Tunnel; then, legs with roots to 'em . . .
no heart at all, brass forehead, and about a quarter of an acre of
fine brains" (470).

Like *Moby-Dick,* Shelley's *Frankenstein* presents a strange sea
voyage into the great unknown as a primary narrative structure.
Walton's obsession with ultimate knowledge drives him toward

the desolate polar region where he meets the questing Franken-stein, who is bent on exacting vengeance by killing the monster he created. As a narrator Walton intermittently reflects the genial and megalomanical qualities of voice that respectively characterize Ishmael and Ahab. At one point Walton seems to prefigure Ishmael's exuberant embrace of the "barbarous," his "everlasting itch for things remote" (*Moby-Dick* 7). Walton reports, "I am practically industrious—pains-taking;—a workman to execute with persever-ance and labour:—but besides this, there is a love for the marvel-lous, a belief in the marvellous, intertwined in all my projects, which hurries me out of the common pathways of men, even to the wild sea and unvisited regions I am about to explore" (21–22). Shortly thereafter, Walton speaks with the obsessive voice that may have reminded Melville of Taji and perhaps pointed ahead to Ahab: "But success shall crown my endeavours. Wherefore not? Thus far I have gone, tracing a secure way over the pathless seas: the very stars themselves being witnesses and testimonies of my triumph. Why not still proceed over the untamed yet obedient element? What can stop the determined heart and resolved will of man?" (23, Shelley's emphasis).

Not only do Shelley and Melville draw on Promethean materi-als and present genial and absolutistic narrative voices, but they also present, in at least a limited sense, cautionary tales that depict the attraction to, and dangers of, one's attempts to recast the funda-mental terms of human existence. Both writers are drawn to the "Exceptional natures" capable of spawning such grandiose aspira-tions (Melville, *Clarel* 1.31.45). What intrigued Shelley about Walton and Frankenstein, and Melville about Ishmael and Ahab (and also Hawthorne and Shakespeare), was the degree to which these figures could strike through commonplace renderings to what Melville called the "vital truth" below the surface (*Piazza Tales* 244). Indeed, Walton's assessment of Frankenstein's exceptional nature evokes Melville's judgment of Shakespeare in "Hawthorne and His Mosses," which was composed in early August 1850. Walton remarks, "Some-times I have endeavoured to discover what quality it is which he possesses, that elevates him so immeasurably above any other person I ever knew. I believe it to be an intuitive discernment; a quick but never-failing power of judgment; a penetration into the causes of things"(29). Echoing this passage, Melville's description of Shakespeare's quality of mind characterizes the "whole corps of thought-divers" (*Correspondence* 121) that Melville so admired: "But it is those deep far-away things in him; those occasional flashings-forth of the intuitive Truth in him; those short, quick probings at the very axis of reality;—these are the things that make Shakespeare, Shakespeare" (*Piazza Tales* 244). And these are the things—the "quick probings at the very axis of reality"—that could well have united Melville's encounters with Plato, Browne, Montaigne, Rabelais, and Burton during the composition of *Mardi* to his al-chemical interaction with Emerson, Shakespeare, Bayle, Browne, Adler, De Quincey, Shelley, and Carlyle (among others) during the gestation and actual composition of *Moby-Dick*.

In mid-July 1850 Melville took his family on vacation to his cousin Robert Melvill's farm in Pittsfield, Massachusetts. This pro-pitious move got Melville away from the summer heat of New York City, returned him to a place where he spent pleasant summer months as a teenager, and placed him near Hawthorne, whom he met on 5 August. Although at this time Melville was saying that his whaling book was almost finished, both his move to the Berkshires and his encounters with Hawthorne, the man and the writer, un-settled his creative life and drove him toward making a book of world-class status. Hawthorne stood as Melville's most immediate model.

Melville's review of Hawthorne's *Mosses* is as close as Melville ever came to composing a self-advertising manifesto. In celebrat-ing the possibilities of American literature, Melville summons him-self forth as the American Shakespeare. Inflamed with the prospect of tragic vision, Melville considers the "great power of blackness" (*Piazza Tales* 243). At the center of Melville's decision to recast his "whaling voyage" must have been his desire to explore this "great power." Out of this desire, the figure of Ahab must somehow have loomed "interweavingly" (*Moby-Dick* 215) with the White Whale—an inventive symbiosis that reshaped the voice telling the tale as well as the symbolic context that contained the tale.

Given the teasing possibilities that attend the question of how Melville came to fuse the vestigial and the re-formed narratives of *Moby-Dick,* it is inviting to view "The Mat-Maker" chapter as an exemplary paradigm for speculating on the ways in which the vestigial narrative provided direction and clues for his reconstruction. This chapter seems to reside at the compositional nexus between old and new. Hayford speculates that "The Mat-Maker" was composed prior to the on-shore relationship between Ishmael and Queequeg (150–51). If this is so, the chapter may have supplied the notion of bringing a tyro Ishmael together with the cannibal Queequeg. It may also have suggested the possibility of extending the symbolic interconnection between phenomenal and noumenal realms, as represented in Ishmael's "Loom of Time," into the nautical and weaving contexts suggested by "Loomings."

In "The Mat-Maker" Ishmael presents a sublime synthesis of material and spiritual processes—a harmony made evident by the interpretive activity of the perceiving mind. Without question Melville derived the image of "the Loom of Time" from Carlyle's *Sartor Resartus.*[8] But his application of this figure constitutes an adaptation from Plato's Myth of Er in Book X of *The Republic.* In telling the tale of the soul's prebirth journey, Socrates fashions an elaborate cosmological image which conflates the structure of a ship with the operation of a loom: "this light is the belt of heaven, and holds together the circle of the universe, like the under-girders of a trireme. From these ends is extended the spindle of Necessity, on which all the revolutions turn. The shaft and hook of this spindle are made of steel. . . . Now the whorl is in form like the whorl used on earth" (2:410). Ship and loom act in unison with the Fates. Unlike Plato, for whom the Fates are absolute, Ishmael argues for the interconnection of apparently disparate elements: "[A]ye, chance, free will, and necessity—no wise incompatible—all interweavingly working together" (215). Melville fuses Carlyle's

Loom and Platonic myth with a narrator who creates meaning in the act of thinking. Melville's narrator is alert to the mind's ability to forge symbolic correspondences, even though the next instant may unravel his synthesis. Indeed, Tashtego sights a whale and Ishmael drops the "ball of free will" (215).

If "The Mat-Maker" chapter provides a nexus between old and new, it then makes sense to examine ways in which key elements of this chapter—the process narrator, the world as loom, the whale as lure—may have been re-formed in relation to Melville's encounters with works by Emerson and Carlyle, both of whom he apparently was reading in the summer of 1850. In the *Mosses* review Melville mentions Emerson with apparent familiarity, and in early September 1850 Melville spent a morning at Hawthorne's home reading an unspecified volume of Emerson's work.[9] Whether around this time or earlier, Melville almost certainly read Emerson's "History," the initial piece in *Essays: First Series*.

At the very least, "History" provides provocative terms that help describe Melville's achievement in developing voice and symbol in *Moby-Dick*. Like Carlyle (and Plato, Montaigne, Browne, Burton, and Coleridge), Emerson identifies an abiding pool of ideas that transcend historical boundaries. As these thoughts impinge on one's consciousness, past and present fuse into a sublime experience of perceptual synthesis: "When a thought of Plato becomes a thought to me,—when a truth that fired the soul of Pindar fires mine, time is no more" (*Essays* 15). Emerson's "History" focuses more on the poetic re-creation in the present "of a very few laws" than it does on the studious contemplation of things past (*Essays* 9). The vital force animating Plato and Pindar generates from the same eternal Soul pervading Nature. What interests Emerson is the way in which ideas become part of a thinker's perceptual present and then are translated into narrative. Emerson's "metempsychosis of nature" allows for the "innumerable variations" of these abiding ideational structures (*Essays* 8 and 9). Consequently, "History" highlights the centrality of story or fable as a means of presenting metaphysical concepts. As Emerson argues, "The philosophical perception of identity through endless mutations of form, makes him know the Proteus" (*Essays* 18). To evoke the figure of Prometheus, then, is for Emerson to give expression to

> universal verities. What a range of meanings and what perpetual pertinence has the story of Prometheus. . . . Prometheus is the Jesus of the old mythology. He is the friend of man; stands between the unjust 'justice' of the Eternal Father, and the race of mortals; and readily suffers all things on their account. (*Essays* 17)

Emerson's conflation of ancient myth and narrative self-fashioning through the "metempsychosis of nature" provides an aesthetic parallel to Melville's tendencies in *Moby-Dick*. Most notably the imperative act of self-naming—"Call me Ishmael" (3)—links present time and Biblical story to the announcement, if not the inception, of the narrator's identity, at the same time that it suggests his status as wanderer, outcast, isolato. Throughout the narrative's unfolding social framework, Ishmael adapts mythic identities to his purposes. When recounting his story by using forms that derive from disparate mythologies, most notably Hebraic and Hellenic, Ishmael appropriates a technique analogous to Emerson's "metempsychosis of nature." Ahab, for example, chases the inscrutable, vicious "Job's whale" (186), an ongoing process which sharply contrasts with Father Mapple's presentation of the subservient whale of Jonah. In "Stowing Down and Clearing Up," Ishmael adapts an element of Hellenic mythology, comparing a sailor's initiation into the world of work to the transmigration of souls. The sailors engage in "the severest uninterrupted labors" only to "go through the whole weary thing again" (429). In a startling observation, Ishmael fuses this "man-killing" process of labor with the eternal recurrence of old souls in new bodies. As Emerson says, "Time is no more" (*Essays* 15). Under the eye of Ishmael, present time is linked to mythic time: "Oh! the metempsychosis! Oh! Pythagoras, that in bright Greece, two thousand years ago, did die, so good, so wise, so mild; I sailed with thee along the Peruvian coast last voyage—and, foolish as I am, taught thee, a green simple boy, how to splice a rope!" (429). Though an incidental perception, this connection is paradigmatic of the myth-making properties of Ishmael's voice—a voice that insistently reshapes fables and forms into new combinations.

Whereas Emerson's "metempsychosis of nature" in "History" provides at least an exemplary parallel for identifying Ishmael's penchant for infusing his story with mythic signification, Thomas Carlyle's wide-ranging dialectical voice in *Sartor Resartus* provides a suggestive foundation for approaching Melville's use of narrative voice in *Moby-Dick*. At one point, Carlyle even mentions the Biblical Ishmael in relation to the acquisition of self-reliance: "[T]hus in the destitution of the wild desert does our young Ishmael acquire for himself the highest of all possessions, that of Self-help" (88). Of special interest would have been Carlyle's insistence on philosophical play, an attribute Melville would have associated with Rabelais and Burton. An appropriate successor to Plato, Montaigne, Browne, and Bayle, Carlyle would certainly have contributed to Melville's sense of the procreant possibilities of the compositional act. In *Mardi*, Melville depicted processes of consciousness as principles of narrative self-fashioning. However uncontrolled a work, *Mardi* first provided a forum within which Melville could link narrative situation and metaphysical speculation. What Melville needed was a way to focus voice and vision. With his emphasis in *Sartor Resartus* on open-ended discussion and dialectical interchange, Carlyle would at least have complemented Melville's growing sense of the aesthetic potential of a narrator who uses the present tense to recount incidents that he is struggling to understand.

Moby-Dick is a fiction in which Ishmael's process narration overcomes distinctions between then and now, as well as there and here, in order to bring the reader to experience the processes animating the narrator's perceptual experience. Like Carlyle, Ishmael conflates retrospection and interpretation. The narrative voice, then, is authoritative insofar as it identifies a field of inquiry—Teufelsdröckh's philosophy of clothes or Ishmael's wonderworld of whaling—*and* provisional insofar as the narrator becomes enmeshed in a slippery interpretive activity. The assimilative process narrator highlights the dialectical play of possibility. In *Sartor Resartus,* two voices—sometimes three—coexist in a comic display of conjecture. Just as Ishmael claims that in "some enterprises . . . a careful disorderliness is the true method" (361), so too does Carlyle's editor attest to Teufelsdröckh's sporadic illogical assays:

> [B]ut of true logical method and sequence there is too little. Apart from its multifarious sections and subdivisions, the Work naturally falls into two Parts; a Historical-Descriptive, and a Philosophical-Speculative: but falls, unhappily, by no firm line of demarcation; in that labyrinthic combination, each Part overlaps, and indents, and indeed runs quite through the other. (26–27)

It is inviting to think of *Moby-Dick* as possessing both "Historical-Descriptive" and "Philosophical-Speculative" centers that are "no wise incompatible" (215), each woven by a teasing voice which appears intermittently as participating actor (both tyro and veteran), detached observer, and omniscient commentator.

A key to the connection between Melville and Carlyle is not only to be found in narrative voice but also in the way in which the narrative voice attempts to make meaning in a world rife with symbolic suggestiveness. In one representative passage, Carlyle writes:

> Rightly viewed no meanest object is insignificant; all objects are as windows, through which the philosophic eye looks into Infinitude itself. . . . All visible things are emblems; what thou seest is not there on its own account; strictly taken, is not there at all: Matter exists only spiritually, and to represent some Idea, and *body* it forth. (55, Carlyle's emphasis)

This passage is echoed in Ahab's "pasteboard masks" speech (164), in his later assertion, "What things real are there, but imponderable thoughts?" (528), and in Ishmael's claim that "some certain significance lurks in all things, else all things are little worth, and the round world itself but an empty cipher" (430). Teufelsdröckh's philosophy of clothes constitutes a comic celebration of how the

outer world of material things is but the woven garment of the
spiritual world. In arguing for the correspondence of Nature and
Soul, Teufelsdröckh depicts a universal fusion of seen and unseen.
Viewed "philosophico-poetically," the world of material forms reflects the ubiquitous hand of the divine weaver (57). In presenting
the relationship of seen and unseen, Teufelsdröckh adopts
Goethe's image of the Loom of Time. The artist's holy office is to
weave the "garment" whereby God is recognized:

> 'Tis thus at the roaring Loom of Time I ply,
> And weave for God the Garment thous seest Him by. (42)

Melville would have recognized that Carlyle's book offers a
quirky reformulation of Platonic Idealism. The editor even mentions Teufelsdröckh's "high Platonic Mysticism" (50). Carlyle's extended exegesis on the philosophy of clothes might have suggested
ways for Melville to vary his application of distinct correspondences between objects and ideas. In *Moby-Dick,* for example,
Melville adapts the image of the loom to multiple contexts. The
very word *loomings* plays on the double meaning of weaving and
nautical vistas. And Melville naturally associates the loom with the
imagery of lines—such as the whale line, which depicts the tenu-
ousness of life, and the monkey rope, which symbolizes the interdependence among mortals. The image of the loom also suggests
literal lines of intersection between phenomenal and noumenal
realms. As already noted, the weaving scene in "The Mat-Maker"
explicitly connects the social contexts of cooperative labor with
the metaphysical contexts of the Loom of Time, an association that
is recast in Pip's cosmic vision in "The Castaway." He sees "God's
foot upon the treadle of the loom" (414), an activity that ironically
separates him from the sane social world of commonplace perceptions. The loom as image complements Ishmael's role as process
narrator. Thus the loom is an appropriate image for a world characterized by the interaction between fixity and flux. The loom, in
effect, *translates* possibility into fixity, process into product.

For Carlyle, the philosophy of clothes and the Loom of Time
provide ways of discussing a dynamic world of constant and co-

herent interplay among disparate forces: "I say there is no . . . separation; nothing hitherto was ever stranded, cast aside; but all, were it only a withered leaf, works together with all: is borne forward on the bottomless, shoreless flood of Action, and lives through perpetual metamorphoses" (54–55). Melville apparently adapts Carlyle's notion of "perpetual metamorphoses" to very different purposes in "A Bower in the Arsacides." In this chapter, Ishmael describes a beached skeleton of a sperm whale, carved "in strange hieroglyphics" (449) and festooned with verdure from "the great world's loom" (450). In this paradigmatic scene of reading, Ishmael confronts the unification of unreadable sign and natural process:

> [T]he industrious earth beneath was as a weaver's loom, with a gorgeous carpet on it, whereof the ground-vine tendrils formed the warp and woof, and the living flowers the figures. All the trees, with all their laden branches; all the shrubs, and ferns, and grasses; the message-carrying air; all these unceasingly were active. Through the lacings of the leaves, the great sun seemed a flying shuttle weaving the unwearied verdure. Oh, busy weaver! . . . the shuttle flies— the figures float from forth the loom; the freshet-rushing carpet for ever slides away. The weaver-god, he weaves; and by that weaving is he deafened, that he hears no mortal voice; and by that humming, we, too, who look on the loom are deafened. (449–50)

In *Sartor Resartus* the "perpetual metamorphoses" ultimately express mankind's ontological relation to an immanent God; Melville's adaptation, however, reflects our experiential separation and cosmic alienation from God. Indeed, it is the very driving force of natural process itself that deafens God to indigent mortals.

The "strange hieroglyphics" of the whale's skeleton indicate Melville's attraction to using Egyptian symbolism to evoke the inscrutable mysteries of the cosmos.[10] He would have been alert to the recurrence of such imagery in his reading of De Quincey, Carlyle, and Emerson. Such encounters would have reinforced Melville's penchant for placing the human perceiver before the inscrutable sign. As early as *Typee*, Tommo confronts the natives' indecipherable totems. In *Mardi* the high priest Aleema is covered with hieroglyphic tattoos. In reading De Quincey, Carlyle, and Emerson, Melville probably noted their similar evocations of the Sphinx. In fact, Emerson's "old fable of the Sphinx," which depicts the dangers that face the strident seeker-after-truth, is actually a version of De Quincey's Sphinx as a sign of what he calls "the Incommunicable." In Emerson's figuration, the Sphinx puts riddles to every passerby: "If the man could not answer she swallowed him alive. If he could solve the riddle, the Sphinx was slain" (*Essays* 18).[11] This description evokes the Jonah story, the devouring maw of Peleg's "monstrousest parmacetty" (72), and Ahab's quest to slay the creature that for him personifies the cosmic riddle. It is Emerson's presentation of this myth that allows its easy adaptation to Melville's purposes. In "The Sphynx" chapter, Ahab directly addresses the severed whale's head. Unlike Emerson's Sphinx, Ahab's "vast and venerable head" is silent (311). Though having witnessed the mysteries of the deep, the whale hangs dead and dumb.

Under the hand of Carlyle in *Sartor Resartus*, the Sphinx excites a similar mystery. To Herr Teufelsdröckh, "The Universe . . . was as a mighty Sphinx-riddle, which I knew so little of, yet must rede, or be devoured. In red streaks of unspeakable grandeur, yet also in the blackness of darkness, was Life, to my too-unfurnished Thought, unfolding itself" (Carlyle 98).[12] Carlyle extends the image to evoke the mystery of human ontology: "The secret of Man's Being is still like the Sphinx's secret: a riddle that he cannot rede; and for ignorance of which he suffers death, the worst death, a spiritual" (41). Ishmael's "one grand hooded phantom, like a snow hill in the air" (7) has associations with "the ungraspable phantom of life"—the ontological and epistemological mysteries layered in "that story of Narcissus" (5). The whale as Sphinx finds a recurrent imagistic corollary in the whale as an unreadable symbol of mystery, especially in the hieroglyphic markings associated with whales in general and Moby Dick in particular. With its "unaccountable masses of shades and shadows," the painting on the wall of the Spouter-Inn elicits Ishmael's puzzled meditation on a creature very like a whale, a "long, limber, portentous, black mass of something hovering in the centre" (12). In "The Prairie" the brow of the whale

possesses the Sphinx-like inscrutability—the very unreadability—
of God Himself: "Human or animal, the mystical brow is as that
great golden seal affixed by the German emperors to their decrees.
It signifies—'God: done this day by my hand'" (346). In embody-
ing the living nexus between phenomenal and noumenal realms,
then, the sperm whale emanates "god-like dignity. . . . For you see
no one point precisely; not one distinct feature is revealed . . . nothing but that one broad firmament of a forehead, pleated with riddles;
dumbly lowering with the doom of boats, and ships, and men."
The whale's brow presents a language utterly foreign: the silent
sounds of the dead Egyptian land. With its haunting surface, the
whale paradoxically declares its genius through "his pyramidical
silence. . . . Champollion deciphered the wrinkled granite hieroglyphics. But there is no Champollion to decipher the Egypt of
every man's and every being's face. . . . how may unlettered Ishmael
hope to read the awful Chaldee of the Sperm Whale's brow? I but
put that brow before you. Read it if you can" (347). Ishmael presents, in effect, the limitations of his powers as process narrator. In
describing himself as "unlettered," he surrenders interpretation to
the reader.

The blank brow of the whale may be viewed as a synoptic image
of the mysterious matrix, or symphony of contrapuntal qualities,
that constitutes *Moby-Dick*. Far from being the narrative of a "whaling voyage," as Melville seems originally to have intended, *Moby-
Dick* offers a grand compendium of competing forces. As he wrote,
Melville became possessed with the idea of making a great book
with a mighty theme. In translating his life experiences into the
process of storytelling, Melville seemed to be trying, whether consciously or unconsciously, to fulfill his own dictates, set forth in
Mardi, for the making of literary monuments. In "Time and
Temples" the narrator proclaims that "to make an eternity, we must
build with eternities" (228). Melville's materials for invention were
frequently literary artifacts—both ancient and contemporary—and
like the Promethean artificer in *Mardi*, Melville in *Moby-Dick* combined invention and creative appropriation to make a book "alike
durable and new" (*Mardi* 229).

6

Moby-Dick and the Forms of Philosophical Fiction

... a riddle to unfold, a wondrous work in one volume.

—*Moby-Dick*

WHEN WRITING TO Hawthorne in the spring and summer of 1851, Melville was heaped and tasked by the colossal chore of finishing his *Whale*. Control and reserve usually characterize his correspondence, but these letters depict an agitated fervor, the effusive discharge of his volatile intellect.[1] As Hershel Parker contends, "Hawthorne did not provide a stylistic model; rather, Melville felt his incalculable influence as psychological exaltation and liberation" ("Herman Melville" 42). In seeking to be impressive and profound, Melville surrendered the public mask of authorship and spoke the moment's fullest truth.

Indeed, Melville believed he was writing the "Gospels in this century" (*Correspondence* 192). But the rankling fact that Truth would not pay—"Try to get a living by the Truth—and go to the Soup Societies"—conditioned his contempt for the marketplace, even as it inspired him to follow the dictates of his genius (191). In fact, Melville's description of "what so strongly characterizes" Hawthorne's work provides a self-reflexive summary of his own sense of mission: the beleaguered artist stands as defiant risk-taker, a warrior of the spirit, possibly a tragic martyr (186). The Prometheus shouting "NO! in thunder" would rather court annihilation than vitiate personal power. By suggesting that Hawthorne expresses "the intense feeling of the visable truth," Melville not only sketches the contours of Ahab's character but also celebrates the high office of fiction writing:

> By visable truth, we mean the apprehension of the absolute condi-
> tion of present things as they strike the eye of the man who fears
> them not, though they do their worst to him,—the man who, like
> Russia or the British Empire, declares himself a sovereign nature
> (in himself) amid the powers of heaven, hell, and earth.

Melville's analysis segues into self-identification; third person gives way to first person: "He may perish; but so long as he exists he insists upon treating with all Powers upon an equal basis. If any of those other Powers choose to withhold certain secrets, let them; that does not impair my sovereignty in myself; that does not make me tributary" (186).

The letters seem to be extensions of their conversations. As Hawthorne himself notes, "After supper, I put Julian to bed; and Melville and I had a talk about time and eternity, things of this world and of the next, and books, and publishers, and all possible and impossible matters" (Leyda 419). In the explosive activity of writing, as in the dynamics of dialogue, Melville wrestles with "ontological heroics" (*Correspondence* 196). Indeed, the very ground of temporal existence offers thin cover to honeycombed depths or a launching pad to astronomical heights. In this endeavor, Melville is drawn less to precept than conundrum. In one perplexing observation, Melville displaces the traditional image of the omnipotent deity. God is baffled by the mysteries of His own Being as well as the exigencies of His creation:

> We incline to think that God cannot explain His own secrets, and
> that He would like a little information upon certain points Him-
> self. We mortals astonish him as much as He us. But it is this *Being*
> of the matter; there lies the knot with which we choke ourselves.
> As soon as you say *Me,* a *God,* a *Nature,* so soon you jump off from
> your stool and hang from the beam. (186, Melville's emphasis)[2]

The Hawthorne letters demonstrate in sporadic forays what *Moby-Dick* realizes within its extended and problematic perimeters. Indeed, Ishmael's compositional act serves as a medium for his protean meditations on "the absolute condition of present things." And for this very reason, the whaling voyage was most welcome. Ishmael gives himself plenty of sea room—the wide ocean, a quest story, an expansive narrative voice. He comprehends how the past becomes intelligible via memory and memory recasts events as story.[3] The act of creating the text fuses past action and present commentary. By repeatedly locating himself in the instant of aesthetic self-representation, Ishmael creates a version of what happened; he translates the amorphous past and thereby engages a dramatically necessary audience. Ishmael makes the broad range of his intellectual life part of his rhetorical encounter with a reader. His strange story encompasses, but is not limited to, the circumstances of the *Pequod*'s journey. As "Etymology" and "Extracts" attest, the story includes not only the inherent mystery of word signs but the narrator's complex recasting of literary antecedents.

The apparently spontaneous nature of Ishmael's account calls attention to *Moby-Dick*'s provisional status as an admittedly incomplete text. When Ishmael exclaims, "God keep me from ever completing anything," he is not offering a disclaimer so much as establishing a compositional principle. The book is indeed a "draught of a draught." Its premise is that any system—whether cetological, narrative, theological, or metaphysical—must be suspended in a state of becoming. Prodigious structures leave their "copestone to posterity" (145). The activity of reading likewise initiates "posterity"—meaning all readers—into the interpretive process of making momentary sense. Ishmael's narrative discontinuities constitute, then, an intrinsic celebration of incompletion.[4] The emphasis remains on literary process rather than finished product: "I try all things; I achieve what I can" (345). Ishmael's formal ruptures suggest that generic expectations are themselves arbitrary structures, valid until they become invalid, useful until they become useless. For example, Ishmael's occasional displays of apparent omniscience, long a problem to baffled commentators, are not a problem to Ishmael. His multiple narrative forms—first-person past and present; third-person omniscient; dramatic—are themselves projections of his attenuated consciousness.

This is not to say that the book depicts Ishmael's solipsistic phantasm, the phenomenology of an isolated consciousness.[5] Rather, the narrating "I"—self-contained like any mind within its own subjectivity—attempts over and over to find a language to contain, however imperfectly, extrinsic events, whether they involve the interactions between other persons, the behavior of whales, the motives of the White Whale, or the ways to chop blubber. In this process, Ishmael often dissolves or subverts his presence as personal narrator or attending actor. How does he purport to know what Ahab thinks? How does he reproduce conversations taking place in three separate boats during a frenetic chase? From one vantage point, such endeavors are inventions, the illusion of literary artifice. More importantly, such situations accentuate the intentionally unstable quality of *Moby-Dick*, especially by way of Ishmael's insistence on literary form-breaking, his refusal to circumscribe his voice and story within conventional forms.

Paradoxically, Ishmael asserts that for "some enterprises . . . a careful disorderliness is the true method" (361). The narrator weaves his words within a state of perceptual flux. The outer world, to the extent that it can be transcribed, retains its character as recalcitrant Other. Ishmael must thereby express his failed, or unfinished, attempt to envelop totality through the experimental expansion of a narrator's province. Ishmael's book contains both his attempt to say what happened and his self-reflexive critique of that attempt. Past experience, then, stands in dialectical relationship to his present meditations. This language experiment liberates him and allows him to proceed in two distinct but related directions: toward psychological analysis of himself and others, and toward metaphysical speculation on phenomenal surfaces as repositories of lurking "significance . . . else all things are little worth" (430). Ishmael's narrative, in other words, is predicated upon the belief that "Truth" can be imperfectly assayed as it applies to persons, phenomena, and "invisible spheres" (195). In this activity, Ishmael expresses a belief in what Lawrence Buell calls the "primacy of the moral imagination" (*New England Literary Culture* 82).

Ishmael's destabilized narrative domain appropriately contains, and expresses, Melville's philosophical purpose in *Moby-Dick*. In *Mardi*, Melville gropes his way through a prolonged quest structure in which characters and islands represent abstract ideas. In *Moby-Dick* the philosophical context derives from the ways in which Ishmael's life-as-lived feeds the life now being written. Melville's informing purpose here is not so much to spin out profoundly derivative thought—the ponderous weight that sank *Mardi*—or even to express "a mighty theme" (456). Rather, he engages those philosophical contexts that fashion an approach to totality. Thus, Ishmael's preoccupation with ontology, epistemology, and cosmology comprise the narrative's sinuous architecture. Like Ishmael's cetology, this model means "simply to project the draught of a systemization" (136).

One aspect of ontology concerns the matter of human essence, the fundamental *what* or nature of being, individual and collective, especially as reflected in its origin, agency, and teleology. Ishmael's process narrative—expressed through his self-actualizing voice—depicts his being in the activity of becoming. Generating from his ontological concerns, Ishmael's epistemological quandaries become dramatized as the problematic "I" perceives and interprets signs, surfaces, and portents.[6] As Hawthorne notes, Melville worried over "all possible and impossible matters" (Leyda 419). Among the more impossible is the ultimate status or meaning of the cosmos, the nature of the universe as it is, or is not, controlled by a transcendent entity. As in "The Mast-Head" and "The Whiteness of the Whale," Ishmael often engages cosmological puzzles by placing the interpreting self at some precarious boundary, a point at which "visible" surfaces give way to intimations regarding the nature of "invisible spheres" (195). Imaginary, or visionary, apprehension displaces sensory experience.

Within the novel, these contexts are seldom dissociated. The nature of Queequeg's being, for instance, cannot be separated from his hieroglyphic tattoos, which are themselves a dead language containing a cosmological key to an unknowable truth. Within a single passage, Ishmael depicts the interpenetration of multiple spheres of existence: the self as text and text as cosmological riddle:

> Many spare hours he spent, in carving the lid [of his coffin] with all manner of grotesque figures and drawings; and it seemed that hereby he was striving, in his rude way, to copy parts of the twisted tattooing on his body. And this tattooing, had been the work of a departed prophet and seer of his island, who, by those hieroglyphic marks, had written out on his body a complete theory of the heavens and the earth, and a mystical treatise on the art of attaining truth; so that Queequeg in his own proper person was a riddle to unfold; a wondrous work in one volume; but whose mysteries not even himself could read . . . and these mysteries were therefore destined in the end to moulder away with the living parchment whereon they were inscribed, and so be unsolved to the last. (480–81)

His body purports to encapsulate both a "complete theory" of cosmology and a "mystical treatise on the art of attaining truth." Outer and inner worlds could be explicated, except for one problem: the language cannot be deciphered. The image of the departed prophet, who was also the originating author, signals the loss of a primal unifying vision. Queequeg is both cosmic orphan and impaired reader, his body a "wondrous work." But while he replicates part of the inscribed figures, he translates, truncates, and defaces the original design. The "mysteries" inscribed on his flesh—indeed, that *are* his flesh—will "moulder," even though the corrupted signs, published on a coffin life buoy, remain as haunting, unreadable images divorced from the life they once might have explained. This passage manifests the entangled complexity of Ishmael's preoccupation with self, phenomena, and cosmos. In fact, the secret of cosmology, described here as an alien, indecipherable text, reflects Ishmael's abiding obsession with problematic mysteries of being.

So far, the chapters in this book have concentrated on the intersection between Melville's own learning and his development of literary techniques that articulate his philosophical concerns. This chapter demonstrates Melville's multilayered application of

Ishmael's philosophical rhetoric—"philosophical" in its pursuit of the "best wisdom" (*White-Jacket* 186) and in its dramatization of ontological, epistemological, and cosmological contexts; and "rhetoric" through its expression as a language system that engages an audience even as it reflexively explores the conditions informing its own making. In *Moby-Dick* Melville recasts the numerous technique and complexes found in *Mardi, Redburn,* and *White-Jacket:* most notably, philosophical dialogue; fables of identity; the construction of texts within the text; the impress of allusion and the dynamics of intertextuality; scenes of reading and essayistic excursions; and the metaphysical quest.

As textual product masquerading as narrative process, the book itself inevitably defies interpretation; both *Moby-Dick* and Moby Dick, the book and the being, are simply too much to grasp. But just as any scholar's language, like Ishmael and Queequeg's sword mat, assumes shape as it brings together disparate, though "no wise incompatible," strands (215), in "The Mat-Maker" Ishmael achieves, more than any commentator, a sublime moment of synthesis as warp and woof evoke the balanced interaction of freedom, fate, and chance. It is a moment in which the humble activity of weaving expresses cosmological harmony, a moment that seems true while it lasts. But the moment's meditation is ruptured: a whale is sighted, and the yarn—"the ball of free will"—drops, proving the very province of chance. In *Moby-Dick* systems are made and unmade; thus, a critical assay on Melville's philosophical rhetoric must share the provisional nature of its subject. The progression through ontology, epistemology, and (briefly) cosmology promises totality, but this is not to be. Such categories are not exclusive; they describe shifting foci that attract Ishmael as he takes soundings of depths that are too deep for anyone's dive.

ONTOLOGY

Ishmael and the Ground of Being

In "The Carpet-Bag," Ishmael uses the past tense to recount his journey. Adrift in New Bedford, and betraying the dour, alienated mood of the social pariah, he wanders the street. Buffeted by the chill wind, he is a spiritual brother of the beggarly Lazarus starving before the warm and well-fed Dives. Here, Ishmael aptly personifies his biblical prototype, the outcast son of a slave. It seems likely that "The Carpet-Bag" belongs to an early stage of composition when Melville apparently envisioned his narrator as a grim, grown-up Redburn, a displaced malcontent trying to get away.[7] As *Moby-Dick* went through its stages of revision and expansion, Melville developed a narrator capable of exploiting the comic possibilities associated with Queequeg and the expansive metaphysical complexes associated with Ahab and the White Whale. Though preceding "The Carpet-Bag," "Loomings" probably was composed at a fairly late stage. At the level of action, "Loomings" is certainly an unnecessary duplicate, for in it Melville takes Ishmael back one giant step to lower Manhattan. But when viewed in the light of Melville's expanded purpose, the chapter becomes integral. The bitter tone and conventional retrospection of "The Carpet-Bag" seem anomalous after the genial, present-tense voice of "Loomings." "Call me Ishmael" establishes the dramatic meeting of narrator and reader.

In naming himself through a directly addressed imperative, the narrator casts the reader as auditor, companion, and interlocutor.[8] No sooner does Ishmael say, "I thought I would sail about a little and see the watery part of the world" than he immerses himself within the compositional moment: "It is a way I have of driving off the spleen" (3). Ishmael jettisons traditional, retrospective narrative, and with it the attempt to fashion the amorphous past into the illusion of reconstructed wholeness—the life revealed in a sequential narrative line. What Peter J. Bellis argues about autobiography applies to Ishmael's process narrative: "the exact dimensions of the writer's experience [must be] lost—autobiographical texts must . . . be fragmentary, haunted by images of an idealized, unified self that is beyond recovery or recreation" (48). In appropriating present-tense narrative, Ishmael reveals what he thinks as he writes. He seeks to be more true, more mimetic, and thus more fragmentary; his tale's contextual truth emerges as he inscribes the

passing moment. In the absence of a fully realized, fully comprehended past self, Ishmael asserts circumstantial authority. His truth
need only reflect his current apprehension. The flux of consciousness, translated into words, grounds and licenses Ishmael's story.

By the time Melville came to write "Loomings," the image of the
biblical Ishmael had given way to the metaphysical wanderer seeking relation. What "Loomings" possesses and "The Carpet-Bag"
lacks, then, is Ishmael's expressed communion with fellow humans.
Ishmael's seabound instinct manifests a collective urge: "[A]lmost
all men in their degree, some time or other, cherish very nearly the
same feelings toward the ocean with me" (3). "[S]eemingly bound
for a dive," the Sunday legion of "water-gazers" perch at the very
limit of land and languish in frustrated longing (4). They forgo
possibility and accept the "clinched" confinement of preexperiential failure. Ishmael enacts the repressed desire to step beyond
quotidian bounds. But instead of manifesting deviant behavior,
Ishmael's act is therapeutic: "With a philosophical flourish Cato
throws himself upon his sword; I quietly take to the ship" (3). His
integral identification with "all men" is not an isolated incident;
nor is it contingent. Rather, he carries this shared impulse into the
arena of action. He rejects suicide for a life-affirming, life-threat-
ening immersion into extremity.

The sea fuses a whole range of phenomenal and mythic associations. Ishmael's narrative technique obliterates the sense of a reconstructed past in favor of experiential immediacy; the scene
taking place is continually recurrent. Ishmael insists on the exact
coincidence of his language and the unfolding scene:

> There now is your insular city of the Manhattoes.... Right and
> left, the streets take you waterward.... Look at the crowds of wa-
> ter-gazers there.
> Circumambulate the city.... Go from Corlears Hook to Coenties
> Slip, and from thence, by Whitehall, northward. What do you see?—
> Posted like silent sentinels all around the town, stand thousands
> upon thousands of mortal men fixed in ocean reveries. (3–4)

Not only does the action unfold *now*, but Ishmael situates the reader *within* the text as participant and observer: "But look! here come more crowds, pacing straight for the water, and seemingly bound for a dive. . . . Tell me, does the magnetic virtue of the needles of the compasses of all those ships attract them thither?" (4). Ishmael's celebration of water gazing as an elemental aspect of human nature—"Yet here they all unite"—integrates action, language, and audience. Water gazing also expresses a psychological process. Water draws all humans to "meditation"—that is, to the very activity that Ishmael inscribes in his compositional moment: "Yes, as every one knows, meditation and water are wedded for ever." His succeeding series of questions make his case appear self-evident, irrefutable, and all-encompassing.

In uniting himself with all humans in the ongoing rhetorical moment, Ishmael couples present time with mythic time, and diachronic process with synchronic fixity. He associates the sea urge of "almost every robust healthy boy" with "the old Persians [who] hold the sea holy" and, most significantly, to "the Greeks [who] give it a separate deity, and make him the own brother of Jove" (5). Ishmael proposes a "key" to all experience. His evocation of Narcissus confirms on a mythic level the elemental nature of water gazing. The "story of Narcissus" images the sea as a double of the human self. Simultaneously, the sea symbolizes the elusive absolute:[9] "Surely all this is not without meaning. And still deeper the meaning of that story of Narcissus, who because he could not grasp the tormenting, mild image he saw in the fountain, plunged into it and was drowned. But that same image, we ourselves see in all rivers and oceans. It is the image of the ungraspable phantom of life; and this is the key to it all" (5). Narcissus perceives what everyone sees—a "tormenting, mild" image, a projection of self as putative other, an attractive lure that teases him beyond the margins of safety. Narcissus naively acts on this urge. By attempting to "grasp" the mysterious other, he falls into the pool and drowns. Crucially, Ishmael realizes that what he, the "water-gazers," and Narcissus see is no more and no less than a self-reflection. As image of the self—the Soul's unfathomable depths and Nature's reflecting pool—the sea suggests the possibility that one might forge a romantic, even transcendent, union of self and phenomena, Soul and Nature. Unlike Narcissus, Ishmael comprehends that the meanings one extracts offer projections of the self. In failing to recognize one's own lineaments in the pool, one mistakes subjective projection for objective fact, a graspable phantom for an ungraspable one. In effect, one posits in oneself an ontological absolute that can subsume all phenomena. Consequently, when Ahab sees "all evil" in Moby Dick (184), he validates his quest for ultimate vindication. He also displaces, or evades, the essential indigence of human nature, replacing it with a fiction of ontological transcendence that takes the form of his rhetorical identification with the gods. Ishmael's "key to it all," on the contrary, allows him to see in nature a reflection of the self; to pursue the "image" beyond the limits of land; and to recognize the contextual, relativistic nature of this "ungraspable phantom."

Thus Ishmael is not an outcast so much as a representational wanderer. His separation from the landlubbers is not a matter of ontological dissociation, of existing—as Queequeg first seems to—on a diminutive level. Ishmael's so-called alienation—his status as "Isolato" (121, Melville's emphasis)—is a matter of action and behavior, a necessary consequence of daring to take the plunge. If Ishmael carries the instinct for water gazing into action, then Bulkington embodies the most extreme version of the questing sailor. In "The Lee Shore" the heroic Bulkington functions as Ishmael's extended alter ego. Bulkington is indeed an "apotheosis" (107). He leaves behind "all that's kind to our mortalities" (106) and dares to seek the "highest truth" (107). Like Ishmael, Bulkington retains an essential connection to the commonalty. Through Bulkington, however, Ishmael makes explicit the philosophical nature of the journey. In rendering the vestigial Bulkington in this momentous way, Ishmael pens, as it were, a brief fable of identity. To go to sea is to open oneself to the prospect of independent thought. According to Ishmael, Bulkington sees "that mortally intolerable truth; that all deep, earnest thinking is but the intrepid effort of the soul to keep the open independence of her sea; while the wildest winds of heaven and earth conspire to cast her on the treacherous, slavish shore" (107). Bulkington's pursuit of "the highest truth, shoreless, indefinite as God" eventually leads him to perish in "that howling infinite." If the landlubbers are "worm-like" and Bulkington is the "apotheosis," then Ishmael locates himself somewhere between these extremes (107).

In celebrating his status as worker and sailor, Ishmael retains his affiliation both with the "water-gazers" and Bulkington. As one of the "kingly commons" (117), Ishmael "requires a strong decoction of Seneca and the Stoics" to accept the oppressive indignities of life before the mast. His enslavement reflects the basic human condition:

> Who aint a slave? Tell me that. Well, then, however the old sea-captains may order me about—however they may thump and punch me about, I have the satisfaction of knowing that it is all right; that everybody else is one way or other served in much the same way—either in a physical or metaphysical point of view, that is; and so the universal thump is passed round, and all hands should rub each other's shoulder-blades, and be content. (6)

Ishmael's flexible, accommodating sensibility allows him to accept the "universal thump" as a necessary condition that federates humanity in physical and metaphysical terms.

In demonstrating Ishmael's representational ontological status, "Loomings" offers an intensive rendering of the novel's major complexes. Ishmael's concluding meditation on causality, agency, and intention—his playful conjecture on "the grand programme of Providence" (7)—reflects his preoccupation with "ontological heroics" (*Correspondence* 196) and human volition. Ishmael is comically ambiguous. On the one hand, he depicts his past experiences as providentially ordained:

> [N]ow that I recall all the circumstances, I think I can see a little into the springs and motives which being cunningly presented to me under various disguises, induced me to set about performing the part I did, besides cajoling me into the delusion that it was a

choice resulting from my own unbiased freewill and discriminating judgment. (7)

On the other hand, he mentions how his motives and his curiosity "helped to sway me to my wish." Ishmael endorses neither fixed fate nor noncontingent freedom; rather, he reflects a shifting emphasis and thereby creates a dialectic among competing possibilities. Indeed, his providential playbill lacks objective warrant: it is a text of his own invention. He reads, as he writes, the unanswerable questions about his life.

Ishmael constantly attempts to push his understanding of ontology beyond the tenuous confines of phenomenal experience. The axiom "Nothing exists in itself" (53) informs Ishmael's unstinting drive to articulate sometimes contradictory explanations of experience. Repeatedly, he formulates versions of the soul's relation to absolute contexts. This endeavor becomes most apparent as he betrays what may seem a baffling inconsistency in his professed theological affiliation. In the early onshore chapters, for example, Ishmael endorses first Platonic, then Christian, and finally pagan attempts to connect the here with the hereafter, the mediate and ultimate disposition of human affairs. In the first two instances, Ishmael's explorations culminate with psychologically therapeutic teleological affirmations. In the third, Ishmael displaces the traditional framework of Christianity, finding in the pagan Queequeg an ironic means of glorifying the Presbyterian God and, more significantly, a model of essential goodness. These alternatives stand in implicit dialectical arrangement, their successive displacement undercutting any one system's interpretive authority. Each formulation is conditioned by Ishmael's particular moment.

In a meditation from "The Chapel" that depicts his psychological deliverance, Ishmael disassociates himself from the grief-stricken mourners who dwell morbidly on "several marble tablets . . . masoned into the wall" (34). These mourners are imprisoned by the "trappings of some unceasing grief" frozen within the death tales inscribed in stone (36). In considering these legends, Ishmael proceeds through a series of unanswered questions: "In what census of living creatures, the dead of mankind are included; why it is that a universal proverb says of them, that they tell no tales, though containing more secrets than the Goodwin Sands . . . why all the living so strive to hush all the dead" (36–37). Ishmael, though, by an infusion of Platonic idealism that transforms the sense of soul-annihilating death, "somehow . . . grew merry again." He construes the prospect of death by whaling as a "promotion." Repeatedly evoking "Methinks," Ishmael presents his instantaneous experience of the matter:

> Methinks we have hugely mistaken this matter of Life and Death. Methinks that what they call my shadow here on earth is my true substance. Methinks that in looking at things spiritual, we are too much like oysters observing the sun through the water, and thinking that thick water the thinnest of air. Methinks my body is but the lees of my better being. (37)

Here Ishmael is appropriating an image directly from Plato. As early scholar H. N. Couch points out, Ishmael's celebration of his "shadow" as his "true substance" parallels a passage in *Phaedo*. Sealts builds on Couch's discovery, demonstrating that "Melville's memory had ranged elsewhere in the *Phaedo* and *Phaedrus*" ("Platonic Tradition" 301–02). Significantly, Ishmael constructs his analogy from the Platonic dialogues most concerned with death and immortality. Underlying Platonic formalism and the doctrine of Ideas is the notion that the physical world is a mere replica of the Forms, the Ontologically Real. When Ishmael affirms the immortality of his "better being," he rejects the "not me" of his body and vindicates the soul's immortal essence. Crucially, Ishmael's celebration of Platonic teleology is contextual rather than characteristic. His speculations regarding the soul's disposition are rarely so effusive and optimistic. When considering the mystery of whiteness, for example, Ishmael eclipses the fundamental import of Platonic idealism, dreading the very thought of "invisible spheres" (195). He suspects that the existential annihilation of the soul lurks beyond the material masks of this world.

Ishmael's consideration of the relation of body and soul also leads him to traditional Christian ground. He views Father Mapple's "act of physical isolation" as effecting "his spiritual withdrawal for the time, from all outward worldly ties and connections" (39). Ishmael not only speaks of Mapple with awe and reverence but affirms Christian orthodoxy: "Yes, the world's a ship on its passage out, and not a voyage complete; and the pulpit is its prow" (40). Father Mapple's sermon, which Ishmael never discusses, locates the human self as subservient to divine authority. While the sermon can be read as a possible corrective to Ahab's pursuit of "a Job's whale" (186), it does not necessarily comprise a moral touchstone. Ishmael's embrace of the Christian gestalt, like his Platonic synthesis, reflects but a momentary point of view. Ishmael never seeks to reconcile his disparate responses. If anything, he flaunts them.

When Ishmael gets down on his knees and worships Queequeg's idol, Yojo, he constructs a false syllogism to parody the self-justifying tendency of the rationalizing animal. He asks himself, "How then could I unite with this wild idolater in worshipping his piece of wood?" (52). After conducting a self-dialogue on how the "magnanimous God of heaven and earth" must feel, he construes joint worship as divinely ordained and benignly efficacious. In a resounding repudiation of a jealous God, Ishmael concludes, "Consequently, I must then unite with him in his [worship]; ergo, I must turn idolator." Mocking orthodoxy, Ishmael embraces a myth of universal federation. His pagan worship expresses his play of alternative visions, his formulation of psychologically therapeutic positions. Each redefinition generates from Ishmael's analysis of the pressing moment. Significantly, pagan worship radically decenters his former cultural affiliation. He rejects the way of the western world, viewing it now as "hollow courtesy" (51).

Crucial to his involvement with pagan ritual is the word "unite." His heretical act derives explicitly from his recently discovered bond with Queequeg. Though originally Queequeg seemed "some abominable savage" (22), throughout the early chapters of *Moby-Dick* Ishmael is learning to familiarize the bizarre and to humanize the alien. Soon realizing that "the man's a human being just as I am" (24), Ishmael eventually recognizes Queequeg's benign inward essence, his "simple honest heart" (50). "You cannot hide the soul," Ishmael notes (49). By embracing Queequeg, Ishmael undercuts the pretensions of Christianity, especially the pernicious tendency to make ontological distinctions based on religious practice. Dismantling the social categories which dictate that a cannibal necessarily has reduced ontological status, he translates Rousseau's concept of the natural primitive into a principle of cross-cultural fraternity.[10] Imbued with stoical self-containment and self-possession "always equal to itself," Queequeg evinces the "calm self-collectedness of simplicity." Ishmael sees that Queequeg's "Socratic wisdom" makes him one of the "true philosophers": "Surely this was a touch of fine philosophy. . . . But, perhaps, to be true philosophers, we mortals should not be conscious of so living or so striving. So soon as I hear that such or such a man gives himself out for a philosopher, I conclude that . . . he must have 'broken his digester' " (50). In Queequeg, Ishmael conflates romantic and pagan contexts. Their union is primarily spiritual, a celebration of human love and "bosom" fellowship. Ishmael also finds a fulfillment of his ontological relation to the "water-gazers." Here Melville celebrates an integral democracy, a union of souls that transcends racial, class, and religious boundaries, locating the source of federation in a natural law of the heart. Though depicting contingent perceptions and relationships, Ishmael nevertheless reveals what is fixed in nature—essential, immutable, an "absolute condition." His relationship to Queequeg, with its attending exploration of fellowship and its refiguration of the savage, constitutes Melville's primary means of displacing Eurocentric claims to ontological supremacy.

Behind this parodic interracial, homosexual marriage is Ishmael's recurrent insistence on the savage, or the cannibalistic, as a phenomenal and psychological constant in human nature. In associating the savagery of the whale hunter and the Iroquois, Ishmael might seem to be evoking the language of imperial power. Instead, he establishes affinity, not disparity, identifying *himself* as savage: "Your true whale-hunter is as much a savage as an Iroquois. I myself am a savage, owning no allegiance but to the King of the Cannibals; and ready at any moment to rebel against him" (270). Such observations are designed to unseat smug pretensions of civilized readers. Using direct address, Ishmael editorializes on cannibalistic nature:

> Go to the meat-market of a Saturday night and see the crowds of live bipeds staring up at the long rows of dead quadrupeds. Does not that sight take a tooth out of the cannibal's jaw? Cannibals? who is not a cannibal? I tell you it will be more tolerable for the Fejee that salted down a lean missionary in his cellar against a coming famine; it will be more tolerable for that provident Fejee, I say, in the day of judgment, than for thee, civilized and enlightened gourmand, who nailest geese to the ground and feastest on their bloated livers in thy paté-de-foie-gras. (300)

Ishmael does not concern himself with the ethics of cannibalism, seeing instead the cannibalistic nature of humans as a given. Ishmael's indictment focuses on civilized sham, the masked denial of basic instinct. To eat pâté is indeed to "feastest on . . . bloated livers," and Ishmael delights in uncovering self-deluding hypocrisy. The "horrible vulturism of earth" includes the human predator (308). The mask of civilization cannot efface this ontological fact.

To Ishmael, human nature oscillates between savagery and "august dignity" (117), involving not a continuum from lower to higher forms but a superimposition of contending qualities. A savage whale hunter is also a noble whale hunter. So much of *Moby-Dick* concerns itself with implicit and explicit demonstrations of how savagery, or "universal cannibalism," is not contingent on social definition (274). Like evil, freedom, and love, savagery reflects metaphysical dimensions of experience. This innate propensity transcends racial and cultural barriers. It is, for example, part of the predatory activity of colonialism—a kind of state cannibalism—to deflect the denomination of savage or primitive and impose noxious attributes on an alien class. Skin color often becomes the simple sign of ontological inferiority. The chain of being, itself a fiction designed to justify the power of a ruling caste, becomes the instrument of exalted self-definition and the warrant for subjugating putative inferiors. Once a class of persons has been branded ontologically inferior and this definition is sanctioned by some doctrinal truism masquerading as extrinsic authority, then any sort of repressive behavior is justified as the perquisite of those in power.[11]

At the center of Ishmael's ontological explorations in *Moby-Dick*, then, is his attempt to uncover the ground of being; to dismantle, so to speak, the artifice of civilization; and to expose the arbitrary aspect of self-serving hierarchical structures. In this activity Ishmael reveals an abiding fascination with origins. He insists on sailing from Nantucket—American whaling's "great original—the Tyre of this Carthage"—and he celebrates American Indians as "aboriginal whalemen" (8). Through this affiliation, Ishmael tries to appropriate a sense of direct experience—experience unsullied by constructs of historical nationalism or technological development. He wishes to confront nature in its primal state. In the march and progress of time, "baby man . . . has lost that sense of the full awfulness of the sea which aboriginally belongs to it" (273). The phrase "aboriginally belongs" connotes an ongoing continuum in which nature remains unvitiated by petty baubles of "science and skill." The roiling sea—or "masterless ocean" (274)—retains primeval domination. This "everlasting terra incognita" (273) is subtle, beautiful, treacherous. When Ishmael meditates on "the universal cannibalism of the sea; all whose creatures prey upon each other, carrying on eternal war since the world began," he contends with the most violent manifestation of earthly cannibalism (274). In order to link his analysis with its counterpart in human experience, Ishmael asks his reader to

> consider them both, the sea and the land; and do you not find a strange analogy to something in yourself? For as this appalling ocean surrounds the verdant land, so in the soul of man there lies

one insular Tahiti, full of peace and joy, but encompassed by all
the horrors of the half known life. God keep thee! Push not off
from that isle, thou canst never return! (274)

To construct a model of human ontology, Ishmael recasts the land-
sea dichotomy established in "Loomings." By identifying the land
as containing "peace and joy" and the sea as holding "horrors," he
displays the serenity of the soul's preexperiential life. To venture
out to sea is to engage the unknowable "horrors" of nature and
self. Such a voyage makes one incapable of reposing in "verdant"
recesses. One might indeed argue that Ishmael offers a refuge from
metaphysical reflection. The "insular Tahiti," however, comprises
a single fable that coexists with many others. Images of "universal
cannibalism" and an "insular Tahiti" provide "strange" analogies
to the diverse attributes of narrator and reader.

Throughout *Moby-Dick,* Ishmael frequently employs this analogical method to demonstrate elemental aspects of human nature.
By drawing one-to-one comparisons between objects in the whaling world and collective human experience, Ishmael attempts to
describe the self by way of its resemblance to other phenomena.
Usually Ishmael forges an analogy after expounding on an object's
function. For example, his description of the unraveling whale line
leads to his reflection on the imminence of death: "All men live
enveloped in whale-lines" (281). In another case, the simple law
determining possession of a harpooned whale establishes the basis
for a series of analogies on "Fast-Fish" and "Loose-Fish." His concluding observation reflects the embattled, conflicted nature of all
people: "And what are you, reader, but a Loose-Fish and a Fast-
Fish, too?" (398). His philosophical rhetoric impels him to univer-
salize such figures and to establish the degree to which ontological
attributes become manifest in social and political behaviors.[12] Even
from a most idiosyncratic instance—the umbilical connection of
Ishmael and Queequeg in "The Monkey-rope"—Ishmael derives
an analogy of human interdependence: "Are you not the precious
image of each and all of us men in this whaling world? That
unsounded ocean you gasp in, is Life; those sharks, your foes; those

spades, your friends; and what between sharks and spades you are in a sad pickle and peril, poor lad" (321). These analogies on objects and incidents possess the general applicability of allegory. At times, though, they devolve into platitudinous preachment, such as when the whale's thick skin suggests to Ishmael a model of stoic equanimity: "Oh, man! admire and model thyself after the whale! Do thou, too, remain warm among ice. Do thou, too, live in this world without being of it" (307).

Ishmael's numerous analogies forge spontaneous connections between the whaling world and the mysteries of human nature, "the tornadoed Atlantic of . . . being" (389). This activity has a slapdash quality and may impose on "things" a stability of definition that the words themselves do not possess. As John W. Rathbun argues,

> Analogies always seem to have an element of improvisation about them. In this sense, Ishmael may well realize that he is in a dilemma. On the one hand, both the romantic and Modernist faith esteem analogy as a revelatory act that transcends the normal resources of language. On the other hand, language itself can seem ephemeral as it dissolves and re-forms human experience while the reality it seeks to describe remains remote and ultimately unattainable and all the time evasive. (8)

Nevertheless, Ishmael believes that "some certain significance lurks in all things, else all things are little worth" (430). To tell his story, then, is to detail such "significance" and to find in "things" projections of the human story.

ONTOLOGY

Ahab and "the larger, darker, deeper part"

When Ishmael asks Captain Peleg the seemingly simple question— "Who is Captain Ahab?"—Melville presents the nexus between Ishmael as tyro actor and process narrator. In depicting the scene,

Ishmael juxtaposes his past ignorance with what he now knows. While the tyro listens to Peleg's fascinating tale of Ahab's dismemberment, the narrator supplies two kinds of information: the testimony of a knowing, presumably authoritative source (Peleg); and the testimony of a presumably authoritative witness turned narrator (Ishmael). As Peleg tells his tale, the narrating voice interpolates a broad range of personal and cultural aspects that evoke, without limiting, the prodigious, if not fabulous, dimensions of Ahab's being. Ishmael seeks to dramatize not only the tyro's induction into Ahab's mystery but the degree to which the mystery itself poses a problem of aesthetic representation.

Well before "[r]eality outran apprehension" and Ahab stands on the *Pequod*'s deck, Ishmael wrestles with the complexities of Ahab's language, origin, and identity (123). For example, "the stately dramatic thee and thou of the Quaker idiom" license Ishmael's attempt to compose a language commensurate with Ahab's stature (73). Along with "receiving all nature's sweet or savage impressions fresh from her own virgin, voluntary, and confiding breast," Ahab comes "to learn a bold and nervous lofty language." Counterpointing the tyro's ignorance is Ishmael's highly rhetorical portrait of Ahab as a unique man of tragic proportions: his "greatly superior natural force . . . [his] globular brain and . . . ponderous heart" complement his tendency "to think untraditionally and independently" (73).[13] As process narrator, Ishmael admits to straying beyond the tyro's incremental experience: "But, as yet we have not to do with such an one, but with quite another" (74). It falls to Peleg to continue sketching Ahab's hyperbolic nature: "He's a grand, ungodly, god-like man. . . . Ahab's above the common; Ahab's been in colleges, as well as 'mong the cannibals; been used to deeper wonders than the waves; fixed his fiery lance in mightier, stranger foes than whales. . . . he's Ahab, boy. . . . stricken, blasted, if he be, Ahab has his humanities" (79, Melville's emphasis).

With these disjunctive narrative modes, Ishmael is not flaunting convention so much as dramatizing how Ahab was a mysterious actor and is now a fictionalized character. During the voyage,

Ahab remains distant and unapproachable. As a sailor, Ishmael never directly engages Ahab. In fact as far as Ahab is concerned, Ishmael is just another contemptible integer in "a mob of unnecessary duplicates" (466). After the *Pequod*'s wreck, Ahab's actions and the related story remain as vestigial fragments amorphously retained within the sole survivor's memory. During the voyage, Ishmael was a marginal participant; now that he "only am escaped alone to tell thee" (573), he exists as a procreant voice. In telling the tale and in casting the fragments in terms of incidents and exposition, Ishmael constructs the arena within which he not only explains himself but addresses the problem of Ahab's "hidden self" (185), whose perplexities can only be rendered as an inspired product of Ishmael's imagination. Here he translates his memories into words:

> But Ahab, my Captain, still moves before me in all his Nantucket grimness and shagginess; and in this episode touching Emperors and Kings, I must not conceal that I have only to do with a poor old whale-hunter like him; and, therefore, all outward majestical trappings and housings are denied me. Oh, Ahab! what shall be grand in thee, it must needs be plucked at from the skies, and dived for in the deep, and featured in the unbodied air! (148)

Similarly, in "The Ship" Ishmael authorizes himself through peremptory declamation: "For all men tragically great are made so through a certain morbidness. Be sure of this, O young ambition, all mortal greatness is but disease" (74). Such assertions reflect an ethos of self-assured interpretive power, and in fact Ishmael is fond of making grand syntheses. His pronouncements, however, must be recognized as hypothetical statements—propositions to be tested within the subsequent narrative. His apparently authoritative assertions coexist with contending attitudes on a continuum extending from utter ignorance, to informed speculation, to qualified knowledge. His story, therefore, conflates provisional and determinate formulations. Ishmael's life-experience authorizes his tale, but what issues from the narrative cannot be dissociated from his invention.

As seen in the Peleg episode, Ishmael's primary technique for exploiting narrative license is his use of the essayistic excursion. Ishmael's present-tense representations of Ahab tend to constitute inquiries into his "larger, darker, deeper part" (185). It is one thing to view Ahab as a monomaniac; it is quite another to examine his unidirectional madness in relation to the great complexity of his character. Taking pains to delineate the ontology of Ahab's madness, Ishmael does not find it "probable that this monomania . . . took its instant rise at the precise time of his bodily dismemberment" (184).[14] Instead, Ahab was steeped in rage and sorrow; then "his torn body and gashed soul bled into one another; and so interfusing, made him mad" (185). Physical and spiritual domains converge to transform the captain. Though able to affect a "firm, collected front," Ahab still "in his hidden self, raved on." The nature of this "hidden self" looms among Ishmael's most vexing hermeneutical problems, for as Ishmael realizes, what he fathoms must be little more than a frustrating prelude to what cannot *be* fathomed. In the end, analytical activity inevitably leads to the exhaustion of analysis. To comprehend the implications of Ahab's "deepeningly contracted" madness—especially how his "great natural intellect" accelerates rather than diminishes his potency—would be a considerable achievement. But as Ishmael admits, it merely brings him to the threshold of a more daunting problem: "Ahab's larger, darker, deeper part remains unhinted" (185).

Ishmael satisfactorily contends with surface behavior, but the "root" of Ahab's "awful essence" is buried beneath multiple layers. By constructing images of excavation, Ishmael delves into the depths of Ahab's being. Ishmael's striking architectural image of the Hotel de Cluny inducts his "nobler, sadder" readers to the netherworld— the lowest layers—of personal and collective identity:

> Winding far down from within the very heart of this spiked Hotel
> de Cluny where we here stand—however grand and wonderful,
> now quit it;—and take your way, ye nobler, sadder souls, to those
> vast Roman halls of Thermes; where far beneath the fantastic tow-

ers of man's upper earth, his root of grandeur, his whole awful
essence sits in bearded state; an antique buried beneath antiqui-
ties, and throned on torsoes! (185)

Ishmael describes Ahab's innermost recesses as a ruined effigy, a
costumed figure, an image that encompasses individual and an-
cestral identities. In this "proud, sad king," Ishmael conflates time,
paternity, the unconscious, and the mystery of origin. In plunging
into such depths, he recognizes a "family likeness" (186), another
allusion to Narcissus. Here the self is not reflected in Nature's pool
but in a "grim sire," the inscrutable patriarch of time, a figure who
will never yield "the old State-secret." Ahab's innermost self must
remain closed. No inquirer can appropriate the secret of another's
being; nor can one transcend the chronological fact of one's own
exile from a putatively primal, unifying self. To mine buried depths
is to find a shattered icon left by mocking gods: "So with a broken
throne, the great gods mock that captive king; so like a Caryatid,
he patient sits, upholding on his frozen brow the piled entabla-
tures of ages" (185).

Ishmael's extended figure depicts the inevitable failure of
one's quest for a fully explicable truth. It is "vain to popularize
profundities," Ishmael exclaims, "and all truth is profound" (185).
At the self's deepest layers, Ishmael discovers an insuperable ignorance of the unconscious self. The buried king personifies this ontological paradigm: it fuses personal and mythic contexts; it applies
to self and other; it offers an approach to the rich lode buried as the
unconscious; and it conceals what the ultimate "State-secret" might
be (186). Characteristically, Ishmael's excursions exhaust what he
thinks he can know in the act of defining—or suggesting—what
he cannot. Neither motive nor being, thanks to the "subterranean
miner that works in us all," are ultimately explicable: "[A]ll this to
explain, would be to dive deeper than Ishmael can go"(187).

In the absence of full understanding, Ishmael fashions a dialectical model that dramatizes the elemental war racking Ahab. After
pouring over maps to track the White Whale's migratory patterns,
Ahab succumbs to "a weariness and faintness of pondering" (201).
His "insufferable anguish" afflicts him in sleep:

[A]nd when, as was sometimes the case, these spiritual throes in him heaved his being up from its base, and a chasm seemed opening in him, from which forked flames and lightnings shot up, and accursed fiends beckoned him to leap down among them; when this hell in himself yawned beneath him, a wild cry would be heard through the ship; and with glaring eyes Ahab would burst from his state room, as though escaping from a bed that was on fire. (201–02)

This lurid description reflects the intensity of Ahab's self-consumption. To enlarge his portrait Ishmael depicts Ahab's schizophrenia as a fierce dialectic. Describing two contending selves, Ishmael speaks of "the scheming, unappeasedly steadfast hunter" that struggles with

the agent that so caused him to burst from [his bed] in horror again. The latter was the eternal, living principle or soul in him; and in sleep, being for the time dissociated from the characterizing mind, which at other times employed it for its outer vehicle or agent, it spontaneously sought escape from the scorching contiguity of the frantic thing, of which, for the time, it was no longer an integral. (202)

Within Ahab, where two beings vie for sovereignty, the "living principle" is no match for the "characterizing mind." His essential self falls hostage to the "frantic thing." The "characterizing mind" had an "unbidden and unfathered birth"—that is, it has no connection to organic human nature and instead possesses a "self-assumed, independent being of its own." Ahab's "intense thinking thus makes him a Prometheus; a vulture feeds upon that heart for ever; that vulture the very creature he creates" (202).

Ishmael also uses representational characters to reflect aspects of Ahab's ontology. On the *Pequod*, Fedallah and Pip embody projections of Ahab's innermost being—Fedallah as the demonic aspect of Ahab's "characterizing mind" and Pip as the mad, maimed, indigent sign and justification of Ahab's purpose. At one point, Fedallah and Ahab inhabit the same shadow: "And Ahab chanced so to stand, that the Parsee occupied his shadow; while, if the Parsee's shadow was there at all it seemed only to blend with, and lengthen Ahab's" (328). Later, Ishmael makes explicit their reciprocity: "At times, for longest hours, without a single hail, they stood far parted in the starlight; Ahab in his scuttle, the Parsee by the mainmast; but still fixedly gazing upon each other; as if in the Parsee Ahab saw his forethrown shadow, in Ahab the Parsee his abandoned substance" (537–38). Toward the conclusion of "The Symphony," after rejecting Starbuck's pleas to end the hunt, Ahab turns from his "human eye" and looks over the rail into the water (544). Here Ahab gazes into another version of Narcissus's pool and "started at two reflected, fixed eyes in the water there. Fedallah was motionlessly leaning over the same rail" (545). By accentuating how Ahab and Fedallah mirror one another, Ishmael completes the shadow/substance trope.

Ahab's affiliation with Pip, unlike Fedallah, might easily be seen as an expression of Ahab's "humanities," his capacity, as it were, for love and affection. But it must be recognized that their relationship is so marginal that it also reflects Ahab's alienation from society. Pip's experience as castaway fits him to be Ahab's counterpart. After his soul is "carried down alive to wondrous depths," Pip watches the "unwarped primal world" and witnesses "God's foot upon the treadle of the loom" (414). From Ahab's perspective, Pip's apparent madness, then, is really a case of perceptual transcendence. He sees through the masks of material causes to the origins of experience, to the activity of the "weaver God" working on the Loom of Time. Ahab sees Pip as "holiness" (522), a conduit of "most wondrous philosophies" (529). While Pip does indeed touch Ahab's "inmost centre" (522), their bond accentuates Ahab's isolation and cosmic rage. Pip impels Ahab more forcefully in his attempted usurpation of the god-realm. He rages at the "creative libertines" who did "beget this luckless child, and have abandoned him."

The gods reflect a final projection of Ahab's ontology. For Ahab, it is an ontological axiom that he participates in the grandeur of divine being. But unlike Fedallah and Pip, the gods are absent figures. They achieve presence only in the fevered tropes of Ahab's self-reflexive rhetoric. Indeed, Ahab remakes the gods in his own image. Through the "unfathered birth" of his "characterizing mind," Ahab locates himself on an equal plain with the immortals. Ahab's "heart-woes" imbue him with "archangelical grandeur," an asocial quality that he also projects on the gods (464). Ahab's "high mortal miseries" stamp him not only with the constricting burdens of the Fall, but with the very signature of the gods themselves. According to Ishmael, Ahab's excessive suffering becomes contorted into a self-proclaimed genealogical connection that goes all the way back to the primal nonexistence of time: "To trail the genealogies of these high mortal miseries, carries us at last among the sourceless primogenitures of the gods. . . . the gods themselves are not for ever glad. The ineffaceable, sad birth-mark in the brow of man, is but the stamp of sorrow in the signers." Ishmael imagines Ahab as reconstructing divine being through the hyperbolic range of his wrenched emotions. Ahab's affiliation with Fedallah, Pip, and the gods reflect his attempts to reject his "humanities"—his actual ontological condition—in favor of a self-ordained myth of Promethean vent.

Ahab's "characterizing mind"—the monomaniacal schemer hunting Moby Dick—shapes the terms of his self-dramatization, including the self-definitions manifest in his speech. Unlike Ishmael, with his expansive, flexible voice and sensibility, Ahab articulates a philosophical rhetoric of narrow definition. His speech and actions usually generate from unwavering principles. In believing that "all evil . . . were visibly personified, and made practically assailable in Moby Dick" (184), Ahab reduces interpretation to a series of redactions and action to a linear, obsessive pursuit of resolution. The primary expression of this closed rhetorical system appears in "The Quarter-Deck," when Ahab engages in a manipulative philosophical dialogue. Through a series of questions and answers, Ahab inflames the crew, extracting their oaths of vengeance. Starbuck, however, resists. Recognizing that the first mate is impervious to his emotional appeals and therefore "requirest a little lower layer" (163), Ahab describes his intense desire for revenge and also explains his metaphysical justification.

As Michael E. Levin argues, Ahab is an inverted Platonist. Like any Platonist, Ahab sees the material world as a sign of invisible forms. Unlike a Platonist, he believes that malice animates the "pasteboard masks" of matter (164). Thus Ahab's pursuit of the White Whale is designed to defeat the "unknown but still reasoning thing" that expresses its nature from behind "the unreasoning mask." Ahab's fixed theory of reality is diametrically opposed to Ishmael's multiple formulations. Ahab declares:

> All visible objects, man, are but as pasteboard masks. But in each event—in the living act, the undoubted deed—there, some unknown but still reasoning thing puts forth the mouldings of its features from behind the unreasoning mask. If man will strike, strike through the mask! How can the prisoner reach outside except by thrusting through the wall? To me, the white whale is that wall, shoved near to me. Sometimes I think there's naught beyond. But 'tis enough. He tasks me; he heaps me; I see in him outrageous strength, with an inscrutable malice sinewing it. That inscrutable thing is chiefly what I hate; and be the white whale agent, or be the white whale principal, I will wreak that hate upon him. (164)

This metaphysical construct justifies his Promethean self-image: "Talk not to me of blasphemy, man; I'd strike the sun if it insulted me. . . . Who's over me? Truth hath no confines." Ahab thus decrees his dispensation from contingency.

While Ahab's self-fashioned deific identity is the most self-empowering dimension of his tortured being, the validity of this godself is assailed by his intermittent recognition of his "humanities." The perceptual gap between god-self and mortal self usually appears as a consequence of the crippling limitations of his body and, less frequently, of his experience of fellowship. His physical infirmities exacerbate his case against the gods, even while manifestly undermining his assertions of cosmic status. Continually, Ahab makes qualifications that dissociate his "proper and inaccessible being" from the maimed evidence of his corporeality (560).

The conflict between Ahab's god-self and his indigent self emerges not only in Ahab's various dialogues but also in his soliloquies and irruptive declamations.[15] In the latter part of the "Sunset" chapter, for instance, Ahab soliloquizes on how the fixations of his will express an absolutistic purpose: "What I've dared, I've willed; and what I've willed, I'll do! . . . Naught's an obstacle, naught's an angle to the iron way!" (168). In the early part of this chapter, in "The Pipe," and "The Sphynx," Ahab speaks in soliloquy and offers his most indigent self-dramatization. At such times he reveals a rich, though repressed, sense of human affection and communal interdependence. In his address to the severed whale's head and his apostrophe to the dying whale, Ahab contends with inscrutable mysteries of creation. In both instances, he mourns the loss of sailors:

> Oh, thou dark Hindoo half of nature, who of drowned bones hast builded thy separate throne somewhere in the heart of these unverdured seas; thou art an infidel, thou queen, and too truly speakest to me in the wide-slaughtering Typhoon, and the hushed burial of its after calm. . . . All thy unnamable imminglings float beneath me here; I am buoyed by breaths of once living things, exhaled as air, but water now. (497)

In these scenes, Ahab appears as a reflective, inquiring, pondering man momentarily loosed from the hell of his "characterizing mind." Eschewing the solipsism that is indigenous to the god-self, Ahab federates with the mothers of drowned sailors and feels empathy enlarged by grief (311).

Like his dialogues and his soliloquies, Ahab's declamations usually reflect his tendency toward self-dramatization and express the dialectic between his god-self and his corporeal self. After his whalebone leg is crushed, Ahab cries, "But even with a broken bone, old Ahab is untouched. . . . Nor white whale, nor man, nor fiend, can so much as graze old Ahab in his own proper and inaccessible being" (560). Despite the vicissitudes of experience, Ahab claims that his essential self remains inviolate. Here Ahab accepts as a given the ideal properties of his being. The anguish of his spirit derives from his rhetorical assessment of the disparity between the "unconquerable captain in the soul" and the pitiable evidence offered by his "craven mate. . . . [my] body" (560). Ahab laments the humiliation heaped on him by the phenomenal world. Ahab rejects any notion that Ishmael's "universal thump" (6) should be passed to him, and he curses social interdependence. His assertions of absolute existence, however, appear to be psychologically compensatory, as when he constructs ontological self-portraits that replace his maimed flesh with a transcendent soul: "Ye see an old man cut down to the stump; leaning on a shivered lance; propped up on a lonely foot. 'Tis Ahab—his body's part; but Ahab's soul's a centipede, that moves upon a hundred legs" (561).

Rhetorically, his declamations are addressed to no one in particular and thereby reinforce his self-willed isolation. At one point, disgusted with having to deal with the carpenter, Ahab apostrophizes, "Oh, Life! Here I am, proud as a Greek god, and yet standing debtor to this blockhead for a bone to stand on! Cursed be that mortal inter-indebtedness which will not do away with ledgers. I would be free as air; and I'm down in the whole world's books" (471–72). In one respect, Ahab's indigent aspect, which he narrowly and mistakenly associates with his body rather than his emotions, makes his quest self-defeating. To be in voice inevitably is to be in body; he can never be like the wind, bodiless as an object but not as an agent (564). In another respect Ahab's insistence on his soul's incorruptible essence establishes the point to which he proceeds. To vindicate this self-image, Ahab must perform his great action. He must, in body, fulfill the soul's mandate. To slay Moby Dick would be to eradicate "all evil," thus altering the fundamental terms of human existence by imposing the dictates of his own soul on the malign forces that control the phenomenal domain.

Ahab's preeminent declamatory speech occurs in "The Candles." With the "corpusants" (506) flaring atop the masts, Ahab articulates his sense of theology ("right worship is defiance"), cosmology and ontology ("In the midst of the personified impersonal, a personality stands here"), and genealogy ("But thou are but my fiery father; my sweet mother, I know not") (507–08). While depicting himself as orphaned, Ahab nevertheless claims a knowable origin by naming his father. In doing so, Ahab becomes superior to the "unbegun" deific principle: "I know that of me, which thou knowest not of thyself. . . . Oh, thou foundling fire . . . thou too hast thy incommunicable riddle, thy unparticipated grief. Here again, with haughty agony, I read my sire" (508). Rejecting a biological patriarchy for a cosmic one, Ahab thus diverts filial obligation into defiant, hateful imperatives.

If in "The Candles" Ahab asserts his cosmic identity, then in "The Symphony" he questions his most basic knowledge of the self. In this remarkable chapter, Ahab's dialogue with Starbuck (with its attending communalism) gives way to soliloquy (with its attending solipsism). Ishmael dramatizes Ahab's shift from the human interdependence imaged by Starbuck to the stark alienation expressed by Fedallah's diabolical gaze. When Ahab wonders, "Is Ahab, Ahab," he is considering the question of agency. Already he has rejected Starbuck's overtures to return home. Now he revolves the chill implications of why he—or some extrinsic force—drives himself so. Though the question is now moot, he continues to examine the schizoid split between the "inscrutable, unearthly" demands of the god-self and the "natural lovings and longings" (545) associated with his "humanities" (79). Now, however, Ahab does not depict himself as equal to the gods. He perceives the gods not (as they hitherto have been) as immanent beings but as mechanical forces outside the self. He questions, in effect, the stability of his identity, the very efficacy of his hitherto deified volition: "Is Ahab, Ahab? Is it I, God, or who that lifts this arm?"[16] He rejects absolute freedom in favor of a mechanistic analogy: "By heaven, man, we are turned round and round in this world, like yonder windlass, and Fate is the handspike" (545). The province of Fate absolves Ahab from having to think seriously of Starbuck's tempting scenario. Instead, he translates his self-generated constructs into a predetermined force that controls human agency. Ahab's most unsettling moment of ontological uncertainty culminates in his most rigid act of self-definition. Paradoxically, Ahab's rhetorical repudiation of self-propelled agency derives from his own volition. Ahab translates, as it were, his own desires into a script of cosmic determinism in which Fate inevitably manifests his most encompassing (and self-restricting) fiction. As Ahab earlier says, "For with little external to constrain us, the innermost necessities in our being, these still drive us on" (165).

Ishmael's celebration of a shared human condition and Ahab's attempt to dissociate himself from such federation comprise *Moby-Dick*'s informing ontological drama. Both characters pursue elemental questions of being, agency, and teleology; they attempt to understand one's essential identity as reflected in the passage from origin to ending. Ishmael presents his ontological concerns by focusing on rhetoric and behavior. To him, being achieves expression through language and action. It may seem that Melville polarizes the voices of Ishmael and Ahab, as he does with *Mardi*'s genialist and solipsistic voices. Crucially, though, Ahab's "humanities" complicate his pursuit of self-deification, his desire to stand on equal terms with the gods. Significantly, the voices and identities of Ishmael and Ahab are not polarized. There are times when Ishmael speaks in the voice of Ahab and Ahab in the voice of Ishmael. Ishmael's admission, "Ahab's quenchless feud seemed mine," points to an underlying affinity between them (179). Indeed, in identifying the demonic quest as an integral element of collective human experience, Ishmael describes the "demon phantom that, some time or other, swims before all human hearts" (237). This cosmic lure, though promising transcendence, leads to frustration or destruction: "while chasing such over this round globe, they either lead us on in barren mazes or midway leave us whelmed." The philosophical quester either embarks on the endless search of Babbalanja or Bulkington or achieves the "utter wreck" (*Mardi* 557) of Taji or Ahab.

Ishmael's access to Ahab's inner life depends on his capacity to use imagination and extend himself into another psyche. When Ishmael claims, for example, "There is a wisdom that is woe; but there is a woe that is madness," he is suggesting that a continuum might well carry one from wisdom to woe to madness; in fact, the three states manifest degrees of a single complex (425). Whereas Pip's passage to madness is a one-way transit, Ishmael and Ahab seem able to move in either direction, though each reflects a primary emphasis: Ishmael's wisdom that is woe, and Ahab's wisdom that is woe becoming madness. In "The Try-Works," Ishmael's admission that he gave himself up to "fire" reflects his felt affinity with Ahab's absolutism (425). On occasion, Ishmael even has aspirations to cosmic status. At the conclusion of Chapter 57 he conflates the figures of Perseus destroying the whale and Prometheus assaulting the heavens, thereby casting himself in terms of titanic action. This hyperbolic act of self-fashioning echoes Taji's rhetoric in "Dreams": "With a frigate's anchors for my bridle-bits and fasces of harpoons for spurs, would I could mount that whale [the constellation Cetus] and leap the topmost skies, to see whether the fabled heavens with all their countless tents really lie encamped beyond my mortal sight!" (271).[17] Similarly, Ahab at times expresses the inquisitive qualities of Ishmael's voice. When confronted with the possibility that the coffin life buoy might symbolize an "immortality-preserver," Ahab propounds a series of open-ended questions: "Here now's the very dreaded symbol of grim death, by a mere hap, made the expressive sign of the help and hope of most endangered life. A life-buoy of a coffin! Does it go further? Can it be that in some spiritual sense the coffin is, after all, but an immortality-preserver! I'll think of that" (528). Ahab's speculation comes to a curt ending: "But no. So far gone am I in the dark side of earth, that its other side, the theoretic bright one, seems but uncertain twilight to me." Ishmaelean speculation gives way to the rhetoric of narrow definition. By aligning himself with darkness, Ahab negates the potentially curative engagement with multiple values and perspectives.

The rhetorical and ontological symbiosis of Ishmael and Ahab has its culminating, and most teasing, manifestation in the important textual crux in "The Gilder." The chapter's long speech beginning "Oh, grassy glades! oh, ever vernal endless landscapes in the soul" might belong either to Ishmael or Ahab (492). Prior to the 1989 Northwestern-Newberry edition of *Moby-Dick,* Melvillian scholars treated this address as Ishmael's. In no edition prior to Northwestern-Newberry do quotation marks bracket the long paragraph, though this reading was considered but rejected in the 1967 Norton Critical Edition (494). In "Discussions of Adopted Readings," the Northewestern-Newsberry editors contend, "The structure of the chapter conclusively shows that the paragraph should be spoken by Ahab, for the chapter moves from Ishmael's definition of the effect of 'times of dreamy quietude' (491.13) in the Pacific upon a rover like himself, to the effect of such scenes upon Ahab, upon Starbuck, and finally upon Stubb" (901). "The Gilder" chapter dramatizes an unfolding scenic tableau structurally parallel to the speeches in "The Doubloon." The Northwestern-Newberry editors suggest that Melville had not "visualized the scene" fully, but it is also possible that either Melville accidentally left out the quotation marks, in which case the speech reflects Ahab's "temporary" refuge (492), or Melville intended the speech to be Ishmael's response to the fact that "such soothing scenes" had only a temporary effect on Ahab. The speech sounds like Ishmael, especially with the images of the Loom of Time: "But the mingled, mingling threads of life are woven by warp and woof: calms crossed by storms, a storm for every calm." Ishmael also seems to be evoked through the depiction of life as repetitive process: "There is no steady unretracing progress in this life; we do not advance through fixed gradations, and at the last one pause. . . . But once gone through, we trace the round again; and are infants, boys, and men, and Ifs eternally." But whereas the content of the speech favors Ishmael, the dramatic context favors Ahab. The chapter unfolds as a series of speeches with the longest one seeming to belong to Ahab, the narrative's most dramatically resonant actor.

The crux of the speech emphasizes a conflation of rhetorical and ontological aspects evident elsewhere in the text. Certainly, the speech addresses the ontological mystery of both Ishmael and Ahab, if not the human collective. The speaker offers a probing meditation on psychological flux and how lost origin predetermines the inscrutability of one's ending. In wondering about the "final harbor, whence we unmoor no more," the speaker images the soul as an orphan, a foundling in search of what only another world can supply: "Where is the foundling's father hidden? Our souls are like those orphans whose unwedded mothers die in bearing them: the secret of our paternity lies in their grave, and we must there to learn it" (492). Whether Ishmael or Ahab (or, given the possibility that Ishmael elides into Ahab in the compositional moment, both characters at once), the speaker here ponders the mystery of human dispossession, linking the mind's wavering motion with the complexities of lost origin, uncertain identity, and teleological suspension. Paternity inscribes one's place in time and society. Without this patriarchy, one is limited to the implications of a name—an Ishmael or an Ahab—and the unfolding tendency of one's being as expressed through language and behavior. The prospective ending, in its potential for revelation, looms as an unreadable future. Significantly, the soul—the absolute and unknowable essence—remains outside the time-space of genealogy and constitutes a word-sign of teasing, alluring nondefinition.

EPISTEMOLOGY

"Mistifying the Gardens of the Deep"

Even though "thousands of hunters" have for millennia been watching whales "spouting all over the sea, and sprinkling and mistifying the gardens of the deep," no individual "down to this blessed minute" has been able to determine "whether these spoutings are, after all, really water, or nothing but vapor" (370). This "noteworthy thing" impels Ishmael's present-tense inquisition—"Let us, then, look at this matter"—into the sperm whale's circulatory system. Given his inability to achieve "absolute certainty" (372) regarding a "plain" event (373), Ishmael qualifies the epistemological possibilities associated with direct experience. The most careful scrutiny only uncovers layers of obfuscation. Addressing this situation, he simulates a dialogue with an exasperated reader: "But why pester one with all this reasoning on the subject? Speak out! You have seen him spout; then declare what the spout is; can you not tell water from air? My dear sir, in this world it is not so easy to settle these plain things. I have ever found your plain things the knotti-est of all" (373). Through this interplay, Ishmael accentuates the experiential immediacy of his pursuits and illuminates his funda-mental epistemological dilemma: to see plain things is hardly to know them. Or to put it another way, a plain thing simply does not exist. To find "plain things" the "knottiest" is not to embrace chaos, absurdity, or emptiness but to recognize the intrinsic mys-tery lurking in phenomena.

"The Fountain" offers a paradigm of Ishmael's abiding episte-mological activity.[18] His recollections of past experience, combined with his research, lead him to plausible hypothesis: "Still, we can hypothesize, even if we cannot prove and establish" (373). While insisting on the provisional nature of knowledge, Ishmael continu-ally casts himself as an accomplished reader. His facility with books appears first in "Extracts" (xvii–xxvii), a series of chronologically arranged quotations that reflect a seemingly "plain" but actually knotty purpose. "Extracts" contains sporadic and, for the most part, misinformed accounts of the Leviathan; it renders not what whales are but what has been written about them. The references, offered piecemeal, do not disseminate "veritable gospel cetology" (xvii). Since the reader engages this collage for the sole purpose of discounting it, Ishmael begins his book by calling into question the authority of earlier texts. Before departing from the Manhattan wharf, he has distanced himself from his literary predecessors. Us-able, or valid, knowledge, however incomplete or problematic, will only be acquired by leaving behind the "Sub-Sub-Librarian" (xvii). What Ishmael advocates is for book learning to be recast in rela-tion to the chaotic actualities of whaling; iconic texts must un-dergo a sea change and become part of the narrator's dynamic narrative process. As Ishmael testifies, "So there is no earthly way of finding out precisely what the whale really looks like. And the only mode in which you can derive even a tolerable idea of his living contour, is by going a whaling yourself" (264). Or, the reader can go whaling with Ishmael.

The materials in "Extracts" contrast with Ishmael's allusive ac-tivity, his primary means of fusing past experience, and his learn-ing. As an extrinsic sign that ruptures the text, an allusion calls attention to the narrator's importation of alien material. At the very least, allusion conflates two language systems. A consciously made allusion presupposes a prospective reader's shared familiarity with the extratextual material. Ishmael assumes that the reader will recognize a name like Kant and comprehend its pertinence. Even a historical name like George Washington—"Queequeg was George Washington cannibalistically developed" (50)—belongs to an amorphously diffused social text in which the late president represents such attributes as honesty, nobility, and leadership. If a reader happens not to know George Washington from Kant, Pyrrho, Thomas Browne, J. Ross Browne, Paracelsus, Gog and Magog, or Manco Capac, then the reader confronts a blank, the result of which is perceptual lacunae and stunted communication.

Ishmael's use of allusion resides at the book's epistemological center. As crucial and pervasive elements of Ishmael's literary world, these allusions become integral to the experience being translated, not only helping Ishmael tell his story but supplying interpretive problems for the reader. Interestingly, the second mate Stubb describes the fecund symbiosis between text and interpreter. Indicating how written texts generate new language systems, Stubb says, "[T]he fact is, you books must know your places. You'll do to give us the bare words and facts, but we come in to supply the thoughts" (433). Ishmael takes "bare words," gives them a new context, and creates new thoughts. His allusions reveal, not a quaint or irritating fascination with name-dropping, but a vital means of orienting himself and his reader to the life-as-lived through the life that is written.

Ishmael's allusions tend to have highly restrictive or expansive application. They function as either synoptic metaphors or dialectical forays; either closed, determinant signs or open, indeterminate complexes. When, for instance, Ishmael cites "Seneca and the Stoics," Solomon, Pythagoras, or the conflict between Locke and Kant, he intends very specific meanings. Seneca suggests stoical forbearance and patient suffering (6), whereas Solomon represents the wise man of sorrow (424). Pythagoras is linked with metempsychosis (429) and Pyrrho with skepticism (374). And the strained "counterpoise" of the sperm whale's head and the right whale's head comically figures the overwhelming difficulty of balancing the intellectual systems of Locke and Kant (327). Here Ishmael skims rather than dives: Locke stands for empiricism and Kant idealism.[19] To fall into "Plato's honey head" is to be overwhelmed by ideality (344). Ishmael's allusion to Cato's suicide seems at first to denote noble self-extinction (3). This image, however, stirs an ensemble of intellectual resonances. Melville knew that Cato, on the night before his suicide, read *Phaedo*, Plato's great meditation on death and immortality. The reading of Plato embellishes and contextualizes Cato's heroic grandeur. One wonders, then, if Ishmael's departure for the sea is an alternative to, or a form of, suicide. If Ishmael does invite death, then he may be doing so in Cato's spirit. As he suggests in "The Chapel" through his own allusion to *Phaedo*, Ishmael construes death as a "promotion" into one's "better being" (37). His many dialectical allusions unsettle the text and excite the play of multiple possibilities. As argued in the preceding chapter, Ishmael's allusions to Carlyle's "Loom of Time" evoke the complex interaction between matter and spirit. Rather than functioning allegorically, as the synoptic metaphors do, the more expansive allusions assume the status of symbolic clusters and initiate problems in reading. Such allusions are epistemological puzzles with few or many missing pieces.

Ishmael's most expansive dialectical allusion—"that story of Narcissus" (5)—unifies the novel's ontological and epistemological centers. To Narcissus, the fountain reflects an alluring image of the self as the apparent other. In seeking to grasp this image, Narcissus falls in and drowns. Significantly, Ishmael universalizes the story, linking its association with elemental being to the making of meaning, the problems of knowing. Each individual replicates the condition of Narcissus. Though suggesting that it is the "same image, we ourselves see in all rivers and oceans," Ishmael makes a crucial qualification: "It is the image of the ungraspable phantom of life; and this is the key to it all." The phantom is neither to be clutched nor comprehended but rather, seen, pursued, and studied. Ishmael indicates the necessity of maintaining a self-protective dissociation between I and it, between subjective perceiver and self-reflecting sign, between the eye-I and nature. Otherwise, one becomes duped by the illusion that the phantom is the other; one thereby becomes destroyed in the manner of Narcissus or Ahab (or Taji or Pierre or Celio or Mortmain).

The novel's "story of Narcissus" offers a cautionary tale about the dangers of absolutizing one's reading of the world text and of failing to recognize the self-projection involved in any reading. According to Ishmael, we know ourselves through the meanings we assign to the dumb blankness of objects. The "key to it all" unlocks the door to shifting meanings and relative values; we encounter a world text, as it were, that fires one's reading and rereading. While Ishmael's concern with ontological unity achieves expression in fixed and determinant analogies that denote attributes of collective human nature, his concern with epistemology leads to the formulation of indeterminate possibilities.[20] All may see the "same image," but its meaning changes from one reader to the next, or even for the same reader from one minute to the next. Thus, the ontological affinity celebrated by Ishmael becomes displaced by the epistemological process generated by the shared nature. The relation of ontology to epistemology might be seen as the relation of essence to performance, being actualized in the process of becoming. The "root . . . grandeur" (185) of ontological affinity, then, is dispersed into psychological and behavioral idiosyncrasy. For Ishmael, the epistemological process inevitably exposes recalcitrant differences.

Ishmael's primary epistemological activity, then, involves the interpretation of signs and surfaces. By focusing Ishmael's philosophical purpose, reading leads to a dramatic engagement with the complexities of knowing, an engagement conditioned by mood and exigency. In the early chapters of *Moby-Dick*, Ishmael presents how he and others carefully scrutinize written texts and vexing surfaces and then considers the cenotaphs that trap the mourners within "unceasing grief" (36). Later, Father Mapple rereads and re-creates the Jonah story, which in his rendition presumes a hierarchical, stable universe with a vengeful deity controlling the whale. Ishmael, however, never explicates Mapple's sermon. Like *Mardi*'s "Voice from the Gods," the sermon functions as a text within the text and offers the reader a critical problem, a problem for the reader's meditation and application. This hermeneutical cluster concludes with Queequeg holding a large book on his lap and "counting the pages with deliberate regularity; at every fiftieth page—as I fancied—stopping a moment, looking vacantly around him, and giving utterance to a long-drawn gurgling whistle of astonishment" (49). As Joel Porte observes, "Queequeg represents the unlettered wisdom of a prelapsarian consciousness uncontaminated by book learning" (211). But Queequeg's arithmetical act of nonreading is being read by postlapsarian Ishmael. He sees through the odd action and Queequeg's "hideously marred" skin—the corporeal text—to the inner essence: "You cannot hide the soul. Through all his unearthly tattooings, I thought I saw the traces of a simple honest heart" (49–50).

After Ishmael signs on, Elijah makes an ambiguous prophecy concerning the slippery matter of whether one's present act inscribes the future, saying, "Well, well, what's signed, is signed; and what's to be, will be; and then again perhaps it wont be, after all" (93). With these words Elijah prefigures Ahab's mystery as well as the novel's abiding concern with the intricacies of Fate and free will. Elijah's formulation makes and unmakes a proposition: what will be, may not. In contending with this "ambiguous, half-hinting, half-revealing, shrouded sort of talk," Ishmael imagines "all kinds of vague wonderments and half-apprehensions." Situating himself not as process narrator but as retrospective actor, Ishmael recounts what he felt upon meeting Elijah and thus appears as the reader's surrogate. Like any reader contained within the linearity of printed words, Ishmael wonders about the connection between present and future time. If reality is a predetermined script, then what will be has already been written, though what that text will mean is another question.

Essentially, Ishmael dramatizes two kinds of reading scenes: examinations of the self, which are reenactments of "that story of Narcissus"; and examinations of surfaces that are extrinsic to the self, which are alien, often unreadable, always decidedly the other. As Ishmael discovers—in pondering Hotel de Cluny as an image of the self or by evoking the hieroglyphic markings on the whale—both types of examinations present a puzzle to behold, an impenetrable mystery. On the contrary, a monomaniacal reader like Ahab believes that images of the self are knowable. Though admitting there "may be naught beyond" the "pasteboard masks" of material forms, Ahab nevertheless projects a determinant and collective meaning on the representational mask. Since to "crazy Ahab" the White Whale signifies "all evil," he thus forges an allegorical explanation of individual and collective human experience. The perceived malignity of God (or the gods) justifies the linear quest to fulfill an unambiguous, redemptive act. Ahab rejects both multiple, or symbolic, readings and the efficacy of other readings.

"The Doubloon" presents the novel's most important scene of reading. This chapter dramatizes Ishmael's "Narcissus" allusion in the form of an extended tableau. Here, Ahab, Starbuck, Stubb, Flask, the Manxman, and Pip pause before the cabalistic coin; each interprets the inscribed figures as self-reflexive forms. Sign mirrors self. Ahab, in particular, extends his egotism over all creation, seeing in the coin a reflection of his self-justifying absolutism: "The firm tower, that is Ahab; the volcano, that is Ahab; the courageous, the undaunted, and victorious foul, that, too, is Ahab; all are Ahab; and this round gold is but the image of the rounder globe, which, like a magician's glass, to each and every man in turn but mirrors back his own mysterious self" (431). By reading his own features on the coin, he creates an analogical basis for applying the figure to the entire world. In echoing Ishmael's "key to it all," Ahab recognizes that each individual will see an idiosyncratic self-reflection. The book's tragedy, however, generates from his refusal to accept the equal status of disparate readers. His interpretation assumes the force of Fate—a self-justifying fiction of a predetermined universal script. He reads the zodiac and concludes: "From storm to storm! So be it, then. Born in throes, 'tis fit that man should live in pains and die in pangs! So be it, then! Here's stout stuff for woe to work on. So be it, then" (432).

This interpretive tableau reinforces the relativistic hermeneutical activity. After the Manxman interprets these signs, Stubb interprets the readers and sums up the fundamental epistemological condition: "There's another rendering now; but still one text. All sorts of men in one kind of world, you see" (434). These readings are not, as Mark Bauerlein contends, "momentarily definitive"; nor do the readers "reach behind the sign to extract its authentic meaning" (25). Far from being definitive, these readings reflect idiosyncrasy. Rather than possessing authentic or fixed value, the coin reflects possible but inconclusive values. A reader always comes between sign and "authentic meaning." If anything becomes "momentarily" defined, it is the reader rather than the coin. Unlike Ahab, who refuses to reconsider his reading of the White Whale, Ishmael revels in the play of possibility. In fact, his process narrative authorizes the single adumbration of a moment's conditional truth, the "certain significance . . . in all things" (430). But "certain" is a double entendre: for Ahab, "certain" denotes fixed value; for Ishmael, "certain" connotes indefinite value, as in the phrase *a certain something*. Ahab's epistemological absolutism stands as a fixed point against which Ishmael explores, and dramatizes, hermeneutical possibility. Ishmael's contradictions, then, do not manifest an intellectual whirlwind like that in *Mardi;* rather, his readings express the activity of mind seeking knowledge in light of the paradoxical precondition that no final or fixed knowledge exists.

Thus Ishmael frequently casts himself as dramatic reader of extrinsic surfaces. He displays his mind at work in the interplay between subject and object, consciousness and phenomena. In "The Spouter-Inn," Ishmael pauses before the "besmoked" and "defaced" (12) but "marvellous" (13) oil painting of a stormy nautical scene: "[I]t was only by diligent study and a series of systematic visits to it, and careful inquiry of the neighbors, that you could any way arrive at an understanding of its purpose" (12). Ishmael finds the "unaccountable masses of shades and shadows" provocative enough to suggest that some artist "had endeavored to delineate chaos bewitched"—a thought, he admits, that might well be creditable. Ishmael attempts to see the painting through its parts and thereby evokes an impression of the whole. As the novel frequently demonstrates, the act of dissection makes it impossible for one to move from partial to holistic knowledge. At the center of the painting, its most vital part, Ishmael recognizes "a long, limber, portentous, black mass of something," an unsettling though alluring *it* that masquerades as the interpretive key. Ishmael presents a series of conditional concepts, all "deceptive" but each a part of his parade of possibilities. Each successive idea displaces the former; collectively, they depict the inscrutability of the painted surface. What is crucial is the dynamic activity of uncovering provisional, even deceptive, meanings. Significantly, he concludes with two questions— "But stop; does it not bear a faint resemblance to a gigantic fish? even the great leviathan himself?"—and a tall-tale of a "final theory": the whole scene depicts an "exasperated whale" jumping a ship and "impaling himself upon the three mast-heads" (13). Ishmael's foray concludes with rhetorical openness and a joke. At best, by evoking the elusive content of this problematic surface, Ishmael reveals himself to be a man of "earnest contemplation, and oft repeated ponderings" (12). He engages the unreadable sign and offers a primer on how one might read the book he is writing, a book that ponders the metaphysical immensity of whales.

Beginning in "Etymology" and "Extracts" and diffused throughout the novel lurks the abiding question of just how one might approach and possibly know whales as a class and Moby Dick as a being. In attempting to map, or schematize, his knowledge of whales, Ishmael can do no better than offer a taxonomy. And in attempting to classify "the constituents of a chaos," Ishmael illuminates the beauties and limitations of taxonomy (134).[21] Having "swam through libraries and sailed through oceans" (136), Ishmael feels authorized to critique his predecessors: "[T]hough of real knowledge there be little, yet of books there are a plenty" (135). In offering his own synthesis, Ishmael draws "but the draught of a draught" (145). Organizing according to the size of books—Folio, Octavo, and Duodecimo—Ishmael applies a broadly Aristotelian form of classification, presenting his materials according to genus, species, and differences. This taxonomy, however, is a crude way of mapping the domain of ignorance. As an epistemological structure, this schemata is a monument to incompletion. The cetological "draught" is continued through Ishmael's chapter by chapter anatomy of parts.[22] Neither taxonomy nor encyclopedia discloses complete knowledge. General and specific treatments reinforce the whale's essential inscrutability.

In his attempts to read the whale, Ishmael exhausts his powers of decipherment. As beings, whales resemble the Sphinx. In "The Sphinx," Ahab addresses the dead whale's pronounced silence. Similarly, Ishmael associates the whale with philosophical conundrum: "If the Sperm Whale be physiognomically a Sphinx, to the phrenologist his brain seems that geometrical circle which it is impossible to square" (348). At one point, Ishmael surrenders his interpretive quest with an exasperated challenge to the reader: "[H]ow may unlettered Ishmael hope to read the awful Chaldee of the Sperm Whale's brow? I but put that brow before you. Read it if you can" (347). Nor can the whale be comprehended through his imperfectly rendered parts: "Dissect him how I may, then, I but go skin deep; I know him not, and never will. But if I know not even the tail of this whale, how understand his head? much more, how comprehend his face, when face he has none" (379). Nor can he interpret the signs that mark his surface: "Like those mystic rocks, too, the mystic-marked whale remains undecipherable" (306). Ishmael's attempts at reading also lead to the reader's exhaustion. The whale reflects the alluring mystery haunting existence. It constitutes a perfect object of philosophical speculation. The whale cures one of provincialism: "[F]or unless you own the whale, you are but a provincial and sentimentalist in Truth" (338). Ishmael's sense of "Truth" has nothing to do with fact or precept but everything to do with inductive probing. By owning to the literal existence of the magnificent whale, one enlists with Ishmael on his wandering excursion into the vexing problems of life and mind: "[T]he great flood-gates of the wonder-world swung open" and the most wondrous of all whales is that "one grand hooded phantom, like a snow hill in the air" (7).

Ishmael never reads the doubloon. His great scene of reading is not focused on a coin but on the "appalling" ethereality of whiteness, Moby Dick's surface shroud, his enigmatic visible layer. "The

Whiteness of the Whale" contains Ishmael's present-tense reading of the multiple forms of whiteness—the general whiteness diffused throughout nature and the specific noncolor of the albino whale.[23] Ishmael engages an elemental dualism: the "accumulated associations, with whatever is sweet, and honorable, and sublime" stand in diametrical opposition to "an elusive something [lurking] in the innermost idea of this hue, which strikes more of panic to the soul than that redness which affrights in blood" (189). As with the claim that the "story of Narcissus" is "the key to it all," Ishmael confers hermeneutical priority on his attempt to put the "mystical and well nigh ineffable" associations of whiteness into "a comprehensible form": "But how can I hope to explain myself here; and yet, in some dim, random way, explain myself I must, else all these chapters might be naught" (188). As he writes, the very worth of his book teeters in the balance. His self-revelatory imperative—"explain myself I must"—becomes invested with the import of existential risk.

With his most reaching extension of the process narrative, he attempts to elucidate the "vague, nameless horror" that emanates from barely conscious recesses of the emotional life. Ishmael's narrative dilemma derives from his attempt to exemplify an animating cause that is immaterial, unconscious, and apparitional, and thereby illuminate personal and collective experience. Ishmael views himself as spokesman for a companionate reader. His "imaginative impressions" have been "shared by most men," though only a "few perhaps were entirely conscious of them at the time" (192). To make his case, he heaps example upon example—the white bear, the white shark, the white steed, the albino man, the white squall, the white hoods, the "marble pallor" and "milk-white fog"—combining them all to suggest how "in its profoundest idealized significance [whiteness] calls up a peculiar apparition to the soul." As he unleashes his play of imagination, with the reader privy to each turn of thought, Ishmael and the reader proceed toward a potentially clarifying truth: "Let us try. But in a matter like this, subtlety appeals to subtlety, and without imagination no man can follow another into these halls" (192).

Like Ahab in "The Quarter-Deck," Ishmael seeks to penetrate the "pasteboard masks" of visible forms, to read through the "mystic sign" and confront "the instinct of the knowledge of the demonism in the world" (194). In his reading of whiteness, Ishmael eclipses the transcendental conviction that Nature and Soul correspond in harmony. He rejects the Platonic faith in absolute beneficence: "Though in many of its aspects this visible world seems formed in love, the invisible spheres were formed in fright" (195). As Milton R. Stern aptly remarks,

> For [Melville], as for Hawthorne and the Transcendentalists, light was the medium of meaning, but for [Melville] that meaning was that there was no absolute spiritual meaning. In and of itself devoid of idea, light becomes momentary, blinding, the agent of that ultimate darkness, the terrifying revelation of zero. . . . the concept of idealist openness led to Melville's central conclusion and conundrum: endless openness is endless closure. (*Contexts for Hawthorne* 32)

In effect, the Absolute becomes decentered, unfixed. How can elements that comfort also appall? Ishmael replaces Ahab's paranoid scheme of malevolent monism with the unsettling prospect that the "invisible spheres" are a yawning abyss.

Toward the end of this chapter, Ishmael's interpretive quandary leads him to offer a series of propositions that suggest without determining the informing cause of this elemental terror. The "indefiniteness" evokes the prospect of the soul's annihilation, the spirit dissolved amid "heartless voids and immensities of the universe" (195). As a color, whiteness reflects, or embodies, a "visible absence" and creates a "dumb blankness, full of meaning, in a wide landscape of snow—a colorless, all-color of atheism from which we shrink." Ishmael paints a universe of emptiness, mystery, and decay: "[A]llurements cover nothing but the charnel-house within." His reading of whiteness stands as a rhetorical and metaphysical counterpoint to Ahab's equation of the White Whale with "all evil." Whereas Ahab's definition is restrictive, Ishmael's excursion is expansive and open-ended. Ahab fixes his eye on one whale; Ishmael

revolves the prospect that "the palsied universe lies before us a leper."
His final example figures the inevitable self-destruction that attends
the intrepid polar traveler, a man who exposes his eyes to the burning brilliance of the Absolute and "gazes himself blind at the monumental white shroud." If extended obsessively, one's reading of
blinding whiteness will become, like Ahab's quest, self-exhausting
and self-defeating.

Ishmael's epistemological tour de force in "The Whiteness of
the Whale" reveals the dynamic play of mind in the accumulation
of hermeneutical possibility. He provides a glimpse of the god-
realm that cancels human activity, a realm in which whiteness is
cognate to the "heartless immensity" that drowns Pip's soul (414).
Ishmael saves his book—his chapter—from the vortex of "naught"
by dramatizing a version of what drives Ahab *and* himself. The
"fiery hunt" purports to be able to dispose of those malicious forces
that lurk beyond the "masks" of matter. Ahab's mistake is that he
fashions metaphors which make his Promethean attempt seem
possible. He translates the whale, for example, into a "wall, shoved
near" (164). Ishmael, on the other hand, depicts the problem in its
actual cosmological terms. His language describes the inscrutable,
inhuman terror contained within, and extending beyond, "dumb
blankness." Ishmael presents a landscape that dwarfs the human.
Rather than finding in the sign of whiteness a single entity that
must be destroyed, Ishmael describes the opening, yawning expanses of an inhuman ideality that destabilizes the imaginative
seeker as a prelude to destroying this seeker. To push through surfaces is to plunge into that abyss—into either chasmal depths or
astronomical enormities. In "The Whiteness of the Whale" the
mimetic depiction of consciousness unfolding carries Ishmael to
the limits of language, the oxymoronic "colorless, all-color of atheism." This "dumb blankness, full of meaning" is nothing more
than an intensified redaction of those unreadable signs that continually beg to be read, which will lead one again and again to rhetorical and performative exhaustion. As Ishmael makes clear, there
are no words that can say what the blind man sees. The albino
whale as "symbol" remains an incomplete accumulation of sensed

and imagined possibilities that lure one, against the power of knowing, toward a "fiery hunt" (195).

COSMOLOGY: A CODA

"There May Be Naught Beyond, But 'Tis Enough"

Melville's reading in Plato reinforced his sense of Christian dualism, the conflict between the city of man and the city of God. From Platonic or Christian perspectives, the problems in the earthly sphere are consequences of history's original catastrophe. The soul is born into exile; Adam and Eve leave the garden. This world stands either as the shadow of eternal Forms or a fragmented ruin of Paradise. In either case, cosmological meaning involves the teleological vindication of the True and the Good. Emerson's dictum in *Nature*—"There is no object so foul that intense light will not make beautiful" (12)—is but his formulation of the Platonic-Christian myth of cosmic benevolence: this universe is immanent with purpose, teeming with the evidence of Providence's plan.

In *Moby-Dick,* Melville denies his narrator transcendent or vatic status and destabilizes this comforting myth, replacing it with an epistemological world of shifting meanings and relativistic values. Melville's engagement with cosmological complexes carries Ishmael and Ahab to the limits of sensory and intuitive knowledge.[24] At this boundary, each attempts to articulate principles of universal order by drawing on diverse mythologies. Ishmael, as we have seen, evokes Platonic, Christian, and pagan formulations to construe conflicting explanations of both the individual's relationship to God and the connection between this world and the next. In "The Mat-Maker," for instance, recasting Plato's Myth of Er from Book X of *The Republic,* Ishmael presents a sublime moment of ontological and cosmological synthesis in which the apparent incompatibility between freedom, fate, and chance becomes resolved by way of an ongoing balanced process. Crucially, this formulation is only valid for the moment. Later, Ishmael presents the Weaver God operating the Loom of Time. Here the Divine Being is impervious to the human condition, deafened by the noisy mechanism of natural process. At one point Ishmael accepts the "universal thump" (6); later he discloses the frightening implications of cosmic emptiness (195).

Ahab is associated not so much with Platonic or Christian mythologies but with the darker, heretical systems that attribute malign motives to deific forces. Even his essential Platonism—"O Nature, and O soul of man! how far beyond all utterance are your linked analogies! not the smallest atom stirs or lives in matter, but has its cunning duplicate in mind" (312)—tends to become inverted as he embraces such exotic mythologies as Gnosticism, Manichaeism, and Zoroastrianism. As Bloom argues, the White Whale signifies "the demiurgical Creation, against which Ahab, like an ancient Gnostic, rebels. . . . To strike through the mask is to break through what the ancient Gnostics called the Kenoma, the cosmological emptiness into which we have been thrown by the Creation-Fall. The *kenoma* is a prison, the wall of which is Moby Dick himself" (*Ahab* 1–2, Bloom's emphasis).[25] Ahab insists that the evil deity can be known through the malice of its agents; by striking the agent, Ahab believes he can destroy the deity. Ahab's cosmological focus needs to be approached through his Promethean-Messianic complex. He aspires not merely to vengeance; he wishes to redefine the basic human condition. Thus, his Prometheanism informs his cosmic millennialism. A single act will eradicate "all evil." Ahab seeks to destroy history in the very process of redeeming it. In "The Quarter-Deck," Ahab's "lower layer" of exploration conflates Platonic, Christian, and Gnostic mythologies. His attraction to the principle of fire culminates in his proclamation that "right worship is defiance" (507). The "Moby Dick" chapter most succinctly expounds his cosmological principle:

> Ahab had cherished a wild vindictiveness against the whale, all the more fell for that in his frantic morbidness he at last came to identify with him, not only all his bodily woes, but all his intellectual and spiritual exasperations. The White Whale swam before him as the monomaniac incarnation of all those malicious agencies which some deep men feel eating in them, till they are left living on with

half a heart and half a lung. That intangible malignity which has been from the beginning. . . . Ahab did not fall down and worship it . . . but deliriously transferring its idea to the abhorred white whale, he pitted himself, all mutilated, against it. All that most maddens and torments; all that stirs up the lees of things; all truth with malice in it; all that cracks the sinews and cakes the brain; all the subtle demonisms of life and thought; all evil, to crazy Ahab, were visibly personified, and made practically assailable in Moby Dick. He piled upon the whale's white hump the sum of all the general rage and hate felt by his whole race from Adam down; and then, as if his chest had been a mortar, he burst his hot heart's shell upon it. (184)

Ahab's actions never live up to his self-image; his cosmology is never vindicated. Such failures only exasperate Ahab's disease, his "woe" that is madness. Ahab's tragedy derives from a fundamental misapprehension of his cosmological condition. He believes that his fiction actually expresses the truth of creation. In *Moby-Dick*, visible and invisible spheres remain distinct. Trapped within his body, Ahab cannot grasp an immaterial antagonist. For Ahab to translate the White Whale into a "wall, shoved near" is to dissolve his combative obsession into metaphor. Likewise, his defiant actions are frequently irrelevant subtractions. He throws away his pipe. He destroys the quadrant. He even asserts the unreality of the phenomenal domain: "Oh! how immaterial are all materials! What things real are there, but imponderable thoughts?" (528). Longing for a direct encounter with the absented gods, Ahab is left to make obsessive preparations. However nugatory his actions, his rhetoric remains self-empowering. He calls the gods names and challenges them to present themselves, and his verbal assaults reinforce his Promethean self-image: "I'd strike the sun if it insulted me" (164). Ironically, his admiration of the wind defines his own quixotic futility:

And yet, 'tis a noble and heroic thing, the wind! who ever conquered it? In every fight it has the last and bitterest blow. Run

tilting at it, and you but run through it. . . . Would now the wind
but had a body; but all the things that most exasperate and outrage mortal man, all these things are bodiless, but only bodiless
as objects, not as agents. There's a most special, a most cunning,
oh, a most malicious difference! (564)

Ahab's intellectual comprehension of the dissociation between visible and invisible spheres never dissuades him from trying to push
through the "masks" and subjugate the "creative libertines" (522)
to the hegemony of his will.

Unlike Ahab, Ishmael does not engage in rhetorical assaults on
any "unknown, but still reasoning thing." Instead, his essayistic
excursions provide the rhetorical form within which he revolves
"the universal problem of all things" (293). Ishmael's explorations
frequently displace the ideal in favor of the social world. For example, in "The Lee Shore," Ishmael claims it is "better . . . to perish
in that howling infinite, than be ingloriously dashed upon the lee,
even if that were safety" (107). In the next chapter, "The Advocate,"
Ishmael offers his first paean to the cetological world of work. Similarly, "The Castaway" is followed by "A Squeeze of the Hand." Here
Ishmael admits that one must "eventually lower, or at least shift,
his conceit of attainable felicity; not placing it anywhere in the intellect or the fancy; but in the wife, the heart, the bed, the table, the
saddle, the fire-side, the country" (416).

"The Mast-Head" presents *Moby-Dick*'s least problematic instance of cosmological crisis. Ishmael describes the incompatibility between a mind fed by the ideal philosophy of the *Phaedo* and a
mind nourished by the nautical specificity of Bowditch's *Naviga-
tor*. Concluding this chapter is Ishmael's corrective fable of identity. Through his "sunken-eyed young Platonist," Ishmael depicts
the self-exhausting excesses of unimpeded idealism. The attempt
to merge phenomenal and noumenal realms promises transcendence but delivers disaster. In pondering the "problem of the universe," the "absent-minded" observer needs literally to watch his
step (158). As "unconscious reverie" reels within, "Descartian vortices" swirl below.[26] "[A]t last," Ishmael reports, "he loses his iden-

tity; takes the mystic ocean at his feet for the visible image of that deep, blue, bottomless soul, pervading mankind and nature" (159). Resonances of Platonic cosmology suffuse the passage. The conflict between matter and spirit—"uprising fin" and "undiscernible form"—culminates in the destruction of the body. "[E]lusive thoughts" dissolve as the "identity comes back in horror." As the "absent-minded youth" falls, he awakens to meet his death; the historical self is consumed in the Cartesian vortex. To gaze too long into the tormenting ocean of ideality and to embrace the illusion of one's cosmic identity is to risk "the fatal contingency" (424).

As Melville remarks in a long letter to Hawthorne, the "'all' feeling"—the blending of self with the Absolute—is beautiful but transient. The sensation involves one's self-projection, a rhapsodic thrill fictionalized as one's passage into the empyrean: "But what plays the mischief with the truth," Melville suggests, "is that men will insist upon the universal application of a temporary feeling or opinion" (194). In *Moby-Dick,* Ishmael's cosmological considerations on the relation between visible and invisible domains, with all attending questions regarding human and divine natures, reinforce his belief in the nontranscendent capacity of human consciousness, the brute factuality of phenomena, and the implacable inviolability of "that howling infinite" (107).

PART THREE

Pierre and *The Confidence-Man:*

"This Guild of Self-Impostors"

7

Excursive Ponderings in *Pierre*

> Now all his ponderings, however excursive, wheeled round Isabel
> as their center; and back to her they came again from every excur-
> sion; and again derived some new, small germs for wonderment.
>
> —*Pierre*

"Throwing Oneself Helplessly Open"

IN MID-NOVEMBER 1851, Melville responded to Hawthorne's "joy-
giving and exultation-breeding letter" (212) and described his "sense
of unspeakable security": Hawthorne "understood the pervading
thought that impelled" *Moby-Dick*. The dissemination of socially
unpalatable truths purged Melville—"I have written a wicked book,
and feel spotless as the lamb"—and thus made possible an inti-
mate union with the perfect reader. Hawthorne's approbation
sanctified this achievement: "I felt pantheistic then—your heart beat
in my ribs and mine in yours, and both in God's." But Melville was
not elated for long, for these "divine magnanimities" soon dissolved, giving way to the fluidity of identity: "[T]he very fingers
that now guide this pen are not precisely the same that just took it
up and put it on this paper. Lord, when shall we be done changing?" (213). It becomes clear that to be purged, to be "spotless as
the lamb," is also to be emptied: "As long as we have anything more
to do, we have done nothing."

Melville's emotional state following *Moby-Dick* paralleled his
uneasiness after *Omoo*. It was not that *Moby-Dick* somehow seemed
deficient but rather that it ceased to be a work in hand. Once again
Melville felt he must validate his authorial identity by attempting
a radically divergent form, making an even deeper dive, plunging

after even more gigantic beasts: "Leviathan is not the biggest fish;—I have heard of Krakens." Far from being exhausted by the rigors of *Moby-Dick,* Melville was keyed up over the prospect of his next artistic venture. He did not begin *Pierre* intending a village-atheist vengeance, a planned assault on the pious good taste of his audience. As Brian Higgins and Hershel Parker observe, he immersed himself in *Pierre; or, The Ambiguities* with every expectation of establishing "his career and reputation more securely than ever before" (*Critical Essays* 2).

But just as *Omoo* marked Melville's departure from "true" narratives in favor of *Mardi's* acute metaphysical agitation, so too did *Moby-Dick* signal the temporary cessation of his "salt-water tales" in favor of *Pierre's* domestic romance.[1] It seems likely that Melville was sincere when he wrote Sophia Hawthorne that his next "chalice" would be a "rural bowl of milk" (146). He was going all out to attract female readers. Melville's third-person narrator was to tell the tale of a young man's discovery of a dark secret and the disastrous consequences that attend his sexually conflicted pursuit of ideal rectitude. The first half depicts events surrounding Pierre's discovery that Isabel is his supposed half sister. The narrator explores Pierre's life of aristocratic grandeur, though not without mocking the "choice fate" (5) that so quickly metamorphoses into Pierre's decline. Rather than judging Pierre in relation to the violated standards of social behavior, the narrator analyzes him in relation to highly refined, erudite psychological and philosophical contexts.

As with *Mardi,* Melville misapprehended the popular appeal, or even the minimal acceptability, of his obsessions. Since his way of appropriating any new form was to reinvent it, he would fuse domestic romance with his own deep-diving pursuit of Krakens, thereby adding to the arena of ladies' fiction his engagement with the elusive "problem of the universe."[2] But Melville's effort was not successful; *Pierre's* collision of incompatible imperatives guaranteed that the book would rattle foremost among Melville's ostensible "botches" (*Correspondence* 191). In broadest terms, the narrative resembles *all* of Melville's books; it is an amalgam of competing intentions, the predominant genre of domestic romance housing such mismatched tenants as Gothic thriller, Bildungsroman, satire, polemic, and myth, all presented by a narrator who variously affirms and condemns the main character, among many others.[3] In more particular terms, Melville appropriated the florid language of domestic romance, while mocking its artificiality and excess. Not surprisingly, Melville overdid it. To devotees of the form, the narrator's language read like a vicious parody.

Adding to *Pierre*'s diverse imperatives is Melville's decision to vent his anger by wrenching the nearly completed book in new directions. Higgins and Parker demonstrate that in the course of composition, Melville became shocked by *Moby-Dick*'s mixed reviews and infuriated by Harper's diminutive economic terms for the work in hand ("Flawed Grandeur" 243). Expanding his text by 150 pages, Melville turned Pierre into a juvenile author, shifting the focus from the details of Pierre's relation to Isabel to a dramatization of Pierre's immature attempt to write a "Mature Work" (*Pierre* 282).

In the first half of the book, the narrator remains detached from Pierre's affective situation. His purpose is to render Pierre's decline in fortune. In its most elemental focus, this story radiates from a philosophical dilemma—the disjunction between practical conduct and ideal precept. This issue envelops both the narrator and Pierre in far-reaching explorations of identity, ontology, epistemology, and genealogy. Questions regarding the confluence of conscious and unconscious motives become expressed through conflicts between freedom and fate, contingency and determinism. As Melville revised and expanded the first version of the manuscript, however, the narrator's affective dissociation from Pierre collapses. As Brodhead rightly contends, "Melville is never more personally involved, or, indeed, more in earnest in his novels than he is in *Pierre*" (*Hawthorne* 165). In the second half, the narrator's earlier examination of Pierre's philosophical problem gives way to the narrator's fervid, self-reflexive excursions on such issues as the failure of philosophy, the nature of the compositional process, and the horrors of the publishing marketplace. In Pierre's expanded story the narrator vents Melville's outrage. As the narrator admits, "[I]t is impossible to talk or to write without apparently throwing oneself helplessly open" (259).

Pierre; or, The Ambiguities incessantly delineates the activity of two minds, as exemplified by the narrator's presentation of, and his increasing involvement with, the exigencies of Pierre's "choice fate." In this "philosophically dramatic and dramatically philosophical novel,"[4] Melville peels back layer upon layer of social and psychological surface and thus extends the ontological and epistemological preoccupations of *Moby-Dick*, especially insofar as metaphors of "depth" evoke psychological and philosophical complexes. Pierre's disaster derives from his narcissistic compulsion to project psychological apprehension as extrinsic philosophical truth.

THE PROVINCE OF FATE

When Pierre pledges that his fiancée, Lucy Tartan, "belong'st to the regions of an infinite day" (4), he not only reveals his own naiveté, but he puts himself in opposition both to the rush of time and the sea drift of psychological flux. Such rhetorical declamations of ideal love complement young Pierre's notion of his mother as an "unattainable being" (5) and his father's memory as "the vestibule of his abstractest religion" (68). Projecting Pierre's fixation with the inviolability of his icons into an image of architectural ruin, the narrator prefigures the inevitable collapse of such constructs:

> In all this, how unadmonished was our Pierre by that foreboding and prophetic lesson taught, not less by Palmyra's quarries, than by Palmyra's ruins. Among those ruins is a crumbling, uncompleted shaft, and some leagues off, ages ago left in the quarry, is the crumbling corresponding capital, also incomplete. These Time seized and spoiled; these Time crushed in the egg; and the proud stone that should have stood among the clouds, Time left abased beneath the soil. Oh, what quenchless feud is this, that Time hath with the sons of Men! (8)[5]

Such mutability of things and persons contrasts with Pierre's idealizations. "Time" is not only the medium of individual failure; it is also the implacable counterpoint to all Ideal forms. Within the phenomenal realm, the hegemony of time is appropriately reflected in Plotinus Plinlimmon's metaphorical application: heavenly time (Chronometricals), where the voice of God is silence, stands in irreconcilable opposition to earthly time (Horologicals), the domain of relative standards, misrepresentation, and deviation. Time necessarily envelops any narrator.

Writing in the diachronic aftermath of Pierre's experience and inhabiting an elevated, presumably knowledgeable, though not omniscient perspective, the narrator at the outset imposes determinate qualifications on Pierre's idealizations. For example, as a "circumscribed youth," Pierre is proud of his patrimony, "little recking of that maturer and larger interior development, which should forever deprive these things of their full power of pride in his soul" (6). Insistently, the narrator signals the impending onset of "that period of remorseless insight," the realization that "this world hath a secret deeper than beauty, and Life some burdens heavier than death" (7). Here the narrator of *Pierre* is echoing the older Redburn, for both retrospectively critique the tyro's follies. Indeed, the "illuminated scroll of [Pierre's] life" is a radically flawed text that translates the past into the iconic script of perfection. Against Pierre's naive presumption, the narrator ranges the evidence of deflating actualities, a force in the narrator's hermeneutic that assumes the status of "Fate": "[W]e shall see if that blessing pass from him as did the divine blessing from the Hebrews; we shall yet see again, I say, whether Fate hath not just a little bit of a word or two to say in this world" (14). The narrator's "I say" places him outside the chronological limits of Pierre's story, establishing early on his detachment from Pierre's plight. As an impartial, knowledgeable witness, he adopts Fate as an explanatory paradigm.

From one perspective, these testimonies to Fate create the tempting pretext for believing that the narrator validates predestined, providential design: Pierre would then be a victim of extra psychological causality.[6] Fate, however, also needs to be understood, in more elastic terms, as reflecting the narrator's apprehension of things as they were—that is, Pierre's past as having already been lived and thus comprehensible as a linear action now subject to the narrator's predominant explanatory trope. Pierre's life experience certainly antedates the narrator's presentation of it. A construct of a retrospective intelligence, Fate thus becomes a synoptic metaphor, the philosophical signifier of narrative containment. Fate not only encompasses the fixed past seen under the guise of predestination but also the power of character itself, especially the force of conscious and unconscious compulsion. The narrator's trope reflects, then, the Heraclitean notion, already presented in *White-Jacket,* that character is Fate.

In its varying significations, this concept offers the narrator a means of contending with the assembled ambiguities. Possessing a knowledge of events to come, he reads backwards from them. Seeing Fate as both a predetermined event and the issue of psychological predisposition, the narrator peruses the "illuminated scroll of [Pierre's] life" and wryly evokes its latent incestuous content: "He who is sisterless, is as a bachelor before his time. For much that goes to make up the deliciousness of a wife, already lies in the sister" (7). The circumstantial absence of a sister prescripts, with the force of necessity, Pierre's unconscious desire to translate an absent, possibly impostor, sister into a present, but fictive, wife. Essentially, Melville's preoccupation with Fate centers the unfolding dialectic between Pierre's iconic imagination and the narrator's interpretation. The concept of Fate helps him retain affective distance from Pierre. Later, as his distance from his subject dissolves, he begins to enmesh himself in the interstices of Pierre's fated condition.

As with his repeated invocations of Fate, the narrator insists on identifying philosophical contexts for comprehending Pierre's passage from ignorance to insight, from aristocracy to democracy, from figurative heights to emotional depths. Significantly, from the outset, the narrator equates psychological growth with philosophical acuity. The narrator remarks, for example, that "Pierre was quite young and very unphilosophical as yet." His family pride is "too fond and foolish . . . and if you tell me that this sort of thing in him showed him no sterling Democrat . . . believe me you will pronounce Pierre a thorough-going Democrat in time; perhaps a little too Radical altogether to your fancy" (13). It is a foregone conclusion that Pierre will lose "that fine footing" (12) and plunge "layer on layer deeper" (38). In falling from his delusive Edenic condition at Saddle Meadows, he will lose the outward signs of his idealized state. Marriage to the "all-understood" Lucy would continue the false Eden of Saddle Meadows (129). The narrator mocks Pierre and Lucy as "two Platonic particles" (27), evoking Aristophanes' myth in the *Symposium,* which views each person as half of a unified primordial whole in search of the displaced complementary mate.[7] The fiction of "Platonic particles" is as simplistic as Lucy's desire for total self-disclosure. She believes there should be no secrets in a world where Pierre is beginning to find nothing but secrets. What she really wants is for Pierre to talk her forebodings away: "Some nameless sadness, faintness, strangely comes to me. Foretaste I feel of endless dreariness" (37).

Though both Pierre and Lucy are disturbed by irruptions of thought, it is Pierre's fear of opening Dante that reflects his dread of opening himself (42). In a highly concentrated flourish, the narrator fuses the Dantean journey into the arena of subterranean thought, the maze of intellection, and the power of inchoate imaginative discovery: "Pierre shrank abhorringly from the infernal catacombs of thought, down into which, this foetal fancy beckoned him" (51). The image of "that face" initiates his "most surprising and preternatural ponderings" (49). In Melville's lexicon, "ponderings" constitutes the central philosophical activity, an act that excites Babbalanja's neurotic vacillation as well as Ahab's megalomaniacal self-assertion. In these two cases, Babbalanja and Ahab each wrestle with the emergence of repressed forces from the lower layers of being. For Pierre, however, simply the birth of the philosophical self seems an invasion: "He felt that what he had always before considered the solid land of veritable reality, was now being audaciously encroached upon by bannered armies of hooded phantoms, disembarking in his soul, as from flotillas of specter-boats"

(49). This phantasmagoric description reflects Melville's abiding notion that the metaphysical quest eventually, inevitably, circumscribes personal power. Not only does Pierre's newfound inner life take hold "of the deepest roots and subtlest fibres of his being" (48), not only does he suffer an ontological revolution, but he begins to comprehend "what all mature men . . . sooner or later know, and more or less assuredly—that not always in our actions, are we our own factors" (51).

Within the novel, the conceit of the bipartite soul and the lovers' delusive sense of "unchangeable felicity" (36) are belied by Pierre's haunting recollection of what Lucy calls "the riddle" of "the dark-eyed, lustrous, imploring, mournful face, that so mystically paled, and shrunk at thine" (37). Lucy—mistakenly, as it turns out—seems the facile representation of blithe, idealized sentiment.[8] Her naive epistemological axiom—"Knows not all, then loves not all" (37)—provides a foil for Pierre's groping, inarticulate, unsettling attraction to the recollected sign of the unknown and unutterable. If Lucy ingenuously describes herself as a facile text, a flat, thin surface—"Read me through and through. I am entirely thine" (40)—then the human face must conversely suggest deeply buried and inscrutable attributes.

In the case of Isabel, who possesses the "one infinite, dumb, beseeching countenance of mystery, underlying all the surfaces of visible time and space" (52),[9] the narrator displaces the myth of "two Platonic particles" in favor of a complex model of subconscious psychological correspondence. Pierre is obsessed not by Isabel's "person" but by her "radiations"—his intimations of forces that are, and have been, locked within himself. Nowhere in Melville's writing does he more presciently depict the involutions of the self-scrutinizing, self-absorbed, outwardly focused but inwardly impelled seeker:

> But his profound curiosity and interest in the matter—strange as it may seem—did not so much appear to be embodied in the mournful person of the olive girl, as by some radiations from her, embodied in the vague conceits which agitated his own soul. *There,*

lurked the subtler secret: *that,* Pierre had striven to tear away. From without, no wonderful effect is wrought within ourselves, unless some interior, responding wonder meets it. That the starry vault shall surcharge the heart with all rapturous marvelings, is only because we ourselves are greater miracles, and superber trophies than all the stars in universal space. Wonder interlocks with wonder; and then the confounding feeling comes. (51, Melville's emphasis)

The narrator immediately goes on to make a critical ontological qualification: "No cause have we to fancy, that a horse, a dog, a fowl, ever stand transfixed beneath yon skyey load of majesty. But our soul's arches underfit into its; and so, prevent the upper arch from falling on us with unsustainable inscrutableness" (51). The narrator here asserts nothing less that the interpenetration of objective and subjective spheres. Inscrutability—God's very Voice of Silence (208)—constitutes the Divine Being disseminated throughout creation as well as immanent (but buried) within the human self. Thus, the narrator seriously qualifies the transcendental insistence on divine immanence as a vehicle of light and insight. The burden of "this strange integral feeling" is that the awakened self, now confounded, must engage the barely sustainable mystery. The narrator later uses the terms "ineffable correlativeness" (85) and "correlative sympathy" (111) to depict such interdependence between phenomenal and noumenal wonders, thereby associating Plato's metaphysical dualism and Romantic correspondence with a radically unstable epistemological process. In short, the self, awakened to "some interior, responding wonder," must rub her or his weary eyes in the "confounding" (51) apprehension of "Ambiguities." Pierre's problems derive from his obsession with truth as fixed and iconic; his drive "to know something definite of that face" (47) emanates from his overwhelming (but unrecognized) compulsion to peel back the deepest layers of himself. Melville thereby conflates the self-projection imaged in *Moby-Dick*'s "story of Narcissus" and the perceptual relativism of "The Doubloon." More like Ahab than like Ishmael, Pierre believes that *it* is extrinsic and graspable.

At first, the very sight of the "mysterious girl" (41) is enough to elicit the unsettling onset of thought. Subsequently two embedded texts—Isabel's letter and her oral memoir—make Pierre conscious of revolutionary imperatives. Even his response to the letter is prescripted by psychological predisposition. Prior to reading it, Pierre "seemed distinctly to feel two antagonistic agencies within him" (63). The narrator continues this duality by offering a dialogue between contending forces. The "good angel" counsels that "by reading thou may'st entangle thyself, yet may'st thou thereby disentangle others," while the "bad angel" warns against self-involvement.[10] To read or not to read—that is the question. Thus, Pierre engages the nexus between antithetical fates. His decision to read is supported by internal blandishments masquerading as divine benediction: "[F]orth from the infinite distances wonderful harmonies stole into his heart; so that every vein in him pulsed to some heavenly swell" (63). However, Isabel's letter, which declares their joint paternity, shatters Pierre's "marble form" of his father and inspires the self-generated fiction that poses as divine mandate (68). Pierre equates the shocking allegation with the impress of Truth—not the ideal light of Glendinning-family perfection but the depraved darkness of psychological perspicuity. The narrator apostrophizes: "[A]nd now, now, for the first time, Pierre, Truth rolls a black billow through thy soul! Ah, miserable thou, to whom Truth, in her first tides, bears nothing but wrecks" (65).

As Merton M. Sealts, Jr., notes, Melville often employs Platonic materials—most notably, earthly objects as shadows of Ideal forms—for distinctly anti-Platonic purposes ("Platonic Tradition" 320–21). Here Melville eclipses the conventional platonic notion of Truth's capacity to elicit joy. Initially, Pierre's intuition obliterates, so to speak, the Ambiguities: "[T]he spontaneous responsiveness of his being left no shadow of dubiousness as to the direct point he must aim at" (87–88). Melville's most notable anti-Platonic transfiguration is the identification of Truth with briefly illuminated darkness. Indeed, the narrator evokes the imagery of the Allegory of the Cave to depict, on the one hand, the capacity of sudden apprehension to displace darkness, and on the other, the power of grief to confirm the shadow of earthly things:

> [A]s it is the magical effect of the admission into man's inmost spirit of a before unexperienced and wholly inexplicable element, which like electricity suddenly received into any sultry atmosphere of the dark, in all directions splits itself into nimble lances of purifying light; which at one and the same instant discharge all the air of sluggishness and inform it with an illuminating property; so that objects which before, in the uncertainty of the dark, assumed shadowy and romantic outlines, now are lighted up in their substantial realities; so that in these flashing revelations of grief's wonderful fire, we see all things as they are; and though, when the electric element is gone, the shadows once more descend, and the false outlines of objects again return; yet not with their former power to deceive; for now, even in the presence of the falsest aspects, we still retain the impressions of their immovable true ones, though, indeed, once more concealed. (88)

By identifying "Truth" with "a black billow," the narrator effectively redefines the Platonic-Christian dualism, providing the context within which Pierre attempts to make his own actions the embodiment of pure divinity. By attempting to "know what *is*, and do what my deepest angel dictates," he thus dooms himself to unmitigated disaster (65, Melville's emphasis). He does not recognize that the conflation of Ideal Truth with human sorrow has already demythologized the god-realm.

Pierre associates the dark Truth of sin and chaos with a paradigm of insurrectionary redemption. In responding to Isabel, Pierre identifies himself with the "god-like population" (106). Characteristically, he propounds a series of if-then mock syllogisms. His hypothetical premises are succeeded by determinate conclusions: "If this night, which now wraps my soul, be genuine as that which now wraps this half of the world, then Fate, I have a choice quarrel with thee" (65). Similarly he fashions if-then scenarios, such as when he crawls beneath the Memnon Stone and dares the "Mute Massiveness" (134) to fall on him. When it does not, he is convinced of his divine warrant.[11] If God does not become one with Pierre, then Pierre will negate God: "If ye forsake me now,—farewell to Faith, farewell to Truth, farewell to God" (107). His deific self-image, however, provides thin cover to the cavernous depths of psychological involution. His willed acts counterpoint the unconscious compulsions of his being. Thus the narrator depicts how Pierre's self-generated Ideal actions become sacrificed to the hegemony of Fate. Pierre fails to see that *he* is the subject in need of redemption; he fails to see that the sin of his father, and all fathers—the very essence of human limitation—has already emerged through his obsessive fixation with the "beseeching countenance of mystery" (52). By mirroring all that Pierre has repressed, Isabel embodies the primal sin that characterizes the timebound domain of all fathers. The Oedipal implications of calling his mother "sister" become played out through Pierre's incestuous attraction to his father's supposed bastard child.

Along with possessing historical and sexual dimensions, Isabel becomes, like Yillah, orphaned, a condition that allows her identity—her intrinsic humanness—to become an extension of her narrative self-fashioning. Yillah is the lead player in Aleema's fiction; Isabel reconstructs her life by way of memory shards: "Scarce know I at any time whether I tell you real things, or the unrealest dreams" (117). Her account fitfully ruptures her characteristic silence. From these fragments she weaves a bizarre, animistic narrative: "I hope one day to feel myself drank up into the pervading spirit animating all things. I feel I am an exile here" (119). Like Yillah, the "unearthly" Isabel articulates the Platonic story of the vagrant soul born from bliss into the prison house of time and language. Retaining a sense of primordial perfection, she longs to dissolve her "individualness" (119) into pantheistic unity. Symbolically, she represents the inscrutable mysteries of being—a self-reflexive ungraspable phantom, a Yillah, a White Whale. It is Pierre's great problem that, like Taji with Yillah, he never reconciles Isabel's human needs with her ethereal attributes. Since her face elicits Pierre's unsettling ruminations, it is appropriate that Isabel reports having lived in what seems a madhouse for deranged philosophers, something like Milton's Lazar House or a walled-in *Mardi:* "Some were always talking about Hell, Eternity, and God; and some of all things as fixedly decreed; others would say nay to this, and then they would argue. . . . Some harangued the wall; some apostrophized the air; some hissed at the air; some lolled their tongues out at the air" (121).

In the book's first half, the narrator's affective dissociation from Pierre's plight emerges through unequivocal judgments. The narrator makes clear that Pierre gets carried away by his "grand enthusiast resolution. . . . Thus, in the Enthusiast to Duty, the heaven-begotten Christ is born; and will not own a mortal parent, and spurns and rends all mortal bonds"(106).[12] Pierre's self-identification with the god-realm proceeds by way of a fictionalized imposition. The cornerstone of the deific fiction is Pierre's belief that he controls contingency, "free to do his own self-will and present fancy to whatever end" (199). Inimical to the province of Fate is Pierre's misinformed fiction of absolute freedom. The narrator analyzes how the limits of mere flesh belie the imperatives of Pierre's spirit: "[T]hough charged with the fire of all divineness, his containing thing was made of clay"(107). The extension of Pierre's egotism over contingency and its association with transcendent power manage to distort Pierre's vision: "That all-comprehending oneness . . . that pertains not to the young enthusiast. By his eagerness, all objects are deceptively foreshortened; by his intensity each object is viewed as detached; so that essentially and relatively every thing is misseen by him"(175). This perceptual failure insures his entanglement with Fate. Unlike Pierre, the deep-diving philosopher recognizes how "strange and complicate is the human soul"(176); as the narrator makes clear, human beings are always acting beyond the "defined" dictates of ego: "For surely no mere mortal who has at all gone down into himself will ever pretend that his slightest thought or act solely originates in his own defined identity" (176).

Within the novel, then, the narrator delineates two philosophical tales: Pierre's self destructive pursuit of ideal conduct, on the one hand, which provides points of reference and departure for the narrator's probing inquiry into the ramifications of this pursuit, on the other. In distinction to Pierre's self-reflexive and closed system of interpretation, the narrator constantly evokes a world beyond the pencil strokes of human delineation. To the narrator the "visible world" is not "common and prosaic" but "steeped a million fathoms in a mysteriousness wholly hopeless of solution" (128). In a passage that combines Ishmael's acceptance of a lower "conceit of attainable felicity" (*Moby-Dick* 416) and the "heartless voids and immensities" of the god-realm, especially the ideal as figured in "The Whiteness of the Whale" (195), the narrator explicitly indicates how Pierre's situation should offer a corrective warning:

> But the example of many minds forever lost, like undiscoverable Arctic explorers, amid those treacherous regions, warns us entirely away from them; and we learn that it is not for man to follow the trail of truth too far, since by so doing he entirely loses the directing compass of his mind; for arrived at the Pole, to whose barrenness only it points, there, the needle indifferently respects all points of the horizon alike. (165)

Pierre's self-deluding fixations counterpoint the narrator's intimations of all that, unknown and unutterable, lies beyond the compass of written words. By foregoing the Olympian detachment of the novel's early scenes, the narrator immerses himself in the inscrutability of Pierre's inner life. The narrator's initial attempt to write a determinate account becomes undone by his own involvement with the problem of storytelling. In delving further into Pierre's predicament, the narrator increasingly moves away from summary determinations about what Pierre knows and does not know and toward nebulous surmises about what the narrator and Pierre cannot know. The narrator grapples with the very problem of interpretation itself, fully recognizing how words—any words— are displacements of silence and growing all too aware of the infinite distance of words from Truth. Indeed, his indeterminacy becomes a compositional principle.

Consequently, the narrator attacks the facile delineations of formula fiction. If life derives from God, then "it partakes of the unravelable inscrutableness of God" (141). To force such complexity into neat plots is to conjure "inverted attempts at systematizing eternally unsystemizable elements." Like God, like the Memnon Stone, all great art is dumb; it fails to make a full account of its own nature. The narrator lambastes conventional forms that set up problems "only to complacently clear them up at last." If the narrator's text offers a mimetic account of Pierre's condition, it must remain incomplete and vexing:

> [Y]et the profounder emanations of the human mind, intended to illustrate all that can be humanly known of human life; these never unravel their own intricacies, and have no proper endings; but in imperfect, unanticipated, and disappointing sequels (as mutilated stumps), hurry to abrupt intermergings with the eternal tide of time and fate. (141)

The great artist, in the act of *failing* to play God, must write a script destined to remain indecipherable. Rather than making his book another integer among the "countless tribes of common novels," *Pierre*'s narrator believes he composes one of "the profounder emanations of the human mind," a novel of philosophical purpose that flaunts generic expectations. As in *Mardi*, Melville remakes his form, seeking to appropriate, though not to contain, the more expansive reaches of human experience. Thus psychology, philosophy, and literary art interpenetrate, with the threads remaining tangled and "unravelable" (141).

The narrator's loss of affective detachment emerges most often in his present-tense essayistic excursions, during which he becomes enmeshed in the very story he narrates. Similarly, Pierre himself dissolves the space between life and art. Even though "infallible presentiment" tells him to accept life's indeterminate nature, Pierre nevertheless sins against the light. He not only construes his questionable entanglement as absolute rectitude, but he treats life as though it were controllable by authorial fiat. After inventing the

"fictitious alliance"—a marriage story—he binds himself to its consequences. He plays the role and becomes entrapped: this "web of
air . . . in effect would prove a wall of iron" (175). His plot of "pious
imposture" (173) confuses passion and idealism, sexuality and in-
nocence, fate and freedom. He tries to live out the very kind of
formula plot that the narrator mocks.

"Impostor Philosophers" and the "Voice out of Silence"

In the narrator's lexicon, Fate is the power that fixes Pierre, and his
story, in place; the dialectical counterpoint to the power of Fate
emerges in the narrator's explicit and implicit demonstrations of
compositional freedom—his wayward speculations that rupture
the progress of Pierre's story. Asserting his independence from all
prescription, in Book XVII, "Young America In Literature," the
narrator rejects "the various conflicting modes of writing history"
in which "there would seem to be two grand practical distinctions.
. . . I am careless of either; both are well enough in their way; I
write precisely as I please" (244). Book XVII along with Book XVIII,
"Pierre, as a Juvenile Author, Reconsidered," are almost certainly
among Melville's late additions to the original 350-page text.[13] In
savaging Pierre as a facile representation of the Young America
movement, the narrator expresses "sincerest sympathy for those
unfortunate fellows"—like Melville himself—who become "pro-
gressively ashamed of their own successive productions—written
chiefly for the merest cash" (249). These two forces, excoriation
and self-reflexivity, impel the narrator through the second half of
the book. In other words, the suspension of the narrator's determinate attitude toward Pierre coalesces with his rejection of romantic convention. To the extent that Pierre himself repudiates
his youthful poetry is the extent to which he is more closely aligned
with the narrator. Pierre's plight becomes, in effect, the narrator's
self-purgative medium. The action provides occasion for the
narrator's seemingly spontaneous excursions, or rants, on a host
of major and minor irritants. In facilitating a prospective (but

finally unfulfilled) catharsis, Pierre emerges as the narrator's other self, a sacrificial surrogate.

With Pierre out of Saddle Meadows, the novel attends to its transplanted motive: "It is impossible to talk or to write without apparently throwing oneself helplessly open" (259). It is *Mardi* all over again, though in *Pierre* Melville lacks the convenient device of trundling his wranglers from island to island, topic to topic. No matter: he devises convenient opportunities for "excursive" ponderings. In depicting Pierre's decline unto death, the narrator conducts inquiries on three related issues: the gratuitous discovery of Plinlimmon's pamphlet; the narrator's related attacks on philosophy; and Pierre's ludicrous attempt at becoming a philosophical novelist.

Plinlimmon's pamphlet "Horologicals & Chronometricals?" offers an extended, discursive redaction of an earlier scene where Pierre joins a discussion between his mother and the Reverend Mr. Falsgrave as they consider whether Delly Ulver, an unmarried woman with a child, should be embraced or banished. Delly's situation dramatizes Pierre's dilemma. The crucial issue is whether the "legitimate child [should] shun the illegitimate, when one father is father to both" (101). Falsgrave vacillates, claiming that moral absolutes are not easily applied to specific cases. Falsgrave's broach, "representing the allegorical union of the serpent and dove," indicates that the entanglement of good and evil is a staple of horological life (102).

Pierre finds and misplaces the pamphlet and, oddly enough, he never understands the import of Plinlimmon's thesis. By pointing to the document's dilapidated, fragmented state, the narrator invidiously prescripts the reader's judgment. The "dried-fish-like, pamphlet-shaped rag" is "metaphysically and insufferably entitled" (207). Indeed, the reader does not encounter it until after the narrator has explained Pierre's incomprehension as a form of repression. The pamphlet illustrates "the intrinsic incorrectness and non-excellence of both the theory and the practice of his [Pierre's] life" (209). Furthermore, the narrator, shortly after proclaiming that "Silence is the only Voice of our God" (204), launches a pontifical assault, both on "enthusiastic" youths who seek to resolve life's mysteries and on any prospective "Talismanic Secret" that purports to reconcile "this world with [the young Enthusiast's] soul." Even before reprinting the fragment, the narrator assails and marginalizes its authority. In the process, he categorically rejects "vain" philosophy and its practitioners as a "guild of self-impostors":

> Now without doubt this Talismanic Secret has never yet been found; and in the nature of human things it seems as though it never can be. Certain philosophers have time and again pretended to have found it; but if they do not in the end discover their own delusion, other people soon discover it for themselves, and so those philosophers and their vain philosophy are let glide away into practical oblivion. Plato, and Spinoza, and Goethe, and many more belong to this guild of self-impostors, with a preposterous rabble of Muggletonian Scots and Yankees, whose vile brogue still the more bestreaks the stripedness of their Greek or German Neoplatonical originals. That profound Silence, that only Voice of our God, which I before spoke of; from that divine thing without a name, those impostor philosophers pretend somehow to have got an answer; which is as absurd, as though they should say they had got water out of stone; for how can a man get a Voice out of Silence? (208)

From the narrator's perspective, the pursuit of divine illumination is a one-way dialogue with silence, projecting into nothingness much as the human voice creates sound amid the encompassing vacuum. The practice of philosophy becomes, then, specious, a confidence game. The brunt of the narrator's attack is focused on how philosophers claim absolute status for verbal, and therefore relativistic, constructs. The promulgation of a "Talismanic Secret" becomes tantamount to repudiating dialectic.

The narrator's rejection, however, should not be construed as itself a determinate precept or as favoring a nihilistic surrender to silence. Rather, the discovery of the pamphlet and the ensuing diatribe accentuates how the narrator insistently presents himself as an adjudicating voice. As with Ishmael's process narrative, *Pierre*'s narrator positions himself in the compositional present, with his account of Pierre's past furnishing successive points of departure. Indeed, the narrator's volatility counterpoints his earlier status as determinate interpreter. Immersed in the story's confounding mysteries, the narrator reveals himself to be a critical reader of the tale he is *now* writing. He seeks to frame rather than explain issues. In fact, he even describes the pamphlet not as an explanatory paradigm but as

> a very fanciful and mystical, rather than philosophical Lecture, from which, I confess, that I myself can derive no conclusion which permanently satisfies those peculiar motions in my soul, to which that Lecture seems more particularly addressed. For to me it seems more the excellently illustrated re-statement of a problem, than the solution of the problem itself. (210)

By suggesting that "such mere illustrations are almost universally taken for solutions," the narrator anticipates those inattentive readers who mistakenly view Plinlimmon's "rag" as an authorized gestalt. The narrator concludes his introduction with open advice: "At the worst, each person can now skip, or read and rail for himself."

The pamphlet's content is thematically synoptic. It articulates (without resolving) the novel's central philosophical problem: How can "Heaven's own Truth" (211) be apprehended and then applied to earthly practice? While distancing himself from endorsing Plinlimmon's position, the narrator allows the thesis to stand as a workable description of Pierre's predicament just prior to his entrance into the city. Melvillian scholarship has inconclusively examined the implications of Plinlimmon's conclusive dichotomy: "That in things terrestrial (horological) a man must not be governed by ideas celestial (chronometrical)" (214).[14] Plinlimmon's smug, utilitarian, sophistical, and cynical explanation, especially his advocacy of "virtuous expediency," operates like *Mardi*'s "Voice from the Gods" as a text within the text. Like the painting in the

Spouter-Inn, Plinlimmon's treatise focuses the hermeneutical process and translates the informing tensions of the narrative into suggestively (and seductively) compressed concepts.

Once installed in the city, Pierre, like the narrator, finds that his sense of certitude has dissolved. Growing increasingly skeptical, solipsistic, even nihilistic, he views absolute virtue as indistinguishable from vice: both are shadows; both are nothing. He presents himself as an ontological nullity—a condition decreed by self-projection masquerading as Fate: "It is the law. . . . That a nothing should torment a nothing; for I am a nothing. It is all a dream— we dream that we dreamed we dream" (274). The pamphlet, had Pierre understood it, would have corrected his informing delusion. Instead, the belief in one chronometrical icon (his father's virtue) simply gave way to his fixation on another (his own deific virtue). Like Taji in "Dreams," Pierre in the city finds himself trapped and exhausted by his excessive inwardness. Repeatedly, his cogitations assail him with intimations of his own folly.

Against the backdrop of Pierre's enervating skepticism, his quest in art is both ridiculous and noble. On the one hand his compositional progress expresses the nadir of his decision to champion Isabel, when she becomes irrelevant to his self-absorbing enterprise. On the other, Pierre attempts to fulfill an artistic imperative—"the burning desire to deliver what he thought to be new, or at least miserably neglected Truth to the world" (283). Pierre's status as a tyro artist dooms him. He is a mere "toddler" (296). The "thoughtful thing of absolute Truth" remains securely sealed within the vacuum of God's Silence (283).

The narrator intermittently regains affective detachment from Pierre's plight only when denouncing what amounts to a redaction of his Saddle Meadows naiveté. Pierre's authorial gambit and the narrator's caricature of it portray the cracked image of Melville himself. Thus Pierre becomes a rueful reflection of the downward declension of Melville's career. Through his narrator's excursions, Melville attacks his own former naiveté, making his own career a text to be dismantled or rewritten.

Just as Pierre is both ridiculous and noble, so too does the narrator's attitude toward philosophical art possess a wrenching, contradictory doubleness. In the very activity of philosophizing, the narrator attacks philosophy for its attempts to construct a final solution to the inherent "universal problem of all things" (*Moby-Dick* 293). Along with his assaults on "this guild of self-impostors," the narrator specifically criticizes Transcendentalists and Utilitarians (262) and satirizes the indigent philosophers in the Church of the Apostles (268).[15] Because they are poor, they "reject the coarse materialism of Hobbes" for the "airy exaltations of the Berkelyan philosophy" (267). In a fit of narcissistic compensation, they starve the body to nourish the soul. The Apostles "had deluded Pierre into the Flesh-Brush Philosophy, and had almost tempted him into the Apple-Parings Dialectics. . . . They went about huskily muttering the Kantian Categories through teeth and lips dry and dusty as any miller's, with the crumbs of Graham crackers" (300). The narrator ridicules the self-deluding and self-exhausting absurdities of rigid absolutists who, in their frantic gyrations of specious theory, reject common sense. In the same spirit, Heraclitus, known among the ancients as "the weeping philosopher," counterpoints Emerson's " 'Compensation,' or 'Optimist' school" (277). Such allusions mock the pathetic dedication to shibboleths.

Similarly, in flaunting his learning even as he satirizes and discounts it, the narrator again reflects Melville's anger with the state of his career. Insistently, his words bear the agitated impress of autobiographical self-exposure. Like Pierre, Melville picked up his learning in a helter-skelter fashion:

A varied scope of reading, little suspected by his friends, and randomly acquired by a random but lynx-eyed mind, in the course of the multifarious, incidental, bibliographic encounterings of almost any civilized young inquirer after Truth; this poured one considerable contributary stream into that bottomless spring of original thought which the occasion and time had caused to burst out in himself. (283)

In *Mardi*, Melville viewed creation as the fusion of acquired learning and original thought. Now, the narrator wishes to dismiss learning, reject influence, and write as he pleases. Thus he carefully distances himself from the forces impinging on Pierre's naive attempt at authorship. Emphasizing what Pierre does not see, the narrator argues that "all mere reading" is an "obstacle" to the creative psyche: "[Pierre] did not see . . . that already, in the incipiency of his work, the heavy unmalleable element of mere book-knowledge would not congenially weld with the wide fluidness and ethereal airiness of spontaneous creative thought" (283). The narrator disavows learning as deductive acquisition in favor of creation as inductive process. One reads in order to escape influence; one builds a scaffold, as it were, only to kick it down. Ironically, the narrator proposes a version of the Platonic ladder to claim that once one achieves Beauty and Power "then books no more are needed for buoys to our souls." The artist of the beautiful graduates, so to speak, into a self-sustaining empyrean:

> [Pierre] did not see, that it was nothing at all to him, what other men had written; that though Plato was indeed a transcendently great man in himself, yet Plato must not be transcendently great to him (Pierre), so long as he (Pierre himself) would also do something transcendently great. . . . [A]ll existing great works must be federated in the fancy; and so regarded as a miscellaneous and Pantheistic whole. (283–84)

The "combined" force could be "provocative" but would only comprise "one small mite, compared to the latent infiniteness and inexhaustibility in himself" (283–84).

Following such hairsplitting, the narrator seems unaware of evoking a distinctly Platonic account of the relation between the ideal existence of art and its material counterpart. Again, Pierre fails to see "that all the great books in the world are but the mutilated shadowings-forth of invisible and eternally unembodied images in the soul; so that they are but the mirrors, distortedly reflecting to us our own things; and never mind what the mirror may be, if we would see the object, we must look at the object itself, and not at its reflection" (284). Like the poet in *The Republic*, the artist fashions but a copy of a copy (Nature), which itself imperfectly replicates the Forms. The work of art bodies forth, and thus distorts, the Ideal original in the soul. The narrator presents a culminating complication of the interaction between Melville's learning and the making of his art. The narrator affirms and repudiates philosophy, even as it animates his depiction of action, image, and psychology. Similarly, he dismisses influence in the very activity of manifesting it. Although in *Mardi*, Melville passionately and disjointedly appropriates a new world of mind, in *Pierre* he passionately and dogmatically asserts his creative independence, drawing all the while on the basic tenet of Plato's aesthetic theory. In essence, then, the narrator's professed hostility to philosophy and influence by no means reveals his independence, only his conflicted, compromised desire for it.

Edgar A. Dryden speculates on the relation between the writer and sham philosophers: "Writing is seen as both an external and internal mining, a digging down toward the 'axis of reality.' But if the writer's method distinguishes him from the impostor philosophers, his product binds him to them. He too builds marble temples from the stones of his experience. For this reason, the wise writer constructs his temples only to destroy them" (*Thematics of Form* 124). *Pierre*, however, does not provide a fit analogy to a destroyed temple. Even while showing the failure of Pierre's art, the book is not destroyed; the words remain as teasing signs. *Pierre* contains the record of the narrator's increasingly attenuated consciousness unfolding in the activity of meditating Pierre's mystery.

Behind the narrator's attacks on philosophical impostors is not a repudiation of metaphysical questioning but an admission of the subject's daunting enormity, especially the narrator's sense of the soul's "tremendous immensity"(284). Pierre is cashiered because he is a tyro wandering lost in the "Switzerland of his soul." The image of mountainous grandeur evokes how impossible it is for any pair of eyes to apprehend the soul's circumference. Indeed, the imagistic counterpart to mountainous grandeur appears in what

Dryden calls "internal mining," especially the downward passage into the pyramid. One finds not a readable sign but vacancy. Pierre's mining leads him only to chasmal emptiness: "[A]ppallingly vacant as vast is the soul of a man!" (285). Dryden sees the pyramid as Melville's most powerful symbol of the inadequacy of all communication:

> Like Hegel, Melville is fascinated by the pyramid because it offers him an external man-made form that represents the 'forms of the natural earth.' It has the appearance of a natural product and yet conceals as its meaning a hollow void, the sign perhaps of the 'horrible interspace' (134) of the Memnon stone and the 'Hollow' (139) of God's hand. . . . The pyramid . . . symbolizes the process of representation itself, for it points to the absence that all signs carry within them. ("Entangled Text" 172)

The vacant center, however, has its cognate in God's inscrutability—the Voice of Silence—rather than in existential nullity. As a searcher, Pierre merely begins to penetrate "the first superficiality of the world" (285). The impostor-philosophers are straw men, propped up and knocked down by the excavating narrator who rejects the "Talismanic Secret" and realizes that the "unlayered substance" cannot be reached even in some imagined bedrock.

In making the soul the subject of his art, and Talismanic Truth his object, Pierre dooms himself. His failure is compounded insofar as he makes himself the subject of his own philosophical novel. Pierre composes diatribes on the failure of art to explain life. Spinoza and Plato are "chattering apes"; Goethe is an "inconceivable coxcomb" (302). Pierre's text extends the narrator's attacks. In seeming to have "directly plagiarized from his own experience," Pierre becomes, like his alter ego Vivia, his own "voluntary jailer" (303), trapped by his own consciousness, his own character. His dedication to Ideal conduct expresses the novel's central paradox. Idealized constructs are invariably self-generated and artificial, "enthusiastic, high-wrought, stoic, and philosophic defenses" (289). They fail to protect "mortal man" from "the final test of a real impassioned onset of Life and Passion upon him." Philosophy thereby lacks therapeutic power and cannot contain or control primal psychological irruptions. The narrator concludes, "For Faith and Philosophy are air, but events are brass. Amidst his gray philosophizings, Life breaks upon a man like a morning"(289). The attempt to contain the Ideal within narrative forms or explanatory tropes simply reinforces the ineluctable fact that human words do not mimic God's Voice.

Pierre constitutes Melville's extended repudiation of the Taji-Ahab pursuit of the Absolute as it plays itself out in a self-reflexive hall of mirrors. Philosophy, especially Ideal philosophy, receives the brunt of the attack, not in its essence, which is never in Plato meant to be taken as a utilitarian corrective to the evils of experience, nor as the ultimate focus that leads individuals to aspire after wisdom; rather, philosophy is attacked in its perverted application, especially as it purports to supply a determinate answer, a skeleton key to horological complexity. The Ideal becomes distorted into Pierre's (or Taji's or Ahab's) limited, contextual, self-serving representation of it. In his elevation of subjective experience into objective warrant, Pierre dismisses the potential efficacy of reasonable alternatives, especially the inductive offices of dialectic, on the one hand, as well as Ishmael's lowered "conceit of attainable felicity," on the other (*Moby-Dick* 416).

Pierre's book becomes a defiant suicide note, an expression of self-cancelling folly: "For the pangs in his heart, he put down hoots on the paper" (339). Ironically, he comes to discover the open-ended nature of his quest. As he writes, "the deeper that he dived," the clearer he sees "the everlasting elusiveness of Truth." Because they are constructed with words, all texts contain "the universal lurking insincerity." In displacing Silence, language displaces the Voice of God. By attempting to depict specific entities, either thoughts or things, the artist plunges into the slough of misapprehension and misrepresentation. In *Pierre* the phenomenal domain, expressed synoptically as Nature, is not immanent with God's message, whether Platonic, Gnostic, or Emersonian. Rather, the narrator contends, "Nature is not so much her own ever-sweet interpreter, as the mere supplier of that cunning alphabet, whereby selecting and combining as he pleases, each man reads his own peculiar lesson according to his own peculiar mind and mood" (342). By recasting the paradigm featured in "The Doubloon," the narrator celebrates inexhaustible creativity. Released from the impossible burden of fashioning Ideal Truth, the artist retains the extensive alphabet of Nature, one's primary resource for expressing the endless and protean languages of self-representation. This is not a proclamation of Melville's solipsism but a procreant symbiosis between Nature as object and "alphabet" (342) and consciousness as subjective perceiver and composer.

The defiant Pierre, though recognizing "the everlasting elusiveness of Truth," is unable to escape the fixed text he has made of his life. He expires as "the fool of Truth, the fool of Virtue, the fool of fate" (358), while the narrator lives on within a language that asserts multiple possibilities for reformulation. Pierre's fated story creates a context within which the narrator depicts an array of determinate and indeterminate interpretations. In presenting Pierre's Fate, the narrator does not inhabit transcendent ground; instead he charts "the endless winding way,—the flowing river in the cave of man; careless whither I be led, reckless where I land" (107). He records unfolding negotiations between what is knowable and inscrutable, between the discordant noises of horological existence and the chronometric voice of an all knowing, but most profound, Silence.

The Confidence-Man: His Masquerade:
"The Most Extraordinary Metaphysical Scamps"

"We are but clay, sir, potter's clay, as the good book says, clay, feeble, and too-yielding clay. But I will not philosophize."
—*The Confidence-Man*

COMPETING VOICES

THE CONFIDENCE-MAN seems most responsive to Melville's studious consumption of Heidegger, Gadamer, Bahktin, and Derrida, especially in its preoccupation with hermeneutics, dialogic play, and logocentric displacement. In terms indebted both to Sartre's depiction of existential angst and the floating signifiers of poststructuralist *differance*, Melville critically assails the once privileged concept of the subject: the Confidence Man's repetition of theatrical display empowers his predatory hegemonics.

As one Melville narrator remarks later, "But aren't it all sham?" (*Billy Budd* 132). Melville both got there first and came later. A reading of the last of Melville's fiction published in his lifetime indicates that the twentieth century has no monopoly on exploring either the limits of signification or the semiotic quagmire attending the relationship between object and sign, voice and writing, being and nonbeing. Nor is Melville, strange and revolutionary as the *The Confidence-Man* may seem, himself the progenitor of fictional and metafictional discourse in which dialogue dramatizes the contentious interplay of unresolved ideational forces.

If he did not get there first, at least Plato was early on the scene. Readers confident of the unexampled reach of modernist and postmodernist inquiries into language as sign would do well to examine

The Republic and *Phaedrus* for their celebration of dialectic and *Cratylus* and *Euthydemus* for the Sophists' exploration of the relativity of language. What may seem quaint, naive, or anachronistic in Plato—for example, Socrates' unshakable confidence in absolute Truth—was to Melville a formidable articulation of the universe's "Problem." In rediscovering Plato, one happens upon arresting resonances of Melville's novel. For example, Plato anticipates, and perhaps even informs, Melville's dramatization of the interplay between philanthropy and misanthropy. In the *Phaedo,* Socrates seems to anticipate the aggrieved tones of the cosmopolitan:

> For as there are misanthropists or haters of men, there are also misologists or haters of ideas, and both spring from the same cause, which is ignorance of the world. Misanthropy arises from the too great confidence of inexperience;—you trust a man and think him altogether true and good and faithful, and then in a little while he turns out to be false and knavish; and then another and another, and when this has happened several times to a man, especially within the circle of his own most trusted friends, as he deems them . . . he at last hates all men, and believes that no one has any good in him at all. (3:231–32)

Socrates could be describing the effect the Confidence Man will have on his subsequently enlightened dupes or the education of the narrative's many sour misanthropes. In truly possessing confidence, Socrates would reject the notion that any number of slights in the phenomenal world could affect the eternal Forms. Shadows, delusion, disappointment—these are the staples of earthly existence. Like the Confidence Man, Socrates teaches that one should never despond. While burlesquing these notions in the novel, Melville never recants his admiration for Socrates the person. The Greek philosopher remains a figure of heroic self-possession and profound wisdom. Similarly, even when most vehemently questioning Platonic idealism, Melville never entirely discounts the existence of the god-realm. It remains an open question, eminently

debatable, apparently unanswerable, which makes even more ur-
gent Melville's primary aesthetic adaptation from Plato—the philosophical dialogue.

In his most single-mindedly philosophical works—*Mardi, The
Confidence-Man,* and *Clarel*—Melville associates travel and talk.
Indeed, the travelogue facilitates the staging of elaborate philosophical exchanges. As in *Mardi,* the literal journeys in *The Confidence-
Man* and *Clarel* provide excuses for metaphysical wrangling,
shifting settings, and diverse interlocutors. In *The Confidence-Man,*
the journey down the Mississippi River is mere plot device; the
essential focus of the novel is ideas expressed within a comedy of
entrapment. Here the master manipulator determines and virtually scripts topics for discussion. Similarly, in *Clarel* philosophical
dialogues generate from complexes within characters, from the
desolate present-day settings, and from pertinent biblical associations.

The Confidence-Man epitomizes the protean possibilities of conversational metaphysics. Here Melville extends the dialogue into
a dialectical theater, a world of changing players. The predominant trope presents the world as a stage in which, as the cosmopolitan points out, "Life is a pic-nic *en costume*" (133).[1] In Melville's
fiction the dialogue is an inherently theatrical medium. As in *Mardi,*
Melville exploits the dramatic immediacy of talk and more talk.
The representational islands create, as it were, ideational stages that
prompt the questers with specific subjects for discussion. In "The
Quarter-Deck" chapter of *Moby-Dick,* Ishmael employs stage directions to reinforce the dramatic context of Ahab's manipulation.
In the first five novels, Melville struggles with—and at times eschews—the conventional limitations of first-person form. In *Mardi,*
Taji's absence from dialectical engagement effectively marries a detached dramatic narration of surface action to the open-ended,
indeterminate play of multiple voices. In *Moby-Dick,* Ishmael's use
of the process narrative frees him from the limits of verisimilitude
and propels him into an arena of self-engendered invention where
what happened provides resource and backdrop for what he now
invents. What happens in *Moby-Dick* is the unfolding activity of

Ishmael's authorial performance. Ishmael's notorious disappearances and his contradictory philosophical excursions reflect not only the discontinuities between genetic stages but the range of his self-authorized, expansive narrative reach.

Following *Moby-Dick,* Ishmael's accommodating, flexible voice disappears from Melville's world, an absence largely conditioned by his subsequent refusal to cast the narrators of his longer fictions—*Pierre, Benito Cereno, Israel Potter, The Confidence-Man,* and *Billy Budd, Sailor*—in the role of first-person participant. Although eventually betraying an agitated, affective involvement in Pierre's plight, the narrator is not an actor. He is decidedly outside the diachronic limits of Pierre's lifeline. At the story's beginning, Pierre is already dead. The narrator's irruptive, present-tense excursions derive from his own problems with writing the story and his own responses to these circumstances and ideas that overwhelm Pierre. This detached narrator has privileged access to Pierre's troubled psyche. He knows more than Pierre does but not enough to arrest his own unquiet surmises. Melville's choice of third-person, nonparticipating narrators seems a formal concession to the Babbalanja-Ishmael insistence on epistemological uncertainty. As the narrators leave the world of fictional action, Melville accentuates the haunting enigma of phenomenal surfaces—surfaces that suggest but cannot reveal a fixed or final essence.

With the succession of third-person narrators and the ur-condition of epistemological uncertainty, Melville also displaces the acting narrator as a partially self-aware subject. Melville is not conceding the death of the subject; rather, one cannot finish peeling back its involuted layers. At the very least, the vagaries of "living character" excite "perplexity as to understanding them" (*The Confidence-Man* 69). In *Benito Cereno* and *The Confidence-Man,* for example, he focuses attention away from the buried depths of the Hotel de Cluny toward the play of competing narrative voices, an aesthetic tête-à-tête among dramatic players. If Ishmael is bent on telling as much as or more than he knows, then the post-Ishmael narrator relates only part of what he knows.

From this perspective, then, the direct antecedent to Melville's narrative performance in *The Confidence-Man* is *Benito Cereno*. Through the fusion of multiple narrative voices and rigidly pre-scribed and applied limits of disclosure, Melville delineates the unfolding action and its vexing implications. The encompassing narrative voice functions as a protocinematic eye that depicts vi-sual surfaces rife with suggestion. For example, the phrase "Shad-ows present, foreshadowing deeper shadows to come" is both a meteorological account and an evocation of subsequent mystery (*Piazza Tales* 46). Significantly, the narrator knows the secrets of the *San Dominick* but does not tell. He teases the reader with ellip-tical sentences that conceal even as they purport to reveal. Remark-ing on Captain Delano's lack of "personal alarms, any way involving the imputation of malign evil in man," the narrator observes, "Whether, in view of what humanity is capable, such a trait im-plies, along with a benevolent heart, more than ordinary quick-ness and accuracy of intellectual perception, may be left to the wise to determine" (47). The "wise" reader is invited to make determi-nations regarding Delano's perspicuity. In order to assist this pro-cess, the narrator provides access only to one mind, the self-blinded, "tranquilizing" consciousness of the American, Captain Delano (70).[2] Put another way, Melville exposes the workings of a psyche imprisoned within an unquestioned ideology, a man whose ap-prehensions are consistently wrong. The retentive narrator elides into Delano's internal monologue, his racist misreading of "the spectacle of disorder"(70). This deposition presents the narrative's third voice. On the one hand it describes events that took place before the protocinematic narrator begins his account and osten-sibly propounds a reliable account of what happened. On the other, the deposition is simply the culturally ordained version that justi-fies Cereno's truth, an egregious masquerade. The self-empowered legal laws determine meaning and value within the social hierar-chy and imbue this hierarchy with divine warrant.

There is a fourth text implied within the "voiceless" (*Piazza Tales* 116) silence of the captured Babo, a script that when spoken or written or in any way given utterance outside the hegemonic forms of American-English-Spanish inscription would tell its own self-justifying morality tale of righteous revolt and liberation. The prospective content of Babo's Declaration of Independence, like the antecedents to Bartleby's silence, paradoxically exists in the blank spaces of unknowable implication.

Crucially, Melville's narrator sets epistemological, ideological, and ontological traps. The reader is cut loose in a world of vexing signs and surfaces, everything from "the shield-like stern-piece" showing "a dark satyr in a mask, holding his foot on the prostrate neck of a writhing figure, likewise masked" to Babo's chalked graffiti scrawl, "'*Seguid vuestro jefe*,' (follow your leader)" (49). To interpret the captured slaves as Evil Arrested is to share complicity in the Delano-Cereno ideology of white, European supremacy. To project Babo's "voiceless" text and indict Eurocentrism is (possibly) to condone the copycat barbarity of the slaves, who, as Sandra A. Zagarell deftly reveals, have no ideology of their own and simply replicate the master-slave power structure (250–52). Indeed, social forms are fluid; a ruling class depends on brute force rather than providential privilege. Melville's implied ontological drama reveals an ugly shade of human sameness, the mottled gray that blends black and white in depraved commonalty. At the outset the protocinematic narrator drops his most telling, and perhaps only, ontological hint: "[I]n view of what humanity is capable." *Benito Cereno* suggests the animating presence of natural, transracial evil that asserts itself in the political drama of power grabs and masquerades, a condition that culminates in the enforced, unstable theatricality of successive versions of enslavement.

In *The Confidence-Man*, Melville accentuates the detachment of *Benito Cereno*'s narrator by subverting its overt topical and ontological dimensions. While providing partial descriptions of dramatic surfaces, the narrator (except, perhaps, in one instance) refuses to enter any character's mind.[3] He is concerned less with the intricacies of ontology than with dramatizing epistemological puzzles. Retentive, detached, mystifying, the narrator of *The Confidence-Man* indulges in cunning equivocation and knavish word-play, intrusively halting the story three times to lecture on the problematic relation between fiction and life, or language and truth.[4] In victimizing his reader with the teasing implications of words, words, words, the narrator obscures the motives, the psyche, and the essential identity of the Confidence Man. He may be the Devil, God, Christ, a Trickster God, or an original genius. Or he may be something else.[5]

The narrator insistently offers ambiguous clues to some "Talismanic Secret"—clues which excite questions that are never answered (*Pierre* 208). With his chalkboard and successive texts on the operations of charity, for example, the deaf-mute—apparently the Confidence Man's first avatar—signals Melville's informing preoccupation with the tangled interplay of writing and interpretation. The deaf-mute finds a crowd gathered around a wanted poster offering a reward for the apprehension of "a mysterious impostor . . . recently arrived from the East; quite an original genius in his vocation" (3).[6] In resembling a "theatre-bill," the placard seems to be describing the Confidence Man and, if so, the masquerade has already begun. The master trickster presents himself as the inoffensive but offending man of silence, an ironic prelude to a host of talky transactions. The deaf-mute's inscriptions—"Charity thinketh no evil. . . . Charity suffereth long, and is kind. . . . Charity believeth all things"—highlight the nexus between confidence and its proof sign, the surrendering of cash (4–5).[7] At the same time, the messages ironically invite rude remarks. The erasable messages contrast with the socially acceptable legend on the barbershop, "No trust": "An inscription which, though in a sense not less intrusive than the contrasted ones of the stranger, did not, as it seemed, provoke any corresponding derision or surprise, much less indignation; and still less, to all appearances, did it gain for the inscriber the repute of being a simpleton" (5).

The phrases, "as it seemed" and "to all appearances," reflect the narrator's characteristic way of undermining the efficacy of his account. Steadfastly avoiding explanations, he dramatizes the equivocal play of possibility. For example, one might guess that the large trunk which bumps the deaf-mute contains the collection of wigs, costumes, and creams used to disguise the Confidence Man. But one can never be sure: one is left with little more than the juxtaposition of two potentially related details. One can make sense or not make sense. One can engage, as it were, the hermeneutical process, either forging determinate readings about what is *really* going on, or construing hints into open-ended conjectures, or identifying the accumulation of vexing uncertainties as constituting the amorphous summation of Melville's impenetrable masquerade.[8] In any case, the words on the page invite the reader into an interpretive labyrinth. In effect, Melville has displaced the "Ishmael" voice and the dialectical permutations of the process narrative. A reader is no longer invited to accompany Ishmael on his interpretive ventures—"Let us try" (*Moby-Dick* 192)—but to engage in the activity alone. As John Bryant indicates, "Melville's use of dialogue generates a complex reading experience which forces us to suspend judgment, read on, re-read, and re-evaluate" ("Allegory and Breakdown" 121). The complexity does not end with the dialogues. The retentive narrator of *The Confidence-Man* only records dialogue as the auditory content of a dramatic situation. He thereby creates a domain of oblique, recalcitrant signification. By displacing even the provisional authority of the subject, Melville creates for his readers a situation analogous to the problem of reading Life. The inscribed surface looms as both object and other.

THE POWER OF PERFORMANCE

The Confidence Man seeks to dramatize his own power of self-possession and thereby control the readings and actions of his interlocutors.[9] Within the novel, self-possession reflects a radical degradation of the one time ennobling romantic exaltation of power. The trickster dominates the first half of the book and he usually succeeds in duping a victim. When thwarted, this master storyteller, dialectician, and actor either wanders off to engage another mark or changes face and tries again. While playing "this game of charity" (12), the trickster imposes his theories and stories on life. He carries a role's demands to completion, whether the part includes the doglike fawning of Black Guinea, or the "round-backed, baker-kneed" crouching of the man from the Philosophical Intelligence Office (114), or the colorful, resplendent fraternizing of the cosmopolitan. The disparity between his philosophical affirmations of love and his artful extractions of money may reflect an underlying cynicism, the monstrous form of the "genial misanthrope" (176). The Confidence Man's exercise of self-possession links his rhetorical professions of community to the deceptive activities of the trickster.

The philosophical dialogue constitutes the trickster's primary means to power. In his campaigns, the Confidence Man uses the dialogue to impose a reductive, determinate gestalt. Paradoxically, dialogic interplay collides with the Confidence Man's imposition of a fallacious polarity between confidence and distrust. One either has confidence or lacks confidence. To lack confidence is to be a philosophical "bear," one who obsessively growls down the bullish euphoria of confidence. In permitting no middle ground, no fine shadings, the Confidence Man recasts Ahab's rhetoric of narrow definition. Having confidence in this configuration leads one to surrender self-control. The trickster asserts power by unmaking another's claim to self-mastery. In responding to Egbert's contention that human beings lack volition, the cosmopolitan affirms the existence of will. In so doing, however, he describes his own capacity for self-determination rather than the virtues of the human masses: "I thought that man was no poor drifting weed of the universe, as you phrased it; that, if so minded, he could have a will, a way, a thought, and a heart of his own" (222). The phrase, "if so minded," separates all self-possessed individuals from the dupes on "this ship of fools" (15). Repeatedly, his independent will achieves expression as verbal power shapes an image of the world. Within the confines of this system, Melville places human beings in a losing situation. If one gives in to altruistic impulses or acts on entrenched philanthropic principles, one is duped; if one denies such impulses or steadfastly retains "confidence in distrust" (108), one is sour and alone. Indeed, the Confidence Man remains isolated within his successive histrionic forms; each dramatic enactment of his will to power precludes the possibility of establishing an "all-fusing" context of social federation (9).

It is the very mastery of role, dialogue, and dialectic that allows the Confidence Man to deconstruct identity. In a number of his transactions, the Confidence Man assails and then dismantles the very notion of a fixed and stable identity.[10] John Ringman, the man with the weed, confuses the kindly merchant, Mr. Roberts, by inventing a story of their past acquaintance. The narrator's report of word play—"Don't you know me?" "No, certainly" (18)—suggests the fragility of Roberts's self-possession. In attempting to restore Roberts's "faithless memory," Ringman exposes "self-knowledge" as a fiction. When Roberts cannot recall Ringman's countenance, the Confidence Man responds, "Can I be so changed? Look at me. Or is it I who am mistaken?" After Roberts responds, "I hope I know myself," Ringman debunks any attempt to privilege the essential stability of the self: "And yet self-knowledge is thought by some not so easy. Who knows, my dear sir, but for a time you may have taken yourself for somebody else?" (19).

As the dialogue progresses, Roberts's increasing distrust of what he knows to be true and his attending loss of self-possession culminate in his failure to complete a number of sentences:

> "Well, to tell the truth, in some things my memory aint of the very best," was the honest rejoinder. "But still," he perplexedly added, "still I—"
>
> "Oh, sir, suffice it that it is as I say. Doubt not that we are all well acquainted."
>
> "But—but I don't like this going dead against my own memory; I—" (19)

As far as the Confidence Man is concerned, identity and memory are "ductile" fictions fashioned within the improvisations of conversation: "You see, sir, the mind is ductile, very much so. . . . We are but clay, sir, potter's clay, as the good book says, clay, feeble, and too-yielding clay. But I will not philosophize" (20). Roberts's self is "quite erased from the tablet. . . . what a blank!" Accepting

Ringman's fabrication, Roberts gives him money to help alleviate his misfortune, a tale of woe which appears to be validated when Roberts later tells the agent for the Black Rapids Coal Company how the agent for the Seminole Widow and Orphan Asylum added details to Ringman's story. The philosophical dialogue and supporting stories create a web of assertion and corroboration that translates life and character into tenuous fictional constructs.

In the first half of the novel, the self-possessed con man makes his way by staging transactions that cynically repudiate connections between word and thing, or language and stable referent. Politically, such dialogues dramatize the absence of individual and communal coherence. Melville's message seems bitterly clear: to have an identity, or the power to control the histrionic form of an identity, is to be divorced from the human mainstream.

Ironically, the Confidence Man can be said to share an affinity only with those characters who have the will to resist his wiles. Substantial opposition to the confidence game comes only from the self-possessed misanthropes, Timon-like isolatoes associated variously with Tacitus, Lazarus, Heraclitus, Diogenes, and Autolycus.[11] The man with the wooden leg and the Kentucky Titan, for example, openly show the very cynicism that seems to impel the Confidence Man's power game. By insisting on the ubiquity of darkness and depravity, by believing in nothing except nonbelief, these Timons retain personal power, but only at the expense of wielding an aggressively reductive sensibility. The man with the wooden leg, for example, construes any behavior as histrionic artifice: "Yes, don't you both perform acts? To do, is to act; so all doers are actors" (31). Ironically again, the agent for the Black Rapids Coal Company reviles the philosophical bears and inversely explains his own tactics:

Why, the most monstrous of all hypocrites are these bears: hypocrites by inversion; hypocrites in the simulation of things dark instead of bright; souls that thrive, less upon depression, than the fiction of depression; professors of the wicked art of manufacturing depressions; spurious Jeremiahs; sham Heraclituses, who, the

lugubrious day done, return, like sham Lazaruses among the beg-
gars, to make merry over the gains got by their pretended sore
heads—scoundrelly bears. (48)

The evocation of Heraclitus is particularly reflective of the Confidence Man's own flux and fluidity. Language is his "Protean easy-
chair" (38). Insistently, he describes the bears as "true types of most
destroyers of confidence and gloomy philosophers, the world
over" (48). Philosophers tend to think, and thought engenders
gloom; confidence is inimical to the deep diving associated with
learning and antiquity:

> And do you know whence this sort of fellow gets his sulk? not
> from life; for he's often too much of a recluse, or else too young to
> have seen anything of it. No, he gets it from some of those old
> plays he sees on the stage, or some of those old books he finds up
> in garrets. Ten to one, he has lugged home from auction a musty
> old Seneca, and sets about stuffing himself with that stale old hay;
> and, thereupon, thinks it looks wise and antique to be a croaker,
> thinks it's taking a stand 'way above his kind. (49)

To venture on "the open ground of reason" is "to indulge in too
much latitude of philosophizing, or, indeed, of compassionating,
since this might beget an indiscreet habit of thinking and feeling
which might unexpectedly betray him upon unsuitable occasions"
(66). Similarly, he counsels that one should avoid not only reason
but "the natural heart"—an open inquiry into the emotional possibilities of human complexity (67). Like poets in *The Republic,*
philosophers on the ship of the world are dangerous. They need to
be kept away from the young and impressionable: "Only [the BRCC
man] deemed it at least desirable that, when such a case as that
alleged of the unfortunate man was made the subject of philosophic
discussion, it should be so philosophized upon, as not to afford
handles to those unblessed with the true light" (66). The "true light,"
of course, is "the secure Malakoff of confidence."

Behind the rhetoric of narrow definition is a desire to escape the vagaries of human nature and impose a pernicious totalitarian order on the free play of consciousness. The Confidence Man narrowly construes "self" in performative rather than ontological terms. To the Confidence Man, philosophy should do nothing more than assert the unwavering existence of an a priori premise. His polarization of confidence and distrust is designed to short-circuit nuance and circumscribe expression. Confidence becomes iconic; dialogue negates dialectic.

The Confidence Man employs the philosophical dialogue not only to undermine identity and entrap his interlocutors but also to pervert the relation of object to idea. In *Moby-Dick,* Ishmael uses analogy to suggest immutable attributes of human nature. What becomes, perhaps, most sophistical in *The Confidence-Man* is the perversion of analogy.[12] Plato's world view hinges on the notion that the material, timebound world is an imperfect copy of the immaterial, eternal realm. The Sophists, however, held that all words and ideas are relative, that each human being is the measure of all things, and that correspondence between sign and referent is arbitrary. In *Phaedrus,* Socrates' discussion of deception could have warned the dupes on the *Fidele* against having undue confidence in mere likenesses. Once again, Socrates seems to be describing the operations of Melville's trickster:

> He, then, who would deceive others, and not be deceived, must exactly know the real likenesses and differences of things. . . . And if he is ignorant of the true nature of anything, how can he ever distinguish the greater or less degree of likeness to other things of that which he does not know? . . . And when men are deceived, and their notions are at variance with realities, it is clear that the error slips in through some resemblances. . . . Then he who would be a master of the art must know the real nature of everything; or he will never know either how to contrive or how to escape the gradual departure from truth into the opposite of truth which is effected by the help of resemblances. (3:425)

Disputing the herb doctor's arguments about the beneficence of nature—"Natur [sic] is good Queen Bess; but who's responsible for the cholera?" (107)—Pitch, the formidable and hirsute Missouri Bachelor, stands as Melville's most complex philosophical bear. This confirmed boy-hater hopes one day that the law will allow him to "go out a boy-shooting" (117). True to form, the man from the Philosophical Intelligence Office uses Socrates' resemblances to make "the gradual departure from truth," presenting himself as a militant man of philosophy and science: "[W]hen deploying into the field of discourse the vanguard of an important argument, much more in evolving the grand central forces of a new philosophy of boys, as I may say, surely you will kindly allow scope adequate to the movement in hand" (121–22). This pseudo official cites false analogy after false analogy. He discusses clean chins and bearded chins, baby teeth and permanent teeth, caterpillar and butterfly. For a while, Pitch holds his own: "Pun away; but even accepting your analogical pun, what does it amount to? Was the caterpillar one creature, and is the butterfly another? The butterfly is the caterpillar in a gaudy cloak; stripped of which, there lies the impostor's long spindle of a body, pretty much worm-shaped as before" (124). Pitch is proficient in uncloaking "this guild of self-impostors" (*Pierre* 208).

But as the Philosophical Intelligence Office man is quick to perceive, Pitch's confident distrust of nature, boys, and men masks a latent desire for belief. The further he strays from his personal experience of boys, the less control he has over his language and convictions, and the less he can "stick to what I say" (117). He falls prey to the "doctrine of analogies" (130). Like bitter wine aging naturally into fine wine, your bad boy will naturally and inevitably become a good man. After admitting that the arguments are "kind of reasonable," Pitch passes from having "conditional confidence" to surrendering "perfect and unquestioning confidence." Pitch pays "my three dollars, and here is my address" (127–28).

The Confidence Man's rhetoric of narrow definition and his strong-armed control of argument create a closed theatrical world that seems true while it lasts. When successfully deployed, his artifice tends to arrest the counterforce of denial, the accumulation of psychological and philosophical experience that qualifies, if not refutes, the consistent fiction of confidence. Even Mr. Roberts, unsettled by wine, teetering with "an imaginative and feminine sensibility," manages an unconfident irruption:

> [T]he wine seemed to shoot to his heart, and began soothsaying there. "Ah. . . . wine is good, and confidence is good; but can wine or confidence percolate down through all the stony strata of hard considerations, and drop warmly and ruddily into the cold cave of truth? Truth will *not* be comforted. Led by dear charity, lured by sweet hope, fond fancy essays this feat; but in vain; mere dreams and ideals, they explode in your hand, leaving naught but the scorching behind!" (67, Melville's emphasis)

Such ostensibly "mad disclosures . . . of the queer, unaccountable caprices of his natural heart" suggest the intractable domain of experience that lies beyond the reach of the powerful masquerade (68). The "cold cave of truth" evokes those conveniently displaced lower layers of being, the dialectical alternative to the confidence game. It is for this reason that the rhetorical artifice of the master trickster is inimical to the brooding interiority of the philosophical bears. For these naysayers, distrust is not simply a static concept or monistic polarity but a process of intellection. *Confidence* has everything to do with maintaining a fiction of stable surfaces and fixed values, while *distrust* rejects appearances in favor of larger, darker, deeper complexities. The bears openly show to the world the very cynicism which lurks beneath the optimistic personae of the artist. These Timons emphasize the limitations of experience.[13]

Interestingly, the retentive narrator betrays an affinity with the bears, but only occasionally, when he absents himself from the action to indulge "the comedy of thought" and to speculate on aspects of the narrative (71). Stepping outside the self-imposed boundaries of the masquerade, in three instances—Chapters 14, 33, and 44—he arrests the story's diachronic progression to offer discursive assays on the relation between fiction and life.[14] These chapters, like the three digressive chapters of *Mardi,* exist not within the past time of reported action but within the compositional present. Such moments qualify, and indeed displace, the closed world of the confidence game. Chapter 14, for example, considers Mr. Roberts's rhetorical inconsistency, his sudden "rhapsody" (68). Like *Mardi's* texts within the text, this chapter questions the Confidence Man's putative authority and evokes a domain of mystery that cannot be contained within the confines of theatrical display. Specifically, Chapter 14 repudiates "consistency" as a valid measure of "living character" (69). As the narrator points out,

> [I]s it not a fact, that, in real life, a consistent character is a *rara avis?* Which being so, the distaste of readers to the contrary sort in books, can hardly arise from any sense of their untrueness. It may rather be from perplexity as to understanding them. But if the acutest sage be often at his wits' ends to understand living character, shall those who are not sages expect to run and read character in those mere phantoms which flit along a page, like shadows along a wall? That fiction, where every character can, by reason of its consistency, be comprehended at a glance, either exhibits but sections of character, making them appear for wholes, or else is very untrue to reality; while, on the other hand, that author who draws a character, even though to common view incongruous in its parts, as the flying-squirrel, and, at different periods, as much at variance with itself as the caterpillar is with the butterfly into which it changes, may yet, in so doing, be not false but faithful to facts. (69–70)

As in *Pierre,* Melville's narrator makes a case for "unravelable inscrutableness" (141). To represent the forms of inscrutability is to offer a mimetic account of what Ishmael calls "this strange mixed affair we call life" (*Moby-Dick* 226). Abstracted from the masquerade, "the comedy of thought" similarly refutes the absolute polarization between confidence and distrust. Like "lesser authors" (70), the Confidence Man perpetrates consistent delineations of character, thus avoiding the "tangled web" of lived experience. He portrays "human nature not in obscurity, but transparency." While either "very pure or very shallow," such theses are irrelevant to the layered mysteries of human nature.

The Confidence-Man, for all its philosophical talk, constitutes a bitter antitext to the expansive reaches of *Mardi* and *Moby-Dick.* By claiming to possess the "Talismanic" key—have confidence and never despond—the Confidence Man peddles the ultimate, simplistic, and therefore most acceptable lie. Indeed, as Chapter 14 makes clear, any single solution is inherently false. To claim an understanding of human nature is to misrepresent the problem. To this extent, then, the narrator puts himself in direct opposition to the Confidence Man:

> Upon the whole, it might rather be thought, that he, who, in view of its inconsistencies, says of human nature the same that, in view of its contrasts, is said of the divine nature, that it is past finding out, thereby evinces a better appreciation of it than he who, by always representing it in a clear light, leaves it to be inferred that he clearly knows all about it. (70)

In Chapter 14, the narrator comes closest to evoking the flexible, accommodating Ishmael, especially his tendency to reject rigid polarizations and propound instead an accumulation of inconsistent possibilities. Doubt, therefore, becomes the hallmark of psychological health, for it presupposes the magnitude of mystery. Indeed, one's commitment to engage in open-ended philosophical surmise reflects one's comfort with shifting allegiances and fine shadings, the actuality of life as a floating solution, a choppy sea of multiple signification. The narrator suggests a depth of experience well beyond the province of this masquerade and the purview of all art. Mere "sallies of ingenuity," especially the attempt to explain "human nature on fixed principles," create the very context for the Confidence Man's success. Even though "the grand points of human nature" are unchangeable, the narrator suggests that, like divine nature, the involutions of "the heart of man" (71) are, were, and will be "past finding out" (70). It seems to be reflective of the Confidence Man's cynical genius that he realizes all this. The ideational fiction of perfect closure is promulgated by way of slippery rhetorical tricks and changed costumes. The Confidence Man's sophistical qualities manifest most fully as his discourse in favor of fixed precept paradoxically reinforces the fluidity of experience and the openness of possibility.[15]

Within the text the fictions of confidence are fragile, tenuous, fleeting. One's conversion to confidence will not last. Sooner or later a dupe will become aware of the swindle, and philanthropic foray will lead to misanthropic recoil. Ironically, confidence is the path to distrust. As darkness falls Pitch recovers from his soporific lapse: "Like one beginning to rouse himself from a dose of chloroform treacherously given, he half divines, too, that he, the philosopher, had unwittingly been betrayed into being an unphilosophical dupe" (129). As he does in the digressive chapters, the narrator alters his rules of revelation. He now seems to provide qualified access to a character's inner life. On the one hand, the narrator remarks that Pitch "audibly mumbles his cynical mind to himself" (129), a notion confirmed later when the cosmopolitan claims to have overheard him talking to himself (133). On the other hand, the narrator presents the content of the meditation not within quotation marks but as indirect discourse or, more accurately, as "uncordial reveries" (130). At the very least, the narrator foregrounds the dissenting meditation of a mind coming to engage intractable mystery: "To what vicissitude of light and shade is man subject! He ponders the mystery of human subjectivity in general" (129)—the very mystery which the narrator examines in Chapter 14, the very "nature" that is "past finding out."

Pitch's "reveries" offer a dialectical counterpoint to the Confidence Man's smoothly shallow explanations. This moment reveals by contrast the intentionally narrow range of the narrator's usual practices—his depiction of what can be seen and heard and his conjectures on what one might *seem* to be thinking. Similarly, the Confidence Man's mastery of dramatic situations leads only to Pyrrhic victories in which so much is left out.

What remain beyond the reach of the Confidence Man's histrionics are the buried depths of "human subjectivity." Melville posits a dissociation between the social, acting self and the lower layers, a condition analogous to Ahab's tortured, schizoid split between his "characterizing mind" and his "eternal, living principle or soul" (*Moby-Dick* 202). Pitch must burrow in order to examine the implications of his defeat:

> But where was slipped in the entering wedge? Philosophy, knowledge, experience—were those trusty knights of the castle recreant? . . . He revolves the crafty process of sociable chat, by which, as he fancies, the man with the brass-plate wormed into him, and made such a fool of him as insensibly to persuade him to waive, in his exceptional case, that general law of distrust systematically applied to the race. He revolves, but cannot comprehend, the operation, still less the operator. Was the man a trickster, it must be more for the love than the lucre. (130)

Pitch, in effect, rereads the encounter and recognizes that the PIO man has a predilection, a "love," for power politics. The trickster's use of analogy, he realizes, is his chief weapon: "The doctrine of analogies recurs. Fallacious enough doctrine when wielded against one's prejudices, but in corroboration of cherished suspicions not without likelihood." Pitch can recognize the cosmopolitan as "another of them. Somehow I meet with the most extraordinary metaphysical scamps to-day. Sort of visitation of them" (136).[16] Pitch does not recognize that the herb doctor, the PIO man, and the cosmopolitan are disguised versions of the same figure. But having once been gulled, Pitch is more than a match. His "Hands off!" attitude reinforces the Timon-like isolation of the philosophical bears (131). By recognizing the cosmopolitan as "Diogenes in disguise. . . . Diogenes masquerading as a cosmopolitan" (138), Pitch suggests the ontological affinity between the bears and the Confidence Man. The play of confidence is but misanthropy in disguise. In fact, the cosmopolitan, when speaking with Charlie Noble, offers a self-reflexive hint of, perhaps, his own inner nature:

> Now, the genial misanthrope, when, in the process of eras, he shall turn up, will be the converse of this; under an affable air, he will hide a misanthropical heart. In short, the genial misanthrope will

be a new kind of monster, but still no small improvement upon
the original one, since, instead of making faces and throwing stones
at people, like that poor old crazy man, Timon, he will take steps,
fiddle in hand, and set the tickled world a' dancing. (176–77)

"THE LAST DREGS OF YOUR INHUMAN PHILOSOPHY"

As a trope, self-possession involves a paradoxical doubleness. At
the level of dramatic action, it signifies one's capacity to control
the progress of one's social performance. In terms of psychological
interiority, self-possession implies the latent presence or dramatic
absence of unacknowledged dimensions of being. On the one hand,
the self achieves expression through role-playing; on the other, the
self remains hidden and unexpressed. Within the diachronic narrative, Melville dissociates the dramatic representation of surfaces
from the revelation of underlying psychological complexes. What
or who the Confidence Man is has rightly vexed generations of
readers. Any determinate ontological designation—God, the
Devil, and so on—involves a speculative leap. In the present argument three related assumptions suggest the Confidence Man's informing cynicism: first, he is aware of how confidence leads to
distrust; second, his cynical misanthropy links him to the grim
self-possession of his surly antagonists, the philosophical bears;
and third, he is speaking self-reflexively when describing the genial misanthrope. As social performers, these Timon-figures enact
the very misanthropy which characterizes their inner lives. They
are in essence what they enact dramatically.

Because the Confidence Man reveals himself only through his
theatrical displays, he can maintain or express self-possession only
within the constrictions of a particular role. In the first half of the
book, the trickster usually succeeds in duping a victim. In the second half, the cosmopolitan, though apparently diddling a shave
from the barber, does not take in a single penny and on two occasions actually pays money. Melvillian criticism has not fully engaged the implications of this failure to extract confidence. With
the appearance of the cosmopolitan, the outer sign of the trickster's
irony disappears. The cosmopolitan's rhetorical expressions of

confidence are never directly undermined by the receipt of cash. To all appearances, the cosmopolitan Frank Goodman is not a con man. Instead, he seems a frank, good man. The most personable avatar of the Confidence Man, Goodman plays the game of charity "to the life" (181). His actions remain consistent with his cosmopolitan philosophy of fellowship. As the controlling ironic context dissolves, and as story and performance, rhetoric and action, merge, the Confidence Man performs those very kinds of charitable action which he burlesqued earlier.

Significantly, the dualism between con man and good man does not translate the terms of Melville's masquerade into an ontological struggle between moral absolutes, with the evil con man opposing the godly good man. That the Confidence Man expresses in his actions the qualities of a good man is not to suggest that he is somehow suddenly regenerated. Rather, Melville indicates that artifice and self-possession create their own forms of entrapment. The role of cosmopolitan circumscribes the possibilities of behavior. Furthermore, the Confidence Man consistently adapts his performance to his various interlocutors. As a con man, he seeks to assert self-possession by duping others into trying a delusive experiment in confidence; as a good man, he maintains self-possession by identifying himself in distinct opposition to a fellow (but diminutive) con artist, Charlie Noble, and the inhumane philosophers, Mark Winsome and Egbert. The artist's apparent goodness emerges with the new dramatic context and is essentially reactive, a response to the performances of other actors. The daytime world of shifting avatars and gullible victims gives way to the nighttime world of an unchanging avatar and highly skilled rhetoricians. When money is not forthcoming, the Confidence Man plays out the dictates of his philosophy. He maintains the integrity of the role by exposing the misanthropic nature of his three major antagonists, who, unlike the philosophical bears, hide their misanthropy beneath self-righteous personae.

As in the first half of the book, Melville's major narrative device is philosophical dialogue. Here it serves to explore three representational fables of identity. Assertions of unity and fellowship initially characterize Frank Goodman's encounters with Noble, Winsome, and Egbert. As the dialogues proceed, and as the treachery of Noble and the coldhearted inhumanity of Winsome and Egbert emerge, the cosmopolitan explicitly defines himself in opposition to them.

At the outset of their conversation, Charlie and Frank appear to agree on everything. As the cosmopolitan notes, "our sentiments agree so, that were they written in a book, whose was whose, few but the nicest critics might determine" (158). But their apparent federation is actually a battle of wits whereby each seeks to undo the other. Charlie engages in the facile ruse of encouraging Frank to drink. Charlie thinks that, with faculties impaired by liquor, Frank will be an easy touch. As Frank drinks and Charlie abstains, Frank befuddles Charlie and comes increasingly to control the conversation. Eventually, the cosmopolitan expresses "the patience of a superior mind at the petulance of an inferior one" (170). Frank's sudden request for a loan completes the "metamorphosis" of Charlie from disguised treachery to open malevolence (179). Charlie becomes a "new creature. Cadmus glided into the snake" (180). After unmasking Charlie, Frank ironically applauds him for playing a role: "[W]hat you say about your humoring the thing is true enough; never did man second a joke better than you did just now. You played your part better than I did mine; you played it, Charlie, to the life" (181). These last words summarize the cosmopolitan's actions in the last half of the book, where his rhetoric and actions merge. Repeatedly endorsing congeniality, he continues to play his role "to the life" as he challenges Mark Winsome and Egbert.[17]

These philosophers are hardhearted absolutists whose brand of self-reliant transcendentalism masks their repudiations of human fellowship. Frank Goodman denounces their misanthropy, twice paying money to register his support for "fellow-feeling" (195). When, for example, the crazy beggar appears before Goodman and Winsome "asking alms under the form of peddling a rhapsodical tract" (194), Winsome starkly rebukes the wretch, for he still seems to possess "a damning peep of sense—damning, I say; for sense in a seeming madman is scoundrelism" (195). The cosmopolitan responds by giving the beggar a shilling and speaking graciously.

Shortly thereafter, Frank Goodman engages Egbert in a purportedly hypothetical dialogue concerning a loan. Frank, playing himself, claims that a loan should be transacted between friends. Egbert, playing Charlie Noble, adamantly refuses and cites the case of the fictional China Aster, a man ruined by accepting a loan from a friend. In this dialogue, allegedly fictive requests and repudiations come to possess the emotional power of actual appeals and denials. Fiction and life merge. Once again the cosmopolitan plays the game "to the life," further establishing his performative identity as a man who plays according to principles of charity and trust. At this point, manifesting the most stable and sympathetic identity in the book, he attacks Egbert and his inhumane philosophy:

> Enough. I have had my fill of the philosophy of Mark Winsome as put into action. And moonshiny as it in theory may be, yet a very practical philosophy it turns out in effect, as he himself engaged I should find. But, miserable for my race should I be, if I thought he spoke truth when he claimed, for proof of the soundness of his system, that the study of it tended to much the same formation of character with the experiences of the world.—Apt disciple! . . . What your illustrious magian has taught you, any poor, old, broken-down, heart-shrunken dandy might have lisped. Pray, leave me, and with you take the last dregs of your inhuman philosophy. And here, take this shilling, and at the first wood-landing buy yourself a few chips to warm the frozen natures of you and your philosopher by. (223)

The cosmopolitan departs in "a grand scorn" and Egbert is left to wonder "where exactly the fictitious character had been dropped, and the real one, if any, resumed."

In his behavior, Frank Goodman becomes an active exemplar of his cosmopolitan philosophy of fellowship. Just as the trickster moves from potential victim to potential victim, so too does the cosmopolitan recast his basic rhetorical trope. Not much more can be known about him. The mask remains firmly in place. In a world limited to the exigencies of social performance, there is no way of telling whether the change from con man to good man involves a transformation of essence, for Melville refuses to peel back the lower layers. Although in *Mardi* and *Moby-Dick* the search for essence drives Melville's unsettled attempt to contain philosophical impulses and imperatives within fiction's very open forms, in *The Confidence-Man* the question of essence barely obtains. This involuted novel reflects the incapacity of the philosophical dialogue, analogy, and dialectic to lead beyond the self-generated, self-frustrating forms of human discourse. The narrator of *The Confidence-Man* is stuck with the limits of the literary. Though images of apocalypse pervade the last chapter, the world does not end. Language can only go so far: a book can neither blow up the world nor obliterate time. As all days do, this day merely ends. The solar lamp burns out; darkness falls; and "the cosmopolitan kindly led the old man away" (251).

Lest one overreact and utterly despond, lest one, while sitting beneath a reading lamp, conclude that the light of the world has been extinguished, the narrator displaces closure with a cryptic, confident intimation: "Something further may follow of this Masquerade." Though reaching a postpunctuation blank, one does not quite exit the theater. The show may yet go on. Or it may not. Throughout the novel, conditional statements are teasing preludes to successive reformulations. The next word may suddenly come forth. Put another way, the end of the novel reinforces the anticlimax and irresolution of the whole. With the prospect of a sequel, Melville suspends teleological definition. Unlike Prospero, neither Melville nor the narrator bury the book. The next book remains an open issue, potentially underhand, even though he never took it up.

Epilogue:
The "Endless Vestibule"

WHATEVER *The Confidence-Man* meant for Melville, it no doubt purged him of pursuing the phantom of fame. He concluded his career as a public fiction writer with the kind of book he must have felt "most moved to write" (*Correspondence* 191), one written to himself. Despite the occasional critical misnomer regarding the so-called years of nonwriting, one must recognize that Melville did not surrender to silence. Specifically, in late 1856, he went traveling. While visiting Hawthorne he talked about his own tortured beliefs and the soul's prospective annihilation; while in Greece he was both miserable and exalted; while within the Pyramids he felt suffocated and paranoid. After coming home, he did not write a travel book and reclaim a popular audience. Instead, he tried lecturing. When this failed, he took up poetry, in slow earnest.

In all his ramblings, rages, and accommodations, Melville never left what Media so aptly calls the "endless vestibule" (*Mardi* 566). With characteristic integrity and intensity, Melville remade himself as a writer and cleared the way for more narrow lines. Over thirty-five years he grappled with the insular poetic vistas of *Battle-Pieces*; the gnarled interstices of *Clarel*; the austerity of *Timoleon*; the nostalgia of *John Marr and Other Sailors*; the rueful, late-blooming love songs of *Weeds and Wildlings*. Out of his poetry came the troubled recastings of *Billy Budd*. This massive body of work falls outside the limits of this study, which is restricted to the fiction published during his lifetime. Melville's second career of private writing and more private living offers a daunting challenge to further "philosophic research" (*Omoo* xv). Melville's late work and his "quality of Grasp" (*Clarel*, "Historical Supplement" 647) provide irrefutable testimony as to how language remained his most potent rejoinder to God's "Silence." To the death, as in the life, he remained intent on tallying "[t]he greatest number of the greatest ideas." Along the winding way, Herman Melville never once lost his voice.

Notes

CHAPTER ONE: Making *Mardi*'s Patchwork

1. For discussions of *Typee,* see Stern, *Critical Essays;* Dimock, *"Typee";* Short; Alberti; and Samson 22–56.

2. For an extended examination of the conditions relating to *Typee*'s publication and textual problems, see "Historical Note" to *Typee.*

3. For excellent discussions of the artistic and thematic contexts of *Omoo,* see Kemper, *"Omoo";* and Samson 57–86.

4. For a summary of the word "philosophy" in Melville's critical lexicon, see Wenke, "'Ontological Heroics'" 567–68.

5. J. Ross Browne apparently took exception to Melville's review. He made his complaint in a letter to Frederick Saunders (Leyda 239).

6. In the preface to *Mardi,* Melville writes,

> Not long ago, having published two narratives of voyages in the Pacific, which, in many quarters, were received with incredulity, the thought occurred to me, of indeed writing a romance of Polynesian adventure, and publishing it as such; to see whether, the fiction might not, possibly, be received for a verity: in some degree the reverse of my previous experience.
> This thought was the germ of others, which have resulted in Mardi. (xvii)

7. See Davis; Sealts, "Melville Reading in Ancient Philosophy"; Sundermann; Howard, *Herman Melville* 112–49; Braswell, *Melville's Religious Thought;* Branch, "The Quest for *Mardi*"; and Bercaw, especially 15–30.

8. On Melville's early life, see also Gilman and Howard, *Herman Melville* 1–40.

9. For further discussion of Melville and religion, see Herbert, Moby-Dick *and Calvinism* 1–68; and Sherrill.

10. In *Pierre,* Melville self-reflexively depicts his protagonist's method of reading. Like Pierre, Melville enjoyed a "varied scope of reading, little suspected by his friends, and randomly acquired by a random but lynx-eyed mind, in the course of the multifarious, incidental, bibliographic encounterings. . . . [T]his poured one considerable contributary stream into that bottomless spring of original thought" (283).

11. See Sealts, *Melville's Reading,* which lists full citations of Melville's reading alphabetically and by number. The numbers are parenthetically included within my discussion.

12. Davis writes,

> These books contained not only the information and discoveries of scientific voyages of exploration, as in Darwin and Wilkes, but also the personal adventures, hairbreadth escapes, and exciting escapades told by voyagers in the South Seas who were interested in arousing the sympathy of the reader for themselves. . . . Although none of these books was used extensively when Melville actually began writing, their purchase appears to have been made at this time by an author engaged in bringing authentic information to whatever narrative he concocted or in looking for materials that would be helpful in setting the direction of that narrative. (51)

13. For a complementary discussion of Melville's creative process in *Mardi,* especially its relation to Edgar Allan Poe's *The Narrative of Arthur Gordon Pym,* see Brodhead, "*Mardi.*"

14. For discussions of Melville's relation to Sir Thomas Browne, see Matthiessen 100–131; Sealts, "Platonic Tradition" 281–99; Vande Kieft; Marovitz, "Melville's Problematic 'Being'" 12–13; and Foley.

15. Here is a representative example of Browne's ranging play of mind:

> Those that held Religion was the difference of man from beasts, have spoken probably, and proceed upon a principle as inductive as the other: That doctrine of *Epicurus,* that denied the providence of God, was no Atheism, but a magnificent and high-strained conceit of his Majesty, which hee deemed too sublime to minde the triviall actions of those inferiour creatures: That fatall necessitie of the Stoickes, is nothing but the immutable Law of his will. (*Religio Medici* 26)

16. Browne discusses the "flux and reflux" of existence:

> I cannot think that *Homer* pin'd away upon the riddle of the Fishermen, or that *Aristotle,* who understood the uncertainty of knowledge, and so often confessed the reason of man too weake for the workes of nature, did ever drowne himself upon the flux and reflux of *Euripus:* wee doe but

learne to day, what our better advanced judgements will unteach us to morrow: and *Aristotle* doth but instruct us as *Plato* did him; that is, to confute himselfe. (*Religio Medici* 78–79)

17. The concept of knowledge as recollection also appears in the opening lines of Sir Thomas Browne's *Pseudodoxia Epidemica:* "Would Truth dispense, we could be content, with Plato, that knowledge were but remembrance; that intellectual acquisition were but reminscential evocation, and new Impressions but the colourishing of old stamps which stood pale in the soul before" (227).

18. Hollander writes, "What a great writer does with direct citation of another's language is quite different from what a minor one may be doing. Similarly, his handling of a commonplace will be radically interpretive of it, while the minor writer's contribution will be more one of handing on the baton, so to speak, of cultivating the topos rather than replanting or even building there" (73).

19. See Wenke, "Melville's *Typee.*"

20. See Chai for a full consideration of Coleridge and other Romantics and their relation to the American Renaissance.

21. In *Phaedrus*, Plato writes,

> The soul or animate being has the care of the inanimate, and traverses the whole heaven in divers forms appearing;—when perfect and fully winged she soars upward, and is the ruler of the universe; while the imperfect soul loses her feathers, and drooping in her flight at last settles on the solid ground—there, finding a home, she receives an earthly frame which appears to be self-moved, but is really moved by her power. . . . The wing is intended to soar aloft and carry that which gravitates downwards into the upper region, which is the dwelling of the gods. (3:404)

CHAPTER TWO: Narrative Self-Fashioning and the Play of Possibility

1. In *New England Literary Culture*, Buell identifies the centrality of romantic art to be not in an ideology of the self-deification of the artist but in a notion of the artist as iconoclastic transformer of existing literary structures, what Buell calls "form breaking": "Romanticism . . . starts with a destructive, ground-clearing impulse that easily moves from the level of mere protest against received forms to the level of an antiaesthetic impulse of protest against the constraints of art itself" (70). The terms of Buell's discourse clarify the nature of Melville's drive to dissociate himself from the narrative form wherein he achieved initial success. In protesting against the limits of the travel narrative, Melville plunged into philosophical romance, which is synonymous in his view with artistic freedom and invention. His pursuit of Truth within this iconoclastic aesthetic, then, must not be seen as representing a search for the practicability of staid, conservative platitudes of mid-nineteenth-century

Christian moralism. Truth seemed for Melville to encompass whatever one found after diving beneath the surfaces of quotidian formulations. Truth came to be grounded in dark, possibly nihilistic, formulations that related to the human domain of instinct, compulsion, vent, and irrationality. Buell goes on to describe the way the iconoclastic artistic impulse emerges: "This impulse is manifested in two principal ways: first, in celebrations of the creative process, as opposed to the aesthetic product, the 'poetic' being located in the realm of experience rather than in the artifact; and second, in Romantic irony, the systematic breaking of the poetic illusion in order to call attention to it as artifice" (70). In the first instance, Melville celebrates the creative process not in terms of the narrator's actions but in the ranging play of his reactions. *Mardi*'s opening sequences, as will be argued, are generally devoid of dramatic activity. In the second case, which is not explicitly within the limits of this study, Melville's political satire reflects Buell's notion of romantic irony.

2. For Melville's view that great literary artists write in a kind of doublespeak— to popular tastes and, simultaneously, to a deeper reader—see "Hawthorne and His Mosses" (*Piazza Tales* 244–45).

3. Melville's concern in *Mardi* with the interpenetration of subject and object places him at the center of Romantic attempts to link the self with the world of experience. In *Biographia Literaria*, Coleridge discusses the basic Socratic dictum,

KNOW THYSELF! . . . And this at once practically and speculatively. For as philosophy is neither a science of the reason or the understanding only, nor merely a science of morals, but the science of BEING altogether, its primary ground can be neither merely speculative nor merely practical, but both in one. All knowledge rests on the coincidence of an object with a subject. (162–63)

For discussions of related issues, see Cascardi; Greenberg; and Chai 308–12.

4. The allusive catalog serves Melville well in *Mardi* and in subsequent works. This technique allows him to combine learned reference with the dialectical play of competing positions. It is a favored technique of Plato, Rabelais, Sir Thomas Browne, and Burton. See Wenke, "'Ontological Heroics'" 569–70, for a discussion of how invoked names tend to function for Melville as synoptic metaphors, which resonate with associational possibilities.

5. In the 1(?) June 1851 letter to Hawthorne, Melville pens a similarly speculative scenario about a congenial afterlife:

It is a rainy morning; so I am indoors, and all work suspended. I feel cheerfully disposed, and therefore I write a little bluely. Would the Gin were here! If ever, my dear Hawthorne, in the eternal times that are to come, you and I shall sit down in Paradise, in some little shady corner by ourselves, and if we shall by any means be able to smuggle a basket of champagne there (I won't believe in a Temperance Heaven), and if we shall then cross our celestial legs in the celestial grass that is forever tropical, and strike our glasses and our heads together, till both musically ring in concert, — then, O my dear fellow-mortal, how shall we pleasantly discourse of all the things manifold which now so distress us, — when all the earth shall be but a reminiscence, yea, its final dissolution an antiquity. Then shall songs be composed as when wars are over. . . . [Y]es, let us look forward to such things. Let us swear that, though now we sweat, yet it is because of the dry heat which is indispensable to the nourishment of the vine which is to bear the grapes that are to give us the champagne hereafter. (191–92)

6. A passage in Burton might well be a direct source for the technique, ideas, and characterization in "Dreams." Burton uses the allusive catalog, but unlike Melville, he celebrates study as a means to exorcise melancholy. Burton's passage is an inversion of Melville's exposition. Burton writes:

Seneca prefers Zeno and Chrysippus . . . before any Prince or General of an Army; and Orontius the Mathematician so far admires Archimedes, that he calls him a petty God, more than a man; and well he might, for ought I see, if you respect fame or worth, Pindar of Thebes is as much renowned for his Poems, as Epaminondas, Pelopidas, Hercules, or Bacchus, his fellow citizens, for their warlike actions. . . . the delight is it which I aim at; so great pleasure, such sweet content, there is in study. . . . Sir Thomas Bodley . . . brake out into that noble speech: If I were not a King, I would be an University man; and if it were so that I must be a prisoner, if I might have my wish, I would desire to have no other prison than that Library, and to be chained together with so many good Authors and dead Masters. (457)

Burton goes on to offer a caution that Taji could well have observed:

Whosoever he is . . . that is overrun with solitariness . . . I can prescribe him no better remedy than this of study, to compose himself to the learning of some art or science. Provided always that his malady proceed not from overmuch study, for in such cases he adds fuel to the fire, and nothing can be more pernicious; let him take heed he do not overstretch his wits, and make a skeleton of himself. (458–59)

7. See Stern, "Towards 'Bartleby'" for a discerning overview of the story's unresolved critical complexes.

CHAPTER THREE: Perpetual Cycling

1. For discussions of explicitly Platonic elements in *Mardi*, see Sealts, "Platonic Tradition"; Sunderman; and Wenke, "'Ontological Heroics.'" While composing *Mardi*, Melville was definitely reading *Phaedo, Phaedrus, Timaeus,* and *Republic,* and he may have been reading *Crito, Apology, Meno,* and *Cratylus*. Sealts establishes that Melville was reading Plato in the Taylor-Sydenham translation, 5 vols., London, 1804.

2. See Sealts, "Ancient Philosophy" 39–47, for a discussion of Melville and Socrates.

3. In November 1856, Hawthorne recorded the substance of his conversation with Melville, casting his friend in terms that adroitly describe Babbalanja:

> Melville, as he always does, began to reason of Providence and futurity, and of everything that lies beyond human ken, and informed me that he had "pretty much made up his mind to be annihilated;" but still he does not seem to rest in that anticipation; and, I think, will never rest until he gets hold of a definite belief. It is strange how he persists—and has persisted ever since I knew him, and probably long before—in wandering to and fro over these deserts, as dismal and monotonous as the sand hills amid which we were sitting. He can neither believe, nor be comfortable in his unbelief; and he is too honest and courageous not to try to do one or the other. (Leyda 529)

4. For a related discussion, see Bickman.

5. For an extended discussion of these islands, see Wenke, "The Isles of Man" 26–31.

6. For a revisionist reading of the myth of American millennialism, see Pease 3–48, 235–75.

7. For a discussion of Serenia and Media and their relations to historical circumstances, see Stern, *The Fine Hammered Steel* 139–49.

CHAPTER FOUR: *Redburn* and *White-Jacket:* "Concocting Information into Wisdom"

1. For a discussion of Melville's knowledge of Emerson, see Sealts, "Emerson's Rainbow."

2. Efforts to argue for Emerson as a major influence on Melville are prone to overstatement. See Baym and Williams.

3. See Duban, "The Translation of Bayle."

4. In "Ancient Philosophy," Sealts remarks that explicit borrowings from Bayle "can be illustrated only by broad comparisons; the technique of citing parallel passages is entirely inapplicable" (196).

5. For a discussion of the reviews, see "Historical Note" to *Mardi* 664–71, and an updated listing of them in Hayes and Parker.

6. See Gilman; Vincent, *Tailoring;* and Heflin.

7. In *Anxiety of Influence,* Bloom writes, "The profundities of poetic influence cannot be reduced to source-study, to the history of ideas, to the patterning of images. Poetic influence, or as I shall more frequently term it, poetic misprision, is necessarily the study of the life-cycle of the poet-as-poet" (7). Hollander observes,

> We might, indeed, propose a kind of hierarchy for the relationship of allusive modes. Actual *quotation,* the literal presence of a body of text, is represented or replaced by *allusion,* which may be fragmentary or periphrastic. In the case of outright allusion . . . the text alluded to is not totally absent, but is part of the portable library shared by the author and his ideal audience. Intention to allude recognizably is essential to the concept. . . . But then there is echo, which represents or substitutes for allusion as allusion does for quotation. . . . In contrast with literary allusion, echo is a metaphor of, and for, alluding, and does not depend on conscious intention. (64, Hollander's emphasis)

8. Hollander provides an appendix on transumption, "the proper name" for "the operation of intertextual echo" (x). See 133–49.

9. See Milton, *Paradise Lost,* Book XII, lines 646–49.

10. It is these exalted moments that soured reviewers. In a review-essay of 1853, Fitz-James O'Brien repudiated the "wild, inflated, repulsive" *Pierre* to praise *Mardi* with a backhanded compliment: "*Mardi,* we believe, is intended to embody all the philosophy of which Mr. Melville is capable, and we have no hesitation in saying that the philosophical parts are the worst" (Leyda 466).

11. For a discussion of Melville and the politics of war, see Adler.

12. This passage anticipates Plinlimmon's pamphlet "Chronometicals and Horologicals," the "set-piece which constitutes the philosophical crux" of *Pierre* ("Historical Note" 407).

13. In *Sartor Resartus,* Carlyle uses the phrase "Armed Neutrality" (222). Though there is no documentary evidence that Melville read Carlyle prior to the summer of 1850, he probably had read all or parts of the book. This phrase may have entered his large "portable library."

14. See Martin, *The Universe of Force,* for a compelling and learned discussion of force as an importation from scientific to aesthetic modes of apprehension and expression.

15. In a letter to Hawthorne, Melville writes,

> There is a certain tragic phase of humanity which, in our opinion, was never more powerfully embodied than by Hawthorne. We mean the

tragicalness of human thought in its own unbiassed, native, and profounder workings. We think that into no recorded mind has the intense feeling of the visable truth ever entered more deeply than into this man's. By visable truth, we mean the apprehension of the absolute condition of present things as they strike the eye of the man who fears them not, though they do their worst to him. (186)

CHAPTER FIVE: *Moby-Dick* and the Impress of Melville's Learning

1. For major genetic studies of *Moby-Dick*, see Stewart; Barbour, "The Composition of *Moby-Dick*"; Milder, "The Composition of *Moby-Dick*"; Barbour, "'All My Books Are Botches'"; and Hayford. For a dissenting point of view, see Post-Lauria.

2. See Melville's letter to Dana (83); *Journals* 3–48; and especially Parker, "*Moby-Dick* and Domesticity."

3. I borrow this phrase from Hawthorne's account of his 1856 meeting with Melville. Exhausted in mind and spirit, Melville took a long tour to seek psychological therapy and lived the events that would latter be recast in *Clarel*.

4. In "More Chartless Voyaging," Marovitz comments on "their remarkably compatible psychological states. . . . Perhaps the most crucial correspondence between them—apart from their mutual willingness to participate in extended discussions on the level of metaphysics—is the fact that both men were in need of rest and change after an extremely trying period of sustained intellectual productivity" (375).

5. See Samson on *Typee, Omoo, Redburn,* and *White-Jacket* 22–172.

6. On Melville and Shakespeare, see Matthiessen 412–17, 423–35; and Olson. Reynolds also discusses the narrative's relation to classic and contemporary texts:

> *Moby-Dick* gives a fully Americanized version of Shakespeare and other classic sources precisely because it democratically encompasses a uniquely large number of antebellum textual strategies. The anecdotal sermon style, the visionary mode, the Oriental dialogue, dark temperance, city-mysteries fiction, sensational yellow novels, grotesque native humor—these are some of the forgotten popular genres that Melville grafts together to forge symbols that possess stylistic plurality as well as broad cultural representativeness. (5)

7. I do not mean to suggest that Melville discovered the image of Prometheus in *Frankenstein*. In fact, he evokes Prometheus as artist and maker in *Mardi* (229).

8. For a brief discussion of Carlyle and Melville, see Howard, "The Unfolding of *Moby-Dick*" 39–43.

9. See Sealts, "Emerson's Rainbow" 269.

10. See Irwin for an extended examination of hieroglyphics in the American Renaissance.

11. Bloom remarks, "Emerson thought that the poet unriddled the Sphinx by perceiving an identity in nature, or else yielded to the Sphinx, if he was merely bombarded by diverse particulars he could never hope to integrate. The Sphinx, as Emerson saw, is nature and the riddle of our emergence from nature, which is to say that the Sphinx is what psychoanalysts have called the Primal Scene" (*Anxiety of Influence* 36).

12. Melville may have borrowed "the blackness of darkness" from Carlyle and included it in his review of Hawthorne (*Piazza Tales* 243), though the phrase also appears in the Book of Job.

CHAPTER SIX: *Moby-Dick* and the Forms of Philosophical Fiction

1. For materials pertaining to the Hawthorne-Melville relationship, see Wilson 1–39; Sophia Hawthorne's letter to Elizabeth Peabody (Leyda 926); Brodhead, *Hawthorne* 1–25.

2. See Marovitz, "Melville's Problematic 'Being'" for an illuminating treatment of this letter; also see Chai for the letter's relation to Spinoza (296–97).

3. For a related discussion of Ishmael as narrator, see Dryden, *Thematics of Form* 81–113.

4. See Cambon for a seminal discussion of *Moby-Dick*'s narrative discontinuities; Martin in *The Destruction of Knowledge* remarks, "It is Ishmael's strong commitment to experience and to instinct and his rejection of a priori philosophical categories that make him the exceptionally effective narrator that he is. . . . He is a new kind of knower, aware of the impossibility of absolute knowledge and aware of the distortion of men's visions that comes from their self-justifying belief systems" (37).

5. See Brodtkorp for his illuminating treatment of the phenomenology of Ishmael's consciousness.

6. Irwin argues, "This post-Kantian doubt of the certainty of knowledge inevitably raises questions that are 'hieroglypical' in nature, whether they pertain to pictographic writing or to the shapes of physical nature or to the form and features of the human body. And these basic questions of meaning inevitably turn out to be questions of origins and ends" (55).

7. Grenburg sees Ishmael as an outcast (95); Dryden sees him as "an outcast in name only" (*Thematics of Form* 87).

8. Railton examines how *Moby-Dick* expresses Melville's conflicted attempts to forge a relationship with his reading public. Ishmael's direct addresses to the reader counterpoint his sense of estrangement: "It shows Melville's desire to enter into a personal relationship with his audience while reserving his right to his own estranged identity" (152).

9. Irwin discusses "doubling" as narcissistic self-making:

> Although we can have no direct knowledge of the simultaneous origin of man and language, for many of these writers [of the American Renaissance] it was an appealing, indeed a compelling, myth to imagine that origin as a form of "hieroglyphic" doubling in which a prelinguistic creature saw the outline of his shadow on the ground or his reflection in water and experienced both the revelation of human self-consciousness (the differentiated existence of self and world) and the revelation of language, the sudden understanding that his shadow or reflection was a double of himself and yet *not* himself, that it was somehow separate and thus could serve as a substitute that would by its shape evoke recognition of what it stood in place of. (61–62, Irwin's emphasis)

Brodhead sees Ishmael's "passionate philosophical surmise" as expressing agitation over ontological mysteries: "As *Moby-Dick* describes it, the most elemental human passion is not love, or ambition, or acquisitiveness, but something more like anxiety—anxiety, specifically, about the ground of our being, an anxiety that drives us . . . to keep worrying the question how the world is framed and governed" (*New Essays* 4).

10. Porter contends that Ishmael "aims to undermine our most basic and fixed assumptions and beliefs, to destablize our culturally inscribed patterns of perception, to decenter our rooted perspective as landsmen. He ought to be a threat. Yet he has usually been regarded by modern readers as genial, tolerant, open-minded" (93–94). In a similar vein, Buell remarks that *Moby-Dick* "is on one level a book about the presumptions of New England cultural imperialism, part of the exposé being the New Englander's discovery of what it means to live in the larger world" (*New England Literary Culture* 178).

11. The larger question generating from the conflict between western and so-called primitive cultures cannot be explored here. See Stern, *Fine Hammered Steel;* Karcher; Dimock, *Empire for Liberty;* Samson; and Alberti. *Benito Cereno* offers Melville's most penetrating exploration of this issue. For an excellent discussion of cultural politics in this narrative, see Zagarell.

12. See Stern's extensive examinations of Melville's politics in *Fine Hammered Steel;* "Melville, Society, and Language"; and *Contexts for Hawthorne.*

13. McIntosh sees Ahab as an "American antitype of many earlier types" (39), among them Jonah, Job, Jesus, Faust, Macbeth, Perseus, and Prometheus. Regarding Ahab, Rathbun argues, "Whether through direct defiance or in league with God's own plan for His demise, the purpose is to alter the teleological course of history and to bring about the final conclusion: God's death, the defeat of evil, and the installation of man as the world's authority" (5). See Bloom's *Ahab* for a range of views.

14. See McCarthy's treatment of madness in Melville's work, especially 65–73.

15. See Porte on Olson, Matthiessen, and Shakespearean soliloquy (194–200).

16. For an illuminating discussion of the suggested reading, "Is it Ahab, Ahab?" see *Moby-Dick* (Northwestern-Newberry) 903.

17. See Sealts's discussion of this passage and its implications regarding philosophical skepticism ("Platonic Tradition" 302–03).

18. See Vincent on "The Fountain" and Melville's borrowings and transformations (*Trying-Out* 286–94).

19. For Sealts's discussion of Locke and Kant, see "Platonic Tradition" (317–19).

20. On the problems of knowing, see Irwin,

> Inasmuch as all human knowledge is a more or less arbitrary unification of experience from the limited perspective of a knowing subject . . . the process of knowledge is in a sense man's discovery of the hieroglyphical outline of his shadow on the world, that image of organic unity derived from the limits of his own body that he projects on the world in order to render it intelligible. (62)

21. Martin argues that the novel "resolves none of the epistemological problems it poses. What's known is truly known—the physiology of whales, the techniques of whaling, the events that men experienced. The rest—the significances and ultimacies—are left to settle any way they will" (*Destruction of Knowledge* 42).

22. See Buell on the cetology chapters ("Sacred Text" 59–61).

23. Martin's discussion of "intellectual frontierism" illuminates Ishmael's sensibility, especially his "striving toward a connection with what is real behind the screen of concepts and categories . . . the liberation of the questing self from the trammels of convention and security" (*Destruction of Knowledge* 3–4).

24. Brodhead remarks, "The energies of literary composition are so interfused with the energies of philosophical surmise in *Moby-Dick* that every stray particular that enters the book is in immediate danger of being seized on and pressed to yield a model of the world" (*New Essays* 5). See also Herbert's discussion of Melville's treatment of "ultimate realities" ("Calvinist Earthquake" 113–14).

25. For further discussion of Melville's use of exotic mythologies, see Vargish; Oates; and Finkelstein.

26. For a discussion of Melville and Descartes, see Mancini.

CHAPTER SEVEN: Excursive Ponderings in *Pierre*

1. For a consideration of Melville's reading in domestic romance, see Sealts, *Melville's Reading* 73–79; Dryden notes that *Pierre* concerns "the problem of derivation: authority and priority, tradition and the individual talent, literary fathers and sons" ("Entangled Text" 150).

2. For an important account of Melville's relation to the literary marketplace and popular forms, see Douglas: "In *Pierre* (1852), Melville presents a savage study of the conspiratorial interaction between genteel religion, feminine morality, and polite literature against the interests of genuine masculinity" (294). In examining Melville's sexual politics, Douglas focuses on his hostility to "the middle-class sentimental-minded feminized reading public" (309); she suggests that the novel "may actually be a parody of the legendary and tempestuous best-sellers cranked out by women like Mrs. E.D.E.N. Southworth in this period. Certainly, Melville makes the sentimental domestic romance into a cage in which he deliberately confines his main character—and himself—both to define the limits of the form and to test the possibility of breaking out and destroying it" (312). Reynolds remarks,

> The truth is that *Pierre* was *too* broadly representative of antebellum popular culture—with all its crippling moral paradoxes—to have wide appeal.... The first half of the novel portrays the Conventional world of pastoralism, domesticity, the angelic exemplar, hopeful religion, military heroism, and innocence. The second half of the novel plunges us into the Subversive world of dark city mysteries, shattered homes, illicit love, social and philosophical radicalism, and bloody crime.... [B]y fusing the two realms he produced a highly explosive mixture that gave little pleasure to either class of readers. (159)

For lucid discussions of *Pierre*'s broad thematic preoccupations, see Watson 162; Berthoff 218; Thorp 192; and Stern, *Fine Hammered Steel* 151.

3. For discussions of *Pierre* and multiple forms, especially satire, see Braswell, "Early Love Scenes" 212; Stern, *Fine Hammered Steel* 162; Milder, "Melville's 'Intentions'"; and also Brodhead, who argues, "The odd combination of straightforwardness and secret mockery inherent in his handling of the style, characters, and characteristic situations is evidence of [Melville's] ambivalence, his desire both to make use of this genre and to assert his independence from it" (*Hawthorne* 164).

4. An anonymous commentator in 1926 writes,

> Melville, it is supposed, has been re-discovered recently. Actually, folk here rave hysterically about 'Moby Dick,' principally, and apparently lack the wit to know that 'Pierre' is one of the most important books in the world, profound beyond description in its metaphysic: in fact, I believe that you yourself would find something to keep your mind hard at work for many a day if you read that philosophically dramatic or dramatically philosophical novel, for it *is* a philosophical novel, reaching to heaven and down to hell in its march to a tragic culmination. (Higgins and Parker, *Critical Essays on Melville's* Pierre 117, emphasis in original)

5. For discussions of stone imagery, see Fleck; and Dryden, *Thematics of Form* 118–26.

6. For another discussion of Fate, see Dillingham 173–86.

7. See Sealts, "Platonic Tradition" 319–20.

8. See Stern's seminal discussion of Lucy (*Fine Hammered Steel* 151–61).

9. For important discussions of Isabel, see Watson 165; Stern, *Fine Hammered Steel* 181–89; and Tolchin 141.

10. Dryden argues, "Isabel's letter . . . seems to provide a context or model that renders intelligible textual details which to this point have been unreadable or misread" ("Entangled Text" 173).

11. Duban contends, "In *Pierre*, intuition is shown as arising from the mind's fabrications of mandates that it projects onto the outside world and reencounters as the 'primitive and sublime sentiment of Duty, engraved by the finger of God on the heart of man'" (*Major Fiction* 166). In seeking to locate *Pierre*'s transcendental affinities, Duban quotes George Ripley.

12. For a wide-ranging discussion of "Enthusiasm," see Simmons.

13. For further discussion of Melville's additions, see Higgins and Parker, "Flawed Grandeur" 256–62.

14. For considerations of Plinlimmon and the pamphlet, see Thorp 195; Stern, *Fine Hammered Steel* 189–95; and Higgins, "[Chronometicals]."

15. For Melville's attacks on Transcendentalism, see Matthiessen 467–73; and Duban, *Major Fiction* 149–91.

CHAPTER EIGHT: *The Confidence-Man: His Masquerade:* "The Most Extraordinary Metaphysical Scamps"

1. For a discussion of theatrical traditions that inform *The Confidence-Man,* see Trimpi.

2. For a discussion of how *Benito Cereno* depicts America's complicity in Old World ideologies and practices, see Zagarell.

3. Bryant summarizes problems relating to narrative surface in *The Confidence-Man:* "So strained is its humor, so generalized its allegorical and satiric sources, so distant its narrator and indefinable its characters, so convoluted its style and involuted its ironies, so elusive its normative values—indeed, so complex is this work that it is even difficult to render a reasonable plot summary without in some sense betraying one's interpretive biases" ("Melville's Problem Novel" 316). Reynolds identifies the novel as "the first full example of the American Subversive Style made intelligent and humane" (560). See especially the introduction to Foster.

4. For discussions of the relationship between language and truth, see Dryden, *Thematics of Form* 151–95; Tichi; Sten; Kemper, "A Knavishly-Packed Deck"; Stein; Ramsey; and Lindberg 15–47.

5. See Madison for her chart depicting the wide spectrum of opinions regarding the Confidence Man's possible identity; for notable discussions of his archetypal qualities, see Shroeder; and Parker, "The Metaphysics of Indian-hating."

6. For considerations of the novel's sources and genesis, see "Historical Note" *The Confidence-Man* 276–310; Branch, "Genesis"; and Bryant, "Melville's Problem Novel" 326–31. Reynolds sees the Confidence Man as an embodiment of "the likable criminal" (303–04).

7. For discussions of the novel's didactic, Christian content, see Quirk; and Bryant, "Allegory and Breakdown."

8. Dryden remarks, "[E]ach newly discovery clue, each new operative pattern or allusion, leads not beneath the verbal surface but across it to another mystery or, more often, to an example which subverts the implications of the original pattern" (*Thematics of Form* 151–52).

9. For discussions of self-possession and self-mastery in *The Confidence-Man*, see Dillingham 297–337; and Wenke, "Melville's Masquerade."

10. For Melville's rendering of the vacuity of identity, see Wenke, "No 'i' in Charlemont"; and Stern, "Melville, Society, and Language" 460–62.

11. On Timonism, see Watson.

12. Franklin suggests that Pitch's "discussion about innate knowledge and innate virtue with the man from the 'Philosophical Intelligence Office' . . . is a carefully constructed parody of Plato's *Meno*" (216).

13. *The Confidence-Man* offers a culmination of Melville's notion of the great artist as one who reveals truth "only by cunning glimpses" ("Hawthorne and His Mosses," *Piazza Tales* 244).

14. For discussions of the digressions and inset chapters, see Dryden, *Thematics of Form* 153–81; and Bryant "Allegory and Breakdown" 115–17.

15. Stern argues, "The limitlessness of illusion is the limitlessness of the unmaking of meanings. The limitlessness of illusion is the limitation of language" ("Melville, Society, and Language" 462).

16. For a discussion of cosmopolitanism, see Bryant " 'Nowhere a Stranger.' "

17. For a summary of critical views on Winsome and Egbert, see Bryant, "Melville's Problem Novel" 330.

Works Cited

Adler, Joyce Sparer. *War in Melville's Imagination.* New York: New York UP, 1981.

Alberti, John. "Cultural Relativism and Melville's *Typee:* Man in the State of Culture." *ESQ: A Journal of the American Renaissance* 36.4 (1990): 329–47.

Anderson, Charles R. *Melville in the South Seas.* New York: Columbia UP, 1939.

Barbour, James. "'All My Books Are Botches': Melville's Struggles with *The Whale*." *Writing the American Classics.* Ed. James Barbour and Tom Quirk. Chapel Hill: U of North Carolina P, 1990. 25–52.

———. "The Composition of *Moby-Dick*." *American Literature* 47 (Nov. 1975): 343–73.

Bauerlein, Mark. "Grammar and Etymology in *Moby-Dick*." *Arizona Quarterly* 46.3 (Autumn 1990): 17–32.

Baym, Nina. "Melville's Quarrel with Fiction." *PMLA* 94 (Oct. 1979): 909–23.

Bellis, Peter J. *No Mysteries Out of Ourselves: Identity and Textual Form in the Novels of Herman Melville.* Philadelphia: U of Pennsylvania P, 1990.

Bercaw, Mary K. *Melville's Sources.* Evanston, IL: Northwestern UP, 1987.

Berthoff, Warner. *The Example of Melville.* Princeton: Princeton UP, 1962. 46–53. Excerpt rpt. as "The Growth of the Mind." *Critical Essays on Herman Melville's Pierre; or, The Ambiguities.* Ed. Brian Higgins and Hershel Parker. Boston: Hall, 1983. 216–21.

Bezanson, Walter E. "*Moby-Dick:* Document, Drama, Dream." *A Companion to Melville Studies.* Ed. John Bryant. New York: Greenwood, 1986. 169–210.

Bickman, Martin. "Melville and the Mind." *A Companion to Melville Studies.* Ed. John Bryant. New York: Greenwood, 1986. 515–41.

Bloom, Harold. Introduction. *Ahab.* New York: Chelsea House, 1991.

———. *The Anxiety of Influence: A Theory of Poetry.* New York: Oxford, 1973.

Branch, Watson. "The Genesis, Composition, and Structure of *The Confidence-Man*." *Nineteenth-Century Fiction* 7 (Mar. 1973): 424–48.

——. "The Quest for *Mardi*." *A Companion to Melville Studies.* Ed. John Bryant. New York: Greenwood, 1986. 123–43.

Braswell, William. "The Early Love Scenes in Melville's *Pierre*." *American Literature* 22 (Nov. 1950): 283–89. Rpt. in *Critical Essays on Herman Melville's Pierre; or, The Ambiguities.* Ed. Brian Higgins and Hershel Parker. Boston: Hall, 1983. 210–16.

——. *Melville's Religious Thought: An Essay in Interpretation.* Durham: Duke UP, 1943.

——. "Melville's Use of Seneca in *Mardi*." *American Literature* 12 (Nov. 1940): 98–104.

Brodhead, Richard H. *Hawthorne, Melville, and the Novel.* Chicago: U of Chicago P, 1976.

——. "*Mardi:* Creating the Creative." *New Perspectives on Melville.* Ed. Faith Pullin. Kent, OH: Kent State UP, 1979. 29–53.

——. "Trying All Things: An Introduction to *Moby-Dick*." *New Essays on Moby-Dick.* Ed. Richard H. Brodhead. Cambridge: Cambridge UP, 1986. 1–21.

Brodtkorb, Paul, Jr. *Ishmael's White World: A Phenomenological Reading of Moby-Dick.* New Haven: Yale UP, 1965.

Browne, J. Ross. *Etchings of a Whaling Cruise.* Ed. John Seelye. Cambridge: Harvard UP, 1968.

Browne, Sir Thomas. *Religio Medici. Sir Thomas Browne: Selected Writings.* Ed. Sir Geoffrey Keynes. Chicago: U of Chicago P, 1966. 1–89.

Bryant, John. "Allegory and Breakdown in *The Confidence-Man:* Melville's Comedy of Doubt." *Philological Quarterly* 65 (Winter 1986): 113–30.

——. "*The Confidence-Man:* Melville's Problem Novel." *A Companion to Melville Studies.* Ed. John Bryant. New York: Greenwood, 1986. 315–50.

——. "'Nowhere a Stranger': Melville and Cosmopolitanism." *Nineteenth-Century Fiction* 39 (Dec. 1984): 275–91.

Buell, Lawrence. "*Moby-Dick* as Sacred Text." *New Essays on Moby-Dick.* Ed. Richard H. Brodhead. Cambridge: Cambridge UP, 1986. 53–72.

——. *New England Literary Culture: From Revolution through Renaissance.* Cambridge: Cambridge UP, 1986.

Burnet, John. *Early Greek Philosophy.* 1892. 1st ed. London: Black, 1930.

Burton, Robert. *The Anatomy of Melancholy.* New York: Tudor, 1927.

Cambon, Glauco. "Ishmael and the Problem of Formal Discontinuities in *Moby-Dick*." *Modern Language Notes* 76 (June 1961): 516–23.

Carlyle, Thomas. *Sartor Resartus: The Life and Opinions of Herr Teufelsdröckh and Heroes and Hero-Worship.* Boston: Dana Estes & Co., n.d. Vol. 14, *Carlyle's Works: Centennial Memorial Edition.*

Cascardi, A. J. "Emerson on Nature: Philosophy beyond Kant." *ESQ: A Journal of the American Renaissance* 30.4 (1984): 201–10.

Chai, Leon. *The Romantic Foundations of the American Renaissance.* Ithaca: Cornell UP, 1987.

Clark, Michael. "Melville's *Typee:* Fact, Fiction, and Esthetics." *Arizona Quarterly* 34 (Winter 1978): 351–70.

Coleridge, Samuel Taylor. *Biographia Literaria or Biographical Sketches of My Literary Life and Opinions.* Ed. John Calvin Metcalf. New York: Macmillan, 1926.

Couch, H. N. "Melville's *Moby-Dick* and the *Phaedo.*" *Classical Journal* 28 (Feb. 1933): 367–68.

Davis, Merrell R. *Melville's Mardi: A Chartless Voyage.* New Haven: Yale UP, 1952.

De Quincey, Thomas. *The Confessions of an English Opium-Eater.* New York: Illustrated Editions, 1932.

Dillingham, William B. *Melville's Later Novels.* Athens: U of Georgia P, 1986.

Dimock, Wai-chee. *Empire for Liberty: Melville and the Poetics of Individualism.* Princeton: Princeton UP, 1989.

———. "*Typee:* Melville's Critique of Community." *ESQ: A Journal of the American Renaissance* 30.1 (1984): 27–39.

Dryden, Edgar A. "The Entangled Text: *Pierre* and the Problem of Reading." *Boundary 2* 7 (Spring 1979): 145–73. Rpt. in *Herman Melville.* Ed. Harold Bloom. New York: Chelsea House, 1986. 155–81.

———. *Melville's Thematics of Form: The Great Art of Telling the Truth.* Baltimore: Johns Hopkins UP, 1968.

Duban, James. *Melville's Major Fiction: Politics, Theology, and Imagination.* Dekalb: Northern Illinois UP, 1983.

———. "The Translation of Pierre Bayle's *An Historical and Critical Dictionary* Owned by Melville." *Papers of the Bibliographical Society of America* 71 (1977): 347–51.

Emerson, Ralph Waldo. "History." *Essays: First Series.* Cambridge: Harvard UP, 1979. Vol. 2 of *The Collected Works of Ralph Waldo Emerson.* Ed. Alfred R. Ferguson and Jean Ferguson Carr. 5 vols. to date, 1971–. 1–23.

———. *Nature, Addresses, and Lectures.* Cambridge: Harvard UP, 1971. Vol. 1 of *The Collected Works of Ralph Waldo Emerson.* Ed. Robert E. Spiller and Alfred R. Ferguson. 5 vols. to date, 1971–. 1–45.

Finkelstein, Dorothee Metlitsky. *Melville's Orienda.* New York: Octagon, 1971.

Fleck, Richard F. "Stone Imagery in Melville's *Pierre.*" *Research Studies* (Washington State University) 12 (1974): 127–30.

Foley, Brian. "Herman Melville and the Example of Sir Thomas Browne." *Modern Philology* 81 (1984): 265–77.

Foster, Elizabeth S. Introduction. *The Confidence-Man: His Masquerade.* By Herman Melville. New York: Hendricks House, 1954. xiii–xcv.

Franklin, H. Bruce. *The Wake of the Gods: Melville's Mythology.* Palo Alto: Stanford UP, 1963.

Gilman, William H. *Melville's Early Life and* Redburn. New York: New York UP, 1951.

Greenburg, Robert M. "Shooting the Gulf: Emerson's Sense of Experience." *ESQ: A Journal of the American Renaissance* 31.4 (1985): 211–29.

Grenberg, Bruce L. *Some Other World to Find: Quest and Negation in the Works of Herman Melville.* Urbana: U of Illinois P, 1989.

Hayes, Kevin J., and Hershel Parker, eds. *Checklist of Melville Reviews.* Evanston, IL: Northwestern UP, 1991.

Hayford, Harrison. "'Unnecessary Duplicates': A Key to the Writing of *Moby-Dick*." *New Perspectives on Melville.* Ed. Faith Pullin. Kent: Kent State UP, 1979. 128–61.

Heflin, Wilson. "*Redburn* and *White-Jacket.*" *A Companion to Melville Studies.* Ed. John Bryant. New York: Greenwood, 1986. 145–67.

Herbert, T. Walter, Jr. "Calvinist Earthquake: *Moby-Dick* and Religious Tradition." *New Essays on* Moby-Dick. Ed. Richard H. Brodhead. Cambridge: Cambridge UP, 1986. 109–40.

———. *Moby-Dick and Calvinism: A World Dismantled.* New Brunswick: Rutgers UP, 1977.

Hetherington, Hugh W. *Melville's Reviewers: British and American, 1846–1891.* Chapel Hill: U of North Carolina P, 1961.

Higgins, Brian. "Plinlimmon and the Pamphlet Again." *Studies in the Novel* 4 (Spring 1972): 27–38. Rpt. as ["Chronometricals and Horologicals"]. *Critical Essays on Melville's Pierre; or, The Ambiguities.* Ed. Brian Higgins and Hershel Parker. Boston: Hall, 1983. 221–25.

Higgins, Brian, and Hershel Parker. "The Flawed Grandeur of Melville's *Pierre.*" *New Perspectives on Melville.* Ed. Faith Pullin. Kent, OH: Kent State UP, 1979. 162–96.

———. "Reading *Pierre.*" *A Companion to Melville Studies.* Ed. John Bryant. New York: Greenwood, 1986. 211–39.

———, ed. Introduction. *Critical Essays on Melville's Pierre: or, The Ambiguities.* Boston: Hall, 1983. 1–27.

Hollander, John. *The Figure of Echo: A Mode of Allusion in Milton and After.* Berkeley: U of California P, 1981.

Howard, Leon. *Herman Melville: A Biography.* Berkeley: U of California P, 1951.

———. *The Unfolding of Moby-Dick.* Ed. James Barbour and Thomas Quirk. Glassboro: Melville Society, 1987.

Irwin, John T. *American Hieroglyphics: The Symbol of the Egyptian Hieroglyphics in the American Renaissance.* New Haven: Yale UP, 1980.

Karcher, Carolyn L. *Shadow Over the Promised Land: Slavery, Race, and Violence in Melville's America.* Baton Rouge: Louisiana State UP, 1980.

Kemper, Steven E. "*The Confidence-Man:* A Knavishly-Packed Deck." *Studies in American Fiction* 8 (Spring 1980): 23–35.

———. "*Omoo:* Germinal Melville." *Studies in the Novel* 10 (Winter 1978): 420–31.

Lawrence, D. H. *Studies in Classic American Literature.* 1923. New York: Viking, 1961.

Levin, Michael E. "Ahab as Socratic Philosopher: The Myth of the Cave Inverted." *American Transcendental Quarterly* 41 (Winter 1979): 61–73.

Leyda, Jay. *The Melville Log: A Documentary Life of Herman Melville, 1819–1891.* 1951. 2 vols. Rpt., with supplement. New York: Gordian, 1969.

Lindberg, Gary. *The Confidence Man in American Literature.* New York: Oxford UP, 1982.

Lopez, Michael. "DeTranscendentalizing Emerson." *ESQ: A Journal of the American Renaissance* 34.1–2 (1988): 77–139.

McCarthy, Paul. *"The Twisted Mind": Madness in Herman Melville's Fiction.* Iowa City: U of Iowa P, 1990.

McIntosh, James. "The Mariner's Multiple Quests." *New Essays on Moby-Dick.* Ed. Richard H. Brodhead. Cambridge: Cambridge UP, 1986. 23–52.

Madison, Mary K. "Hypothetical Friends: The Critics and *The Confidence-Man.*" *Melville Society Extracts* 46 (May 1981): 10–14.

Mancini, Matthew. "Melville's 'Descartian Vortices.'" *ESQ: A Journal of the American Renaissance* 36.4 (1990): 315–27.

Marovitz, Sanford E. "Melville's Problematic 'Being.'" *ESQ: A Journal of the American Renaissance* 28.1 (1982): 11–23.

———. "More Chartless Voyaging: Melville and Adler at Sea." *Studies in the American Renaissance.* Ed. Joel Myerson. Charlottesville: U of Virginia P, 1986. 373–84.

Martin, Ronald E. *American Literature and the Destruction of Knowledge: Innovative Writing in the Age of Epistemology.* Durham: Duke UP, 1991.

———. *American Literature and the Universe of Force.* Durham: Duke UP, 1981.

Matthiessen, F. O. *American Renaissance: Art and Expression in the Age of Emerson and Whitman.* 1941. New York: Oxford UP, 1968.

Melville, Herman. *Billy Budd, Sailor (An Inside Narrative).* Ed. Harrison Hayford and Merton M. Sealts, Jr. Chicago: U of Chicago P, 1962.

———. *Clarel: A Poem and a Pilgrimage in the Holy Land.* Evanston, IL: Northwestern UP/Newberry Library, 1991. Vol. 12 of *The Writings of Herman Melville.* Ed. Harrison Hayford et al. 15 vols. to date. 1968–.

———. *The Confidence-Man: His Masquerade.* Ed. Hershel Parker. New York: Norton, 1971.

———. *The Confidence-Man: His Masquerade.* Evanston, IL: Northwestern UP/ Newberry Library, 1984. Vol. 10 of *The Writings of Herman Melville.* Ed. Harrison Hayford, Hershel Parker, and G. Thomas Tanselle. 15 vols. to date. 1968–.

———. *Correspondence.* Evanston, IL: Northwestern UP/Newberry Library, 1993. Vol. 14 of *The Writings of Herman Melville.* Ed. Lynn Horth. 15 vols. to date. 1968–.

———. *Journals.* Evanston, IL: Northwestern UP/Newberry Library, 1989. Vol. 15 of *The Writings of Herman Melville.* Ed. Howard C. Horsford with Lynn Horth. 15 vols. to date. 1968–.

———. *Mardi and A Voyage Thither.* Evanston, IL: Northwestern UP/Newberry Library, 1970. Vol. 3 of *The Writings of Herman Melville.* Ed. Harrison Hayford, Hershel Parker, and G. Thomas Tanselle. 15 vols. to date. 1968–.

———. *Moby-Dick: or, The Whale.* Ed. Harrison Hayford and Hershel Parker. New York: Norton, 1967.

———. *Moby-Dick or The Whale.* Evanston, IL: Northwestern UP/Newberry Library, 1988. Vol. 6 of *The Writings of Herman Melville.* Ed. Harrison Hayford, Hershel Parker, and G. Thomas Tanselle. 15 vols. to date. 1968–.

———. *Omoo: A Narrative of Adventure in the South Seas.* Evanston, IL: Northwestern UP/Newberry Library, 1968. Vol. 2 of *The Writings of Herman Melville.* Ed. Harrison Hayford, Hershel Parker, and G. Thomas Tanselle. 15 vols. to date. 1968–.

———. *The Piazza Tales and Other Prose Pieces 1839–1860.* Evanston, IL: Northwestern UP/Newberry Library, 1987. Vol. 9 of *The Writings of Herman Melville.* Ed. Harrison Hayford et al. 15 vols. to date. 1968–.

———. *Pierre; or, The Ambiguities.* Evanston, IL: Northwestern UP/Newberry Library. Vol. 7 of *The Writings of Herman Melville.* Ed. Harrison Hayford, Hershel Parker, and G. Thomas Tanselle. 15 vols. to date. 1968–.

———. *Redburn: His First Voyage.* Evanston, IL: Northwestern UP/Newberry Library, 1969. Vol. 4 of *The Writings of Herman Melville.* Ed. Harrison Hayford, Hershel Parker, and G. Thomas Tanselle. 15 vols. to date. 1968–.

———. *Typee: A Peep at Polynesian Life.* Evanston, IL: Northwestern UP/Newberry Library, 1968. Vol. 1 of *The Writings of Herman Melville.* Ed. Harrison Hayford, Hershel Parker, and G. Thomas Tanselle. 15 vols. to date. 1968–.

———. *White-Jacket or The World in a Man-of-War.* Evanston, IL: Northwestern UP/Newberry Library, 1970. Vol. 5 of *The Writings of Herman Melville.* Ed. Harrison Hayford, Hershel Parker, and G. Thomas Tanselle. 15 vols. to date. 1968–.

Michael, John. *Emerson and Skepticism: The Cipher of the World.* Baltimore: Johns Hopkins UP, 1988.

Milder, Robert. "The Composition of *Moby-Dick:* A Review and a Prospect." *ESQ: A Journal of the American Renaissance* 23 (Summer 1977): 203–16.

———. "Melville's 'Intentions' in *Pierre.*" *Studies in the Novel* 6 (Summer 1974): 186–99.

Milton, John. *Paradise Lost.* Ed. Merritt Y. Hughes. New York: Odyssey, 1957.

Montaigne, Michel de. *The Complete Essays of Montaigne.* Trans. Donald M. Frame. Palo Alto: Stanford UP, 1958.

Oates, J. C. "Melville and the Manichean Illusion." *Texas Studies in Literature and Language* 4 (Spring 1962): 117–29.

Olson, Charles. *Call Me Ishmael.* New York: Reynall and Hitchcock, 1947.

"One of the Most Important Books in the World." Cited in Christopher Morley, "The Bowling Green." *Saturday Review of Literature* (New York) 2 (May 1926):

755. Rpt. in *Critical Essays on Melville's Pierre; or, The Ambiguities*. Ed. Brian Higgins and Hershel Parker. Boston: Hall, 1983. 117.

Parker, Hershel. "Herman Melville." *American History Illustrated* Sept.–Oct. 1991: 28–47.

———. "The Metaphysics of Indian-hating." *Nineteenth-Century Fiction* 18 (Sept. 1963): 165–73.

———. "*Moby-Dick* and Domesticity." *Critical Essays on Herman Melville's Moby-Dick*. Ed. Brian Higgins and Hershel Parker. New York: Hall, 1992. 545–62.

Pease, Donald. *Visionary Compacts: American Renaissance Writings in Cultural Contexts*. Madison: U of Wisconsin P, 1987.

Plato. *The Works of Plato*. Trans. B. Jowett. 4 vols. New York: Tudor, n.d.

Porte, Joel. *In Respect to Egotism: Studies in American Romantic Writing*. Cambridge: Cambridge UP, 1991.

Porter, Carolyn. "Call Me Ishmael, or How to Make Double-Talk Speak." *New Essays on Moby-Dick*. Ed. Richard H. Brodhead. Cambridge: Cambridge UP, 1986. 73–108.

Post-Lauria, Sheila. "'Philosophy in Whales . . . Poetry in Blubber': Mixed Form in *Moby-Dick*." *Nineteenth-Century Literature* 45 (Dec. 1990): 300–316.

Quirk, Tom. *Melville's Confidence Man: From Knave to Knight*. Columbia: U of Missouri P, 1982.

Railton, Stephen. "'You Must Have Plenty of Sea-Room to Tell the Truth in': Melville's *Moby-Dick*." *Authorship and Audience: Literary Performance in the American Renaissance*. Princeton: Princeton UP, 1991. 152–89.

Ramsey, William M. "The Moot Points of Indian-Hating." *American Literature* 52 (May 1980): 224–35.

Rathbun, John W. "*Moby-Dick*: Ishmael's Fiction of Ahab's Romantic Insurgency." *Modern Language Studies* 21 (Summer 1991): 3–9.

Reynolds, David S. *Beneath the American Renaissance: The Subversive Imagination in the Age of Emerson and Melville*. New York: Knopf, 1988.

Samson, John. *White Lies: Melville's Narratives of Facts*. Ithaca: Cornell UP, 1989.

Sealts, Merton M., Jr. "Herman Melville's Reading in Ancient Philosophy." Diss. Yale U, 1942.

———. "Melville and Emerson's Rainbow." *ESQ: A Journal of the American Renaissance* 26.2 (1980): 53–78. Rpt. in *Pursuing Melville, 1940–1980: Chapters and Essays by Merton M. Sealts, Jr*. Madison: U of Wisconsin P, 1982. 250–77.

———. "Melville and the Platonic Tradition." *Pursuing Melville, 1940–1980: Chapters and Essays by Merton M. Sealts, Jr*. Madison: U of Wisconsin P, 1982. 278–336.

———. "Melville's 'Neoplatonical Originals.'" *Modern Language Notes* 67 (Feb. 1952): 80–86.

———. *Melville's Reading*. 1966. Columbia: U of South Carolina P, 1988.

Shelley, Mary W. *Frankenstein: or, The Modern Prometheus*. Ed. M. K. Joseph. London: Oxford UP, 1969.

Sherrill, Rowland A. "Melville and Religion." *A Companion to Melville Studies.* Ed. John Bryant. New York: Greenwood, 1986. 481–513.

Short, Bryan C. "'The Author at the Time': Tommo and Melville's Self-Discovery in *Typee.*" *Texas Studies in Literature and Language* 31 (Fall 1989): 386–405.

Shroeder, John W. "Sources and Symbols for Melville's *The Confidence-Man.*" *PMLA* 66 (June 1951): 363–80.

Simmons, Nancy Craig. "Why an Enthusiast?: Melville's *Pierre* and the Problem of the Imagination." *ESQ: A Journal of the American Renaissance* 33.3 (1987): 146–67.

Stein, William B. "Melville's *The Confidence-Man:* Quicksands of the Word." *American Transcendental Quarterly* 24.4 (1974): 38–50.

Sten, Christopher W. "The Dialogue of Crisis in *The Confidence-Man:* Melville's 'New Novel.'" *Studies in the Novel* 6 (Summer 1974): 165–85.

Stern, Milton R. *Contexts for Hawthorne: The Marble Faun and the Politics of Openness and Closure in American Literature.* Urbana: U of Illinois P, 1991.

———. *Critical Essays on Melville's Typee.* Boston: Hall, 1982.

———. *The Fine Hammered Steel of Herman Melville.* Urbana: U of Illinois P, 1957.

———. "Melville, Society, and Language." *A Companion to Melville Studies.* Ed. John Bryant. New York: Greenwood, 1986. 433–79.

———. "Towards 'Bartleby the Scrivener.'" *The Stoic Strain in American Literature.* Ed. Duane J. Macmillan. Toronto: U of Toronto P, 1979. 19–41.

Stewart, George R. "The Two *Moby-Dicks.*" *American Literature* 25 (Jan. 1954): 417–48.

Sunderman, K. H. *Herman Melville's Gegankengut: Eine kritische Untersuchung seiner weltanschaulichen Grundideen.* [The scope of Melville's thought.] Berlin: Collignon, 1937.

Thorp, Willard. *Herman Melville: Representative Selections.* New York: American Book, 1938. lxxv–lxxxii. Rpt. as ["Melville's Quest for the Ultimate"]. *Critical Essays on Melville's Pierre; or, The Ambiguities.* Ed. Brian Higgins and Hershel Parker. Boston: Hall, 1983. 191–96.

Tichi, Cecelia. "Melville's Craft and the Theme of Language Debased in *The Confidence-Man.*" *ELH: A Journal of English Literary History* 39 (Dec. 1972): 639–58.

Titus, David K. "Herman Melville at the Albany Academy." *Melville Society Extracts* 42 (May 1980): 4–10.

Tolchin, Neal L. *Mourning, Gender, and Creativity in the Art of Herman Melville.* New Haven: Yale UP, 1988.

Trimpi, Helen P. "Harlequin-Confidence Man: The Satirical Tradition of Commedia Dell'Arte and Pantomime in Melville's *The Confidence-Man. Texas Studies in Literature and Language* 16 (Spring 1974): 147–93.

Vande Kieft, Ruth M. "'When Big Hearts Strike Together': The Concussion of Melville and Sir Thomas Browne." *Papers on Language and Literature* 5 (Winter 1969): 39–50.

Vargish, Thomas. "Gnostick Mythos in *Moby-Dick. PMLA* 81 (June 1966): 272–77.

Watson, Charles N., Jr. "Melville and the Theme of Timonism: From *Pierre* to *The Confidence-Man.*" *American Literature* 44 (Nov. 1972): 398–413.

Watson, E. L. Grant. "Melville's *Pierre.*" *New England Quarterly* 3 (Apr. 1930): 195–234. Rpt. in *Critical Essays on Melville's Pierre: or, The Ambiguities.* Ed. Brian Higgins and Hershel Parker. Boston: Hall, 1983. 161–84.

Wenke, John. "Melville's *Mardi* and the Isles of Man." *American Transcendental Quarterly* 53 (Winter 1982): 25–41.

———. "Melville's Masquerade and the Aesthetics of Self-Possession." *ESQ: A Journal of the American Renaissance* 28.4 (1982): 233–42.

———. "Melville's *Typee:* A Tale of Two Worlds." *Critical Essays on Melville's Typee.* Ed. Milton R. Stern. Boston: Hall, 1982. 250–58.

———. "No 'i' in Charlemont: A Cryptogrammic Name in *The Confidence-Man.*" *Essays in Literature* (Macomb, IL) 9 (Fall 1982): 269–78.

———. "'Ontological Heroics': Melville's Philosophical Art." *A Companion to Melville Studies.* Ed. John Bryant. New York: Greenwood, 1986. 567–601.

Williams, John B. *White Fire: The Influence of Emerson on Melville.* Long Beach: California State UP, 1991.

Wilson, James C. *The Hawthorne and Melville Friendship: An Annotated Bibliography, Biographical and Critical Essays, and Correspondence Between the Two.* Jefferson: McFarland, 1991.

Wright, Nathalia. *Melville's Use of the Bible.* Durham: Duke UP, 1949.

Zagarell, Sandra A. "Reenvisioning America: Melville's 'Benito Cereno.'" *ESQ: A Journal of the American Renaissance* 30.4 (1984): 245–59.

Index